Animating History:
The Biographical Pulse

David H. Burton

Saint Joseph's University Press

Philadelphia

ORIGINAL PUBLICATION DATA

"History, Hubris and the Heisenberg Principle" *Thought*, March, 1975, pp. 84–93

"Theodore Roosevelt's Social Darwinism and Views on Imperialism," *Journal of the History of Ideas*, Jan–March, 1965, vol. XXXVI, pp. 108–118

"John Adams," *An Anglo-American Plutarch*, University Press of America, Lanham, Md., 1990, pp. 39–50

"E.A. Robinson," *Thought*, Winter, 1969, pp.565–580

"Winston Churchill," *An Anglo-American Plutarch*, University Press of America, Lanham. Md., 1990, pp. 256–271

"Franklin Roosevelt," *An Anglo-American Plutarch*, University Press of America, Lanham, Md., 1990, pp, 272–285

"Clara Barton," *An Anglo-American Plutarch*, University Press of America, Lanham, Md. 1990, 118–128

"Mary Ritter Beard," *An Anglo-American Plutarch*, University Press of America, Lanham, Md., 1990, pp.162–171

"The Anglo-American Rapprochement" *Transactions of the American Philosophical Society*, 1973

Historic Friendships, "The Friendship of Justice Holmes and Canon Sheehan, *Harvard Library Bulletin*, April 1977 vol. XXV, pp. 155–169, Holmes, Pollock, Laski, *Proceedings, American Philosophy Society*, Vol. 119, Number 2, April 16, 1975, pp. 132–145

Jesuit Presence, "The Jesuit As American Patriot: Fathers Robert Harding and Robert Molyneux," *Pennsylvania History*, Vol. XLVIII, No, 1 January, 1981, pp.51–61.

"Justice Holmes and the Jesuits," The *American Journal of Jurisprudence*, volume 27, 1982, pp. 32–45

Chief Justice Taft, "Chief Justice William Howard Taft," *William Howard Taft in the Public Service*, Robert E. Krieger Publishing Company, Malabar, Florida, 1986, pp. 121–141.

Private Burton, "Unit," previously unpublished.

All the foregoing material is published with the permission of the copyright owners.

This publication was supported by a grant from the Earhart Foundation.

Library of Congress Cataloging-in-Publication Data

Burton, David Henry, 1925-
  Animating history : the biographical pulse / David H. Burton.
    p. cm.
  Includes bibliographical references and index.
  ISBN 0-916101-75-4 (alk. paper)
  1. Biography as a literary form. 2. Biography--20th century. 3. Celebrities--Anecdotes. I. Title.

CT21.B87 2007
808'.06692--dc22

2006038371

Published by Saint Joseph's University Press
5600 City Avenue, Philadelphia, Pennsylvania 19131-1395, www.sju.edu/sjupress/

Dedication

To

The Benefactors of the Burton History Fund

CONTENTS

PREFACE

By its very nature this preface should be brief, attempting as it does a commentary on my own work. What I intend to show in this collection taken from my writings is the interaction of people and ideas, as, at the same time, the grouping of selections assumes relationships of people and events. Considered altogether the collection appeals to lives observed as a source of historical insight. Yet this bias depends intrinsically on the historical era. History, therefore, remains very close to the center of each piece.

My attachment to a biographical approach to both intellectual and political history, and to diplomatic and gender history, comes as a result of viewing the past as people-dominated. It does not eschew a history of movements or of grand patterns. It only takes them for granted and in doing so elevates the persons involved to a level of importance possibly otherwise obscured. Sidney Hook has written of "heroes in history," describing them as event-makers. I have chosen a wider angle of focus in order to discover not only event-makers, but men and women who, through their lives have perhaps reflected historical change, being careful not to claim too much for them. Where there are event-makers to be found in these pages, be it Theodore Roosevelt or Clara Barton, there is no reason to deny them their rightful place in history. In sum, it is hard to imagine history without people, famous or obscure, and equally heard to make sense of people outside of the history of their times.

In somewhat the same sense it is difficult to determine how this retrospective would have come into print without the help and encouragement of the Earhart Foundation which, on several occasions, including the present study, has generously supported my work over the years. My thanks as well to Brice Wachterhauser, Provost of Saint Joseph's University, for his interest and support, to David Contosta who brought his practiced, scholarly eye to bear on the manuscript, and to Carmen Croce, Director of Saint Joseph's University Press, who from start to finish worked steadfastly to bring this collection to fulfillment.

INTRODUCTION

In writing the entries in this collection, training and taste have been influential factors. This is especially so as work progressed, widening and deepening an appreciation of the roles played by three prominent figures in the history of the United States with the onset of the American century. Theodore Roosevelt, Oliver Wendell Holmes, and William Howard Taft, each in his own way, was among the event-makers, yet there developed an increasing awareness of how much they depended on others to achieve their objectives and, to be sure, when they failed to harness history to suit their purposes. They entwined, encompassed, and entered into the lives of many people and these "others" might have stories of their own worth knowing about. One example may suffice to graph this connectiveness. In 1898 during the Spanish-American War Colonel Theodore Roosevelt encountered Clara Barton of the American Red Cross while they were both serving their country in Cuba. It was a friendly meeting, each admiring the work of the other. After the war, TR publicly praised the leadership of Barton and as required by law she gave President Roosevelt annual reports of Red Cross activities which he heartily approved. But when a movement was afoot to oust her from the Red Cross headship, Roosevelt turned his back on her, accepting at face value charges of financial wrongdoing levied against her by those intent on taking charge of the organization. Roosevelt deliberately and maliciously ignored her. It was a most ungallant act, helping to bring about Barton's resignation. Roosevelt biographers have never even made mention of this affair. But is this incident of any historical significance? It is certainly important in writing the story of the American Red Cross which itself is, by definition, history, not biography.

The writing of history is in many respects a highly personalized undertaking. To prescind from the familiar issue of distinguishing between objective and subjective historical accounts, it is, after all, the work of men and women and not of zombies. Of course there is history as propaganda or special pleading or apologia or of time and place. But the personal cannot be eliminated from the process. It is with such considerations as these in mind that the selections included in this testament to the place of biography in historiography are offered. They are chosen from work which has appeared in scholarly journals and as chapters in books and reflect a range of interests from Progressive Politics to the special relationship between America and Britain to Constitutional Law. There is to be found a unity of intention, namely, men and women who, in their various and separate ways, lived lives of purpose and fulfillment. In the big picture not all the individuals found herein are of the greatest importance. But great or not, their lives appealed to me as worthy of study, an effort to understand not only who they were but how they mattered in the unfolding of the human experience we speak of as the historical record. It has been my good fortune to meet these men and women, so to speak, an enriching process which makes the teaching of history that much more engaging. It justifies the effort, sometimes at great expense of time and attention, to enter their worlds in order to better understand both them and us.

The public lives of Theodore Roosevelt, Oliver Wendell Holmes, and William Howard Taft form a concentric circle in and of themselves. But attention should be given to other, less high profile individuals with whom these men interacted. TR in particular enjoyed a particularly wide range of associations, from E.A. Robinson, the American poet, to the British diplomat, Cecil Spring Rice. Holmes also profited from a diversity of friendships which included the Irish priest-savant Canon Sheehan and Sir Frederick Pollock, a leading authority on English law and practice. Taft frequently consulted his brother, Charles Phelps Taft, and was close to President McKinley. And as it happened, he was an intimate of both Roosevelt and Holmes. In singular ways this trio of national leaders were influenced by each other and by others as well. All three have been the subject of biographies – great lives observed – as proper tools for investigating the past. In fact, given the critical importance of Roosevelt, Holmes, and Taft in our history, reliance on their biographies is indispensable for understanding them and their times.

"Read no history, only biography, for in biography there is life without theory," was a rule of thumb attributed to Queen Victoria's favorite prime minister, Benjamin Disraeli. His contemporary, Benjamin Jowett, master of Balliol, has put it another way, rather perversely, though his comment may well have merit. "Do tell us his faults, surely that is the most interesting thing about him." Better to listen to H.H. Asquith who found that biography "brings comfort, it enlarges sympathy, it expels selfishness, it quickens aspiration." More to the point Allan Nevins, a greatly respected historian himself, has written that biography "humanizes the past, while at the same time it enriches the present by showing us life with a vividness and a completeness that few experience in life itself." And he observes further, "To men who lack imagination, history is difficult to visualize, while biography brings them the past in concrete, real and vivid terms. To men who have known little of life or who have dwelt in narrow environments, history is often meaningless confusion, while reading a series of biographies holds out all the richness that human existence can present." The case for biography as history is indeed a strong one.

A word or more may be in order regarding the organization of the selections chosen to reveal the thesis of biographer as historian. Pairings represent the full range of the author's historical interests found in his published books and articles. The first entry is designed to challenge conventional thinking about biography. Other pairings within categories may appear off track, such as John Adams and E.A. Robinson, or Clara Barton and Mary Ritter Beard, but that is all the better for arguing the case of the critical importance of men and women in order to grasp the reality of the past. Other pairings, in contrast, are perfectly obvious, that of Winston Churchill and Franklin Roosevelt. The literary record found in the correspondence of Oliver Wendell Holmes, like that of Canon

Sheehan, reveals aspects of his thinking not otherwise accessible, thereby adding meaning to his Court rulings. Historic friendships between men of parts have often had an impact on public policy, as the relationship between Theodore Roosevelt and Cecil Spring Rice makes clear. A Jesuit Presence brings out the kinship between men in orders who are separated by a century and more of the American experience. Finally some mention should be made respecting biography and autobiography. The entries dealing with Chief Justice Taft and Private Burton spell out how vast the difference between the great man and everyman can be.

In an analysis of lives meaningful to historical understanding, the genre has two species, biography and autobiography. And within each of these there are sub-species, as in thematic or time period or the dominating event of a given life. Autobiography is much the rarer species, and when it is available it is almost certain to reveal the inner self of the person to a degree beyond the ken of a second party. Theodore Roosevelt's *An Autobiography* is a case in point just as it is in "Unit," the account of a private soldier of the line. Indeed such investigation and conclusions evoke the psycho-biographical. How vital may this be in making for historical discernment? Such findings may not always be essential but they must always be treated as germane, providing insights into the mind and spirit of the person which would not otherwise be seen.

INTERFACING
SCIENCE AND BIOGRAPHY

From the early modern period onward scientific figures have had an influence on history and more germane, on the writing of history and biography. It requires only a passing reference to Galileo or Newton in early times and Darwin or Einstein in the more immediate past to appreciate the impact of ideas on events, and by implication, how historical biography has been influenced by thinking. In the late nineteenth century Darwin stood forth as the dominant scientific figure. When "the vogue of Social Darwinism" as Richard Hofstadter has phrased it, passed, his disciples continued to fight a rear-guard action, only to succumb to the will of pragmatism represented best perhaps by the thinking of William James. "History, Hubris and the Heisenberg Principle" takes up the issue of how a principle derived from physics may be applied to historical biography, rendering that genre less deliberately subjective and therefore more scientifically defensible. "Theodore Roosevelt's Social Darwinism And Views on Imperialism" in turn examines in some depth the conflict between traditional values which have been asserted over the centuries and the contentions of Herbert Spencer and William Graham Sumner, hard line Darwinists, who argued that progress is achieved only through struggle for survival. Roosevelt proves to be a prime example of a personal inner contention between new and old ways of thinking and acting morally both in private life and in the discharge of public responsibilities. The interfacing of science and biography becomes thereby more readily understood and this is well to bear in mind in the uses of biography for the study of history.

WERNER HEISENBERG

I

The Application of Scientific Principles to past human experience, though it can promise much by way of historical appreciations, must proceed, none the less, with cautious selectivity. The tools of the historian are many and varied. The increasingly scientific temper of the modern age has affected the understanding of history and has added significantly to methods and procedures which historians reliably use. Yet science has been made to do service to history rather than absorbing that essentially humanistic discipline. History remains, in consequence, an account of man in all his variations, based on as many different methods. In the application of a specific scientific principle to a particular historical problem the historian does well to assume a basic laboratory attitude. He is engaged in a real experiment in which the results obtained are generally but not always predictable. The experiment is conducted to achieve the more exact definition of the condition involved, to refine a principle ever more closely, or to refute a proposition—all of which, for the historian, can be translated as a fuller understanding of the past. By applying the Heisenberg Principle of Uncertainty to the hubris of Theodore Roosevelt over the last ten years of his life a test case can be developed which may or may not—for the spirit of the inquiry must be preserved—lead to a more informed view of Roosevelt's post-presidential years. At the same time, and underlying the experiment, the uses of a scientific method when related to history in general and to biography as history in particular will receive some elucidation.[1]

Taking leave of the presidency in March, 1909, Theodore Roosevelt possessed hubris unlimited. As the youngest man to have become president his efforts in office had been altogether successful. Failures, as witnessed in his inability to achieve a downward revision of the tariff, and mistakes, including his handling of the Brownsville episode and his response to the Panic of 1907, were more than offset, both in his own view and in the nation's estimate of his stewardship, by that series of triumphs which were his in domestic matters and foreign affairs. He faced his post-presidential future, in consequence, with an assertive self-confidence, an attitude lightly worn but deeply embedded. After all, had he not set the nation on a new Progressive course which his successors would do well to follow, and had he not placed America in the front rank of the nations of the world, from which position it could hardly retreat?

The frustrations and failures of Roosevelt's post-presidential career therefore were hardly predictable. His own devotion to the Progressive cause splintered the Republican Party to which he had been singularly faithful over three decades, while the success of Woodrow Wilson as a Democratic Party reformer seemed to dull the luster of Progressivism for him. The onset of World War I at just about the time Wilson's reform program came to a peak no doubt accounted for some of Roosevelt's lessening concern for rights at home and his increasing commitment to The Right abroad. In any case, the hubris of his Progressive faith was lost, never to be rekindled. In similar fashion the astonishing confidence he had exhibited in what he termed "the world movement"—the spread of the so-called superior nations over the undeveloped reaches of the earth—World War I shattered totally. Once the imperialist Powers became locked in their dance of death, Western imperialism had signed the warrant of its own demise. By 1918 Theodore Roosevelt's hubris was deflated, incongruous in a world grim with destruction, defeat and death. Roosevelt was aware of this and disturbed. Confidence in himself and in his political prescriptions had been the stock in trade of his success as a public man. Hubris had succumbed to forces much larger than Roosevelt, or any man. True to his instinct, he began to indulge in demands for a highly nationalistic post-war world, uttering his nostrums with an undeniably hubristic inflexion. But death intervened.[2]

II

Of the diverse historical subjects to which the Heisenberg Principle might be applied, biography is one of the most promising. In consistency with the large outlines of the quantum theory, the historian attempts to measure the position and the momentum of an object. The public life of an important individual is much easier to associate mentally with an "object" and thus somewhat easier to deal with experimentally, than a system of ideas or a major historical movement. For the purposes at hand it becomes unnecessary to give an exact formulation of Heisenberg's Principle; the language in which it is stated is highly technical. The spirit of the Principle is an easier matter.[3] Essentially it is that there are real limitations to the accuracy with which a physical condition can be described. This comes about, not because of error which may arise due to faulty measuring apparatus, much less to improper techniques, but because of the practical impossibility of simultaneously stating the exact position and momentum of the object in question. The reason for this is the aspect which so intrigues the historian inasmuch as it brings him face to face with the perennial problem of historical subjectivity, and this in a curious and unsuspected way. Specifically, a rigorous use of the Heisenberg Principle would show that the position of the object to be measured may be stated as accurately as we choose but there is sacrificed, by a compensatory amount, the possibility of measuring precisely the momentum of the object. Taking this reasoning one step further, it can be seen that if the position of the object is measured with perfect accuracy, the possibility of making any accurate measurement of its momentum approaches zero. A perfect measurement of position entails less than a perfect assessment of momentum.[4] Rendering the Principle and its application to the problem of historical judgments can be done fairly simply, and with a degree of relevance, if it be kept in mind that for the scientist momentum includes both velocity, i.e., speed in a specific direction, and mass, or the historical "weightiness" of the object. If the historian prefers to give a full and final judgment as to the attitude(s) of the biographical object at a given time, then velocity (energies expanded) and mass (thoughts and actions leading to the position being evaluated) must suffer some inaccuracy of statement. If, however, the historian is judging momentum, then positions along the way will be somewhat blurred. Perhaps all this can be better appreciated by reverting to the world of the physicist momentarily, because its justification is to be found in an analysis of the meaning of our conceptions of the physical world stimulated by Einstein's relativity theory. To the scientist, a body or object, has position or momentum only in so far as either of these qualities can be measured. If momentum alone is measured, for example, the object lacks position as scientifically determined. Of course the reverse of this analysis also applies. The argument can now lead back to possible historical utility. Historians, depending on their purpose and methods, tend either to write about position or momentum. As a matter not of style alone, historians pass back and forth between stressing the processes of historical change or descriptions of a past which is more or less fixed. Perhaps it can even be suggested that the tendency to proceed in such a fashion is a necessary elucidation of what the quantum theory has been saying about the character and structure of the atom over the past several decades, though so broad a claim is beyond the intention of the present essay. What is worth noting, however, is that the historian does tend to emphasize either position or momentum in writing, and by choosing one or the other brings a kind of inevitable subjectiveness to his work. This is not the conventional subjectivity dictated by a rooted prejudice or principle but a logical, scientific subjectiveness.

In attempting to transcribe a concept such as Heisenberg's Principle to historical investigations one or more caveats are in order. Sustained effort may be required to think consistently of human actions, with all their subtleties and shadings of motivation and unpredictability of consequences, as the "object" of an experiment, while the measurement of either position or momentum, rendered in prose rather than mathematics, obscures the scientific lines along which experiments conventionally proceed. Since the Heisenberg Principle holds that in the laboratory objects of large mass can be measured with greater accuracy than objects of less weight, the total life of the biographical subject should be thought of in terms of a greater mass while the increasingly more specific thoughts, motivations, and actions of the subject, since they represent matter of less moment, become correspondingly difficult to assess. At least with regard to the total biography the scientist would say, applying the Heisenberg Principle, that there will be no intrinsic limitation to measuring the object of the greater mass, although the actual evaluation, which means coming to some final assessment of the historical significance of the biographical subject, may be difficult to make. This is a proposition to which historians would subscribe, quite apart from the Heisenberg Principle, for few considerations are more fiercely debated than the reputations of many leading historical personages, Theodore Roosevelt among them. This proposition is, none the less, a partial and qualitative statement of the content of the Heisenberg Principle, and one that makes sense.

Furthermore, few if any reputable historical studies deal exclusively with position as opposed to momentum. But depending on what the author is seeking to do, the strong probability exists that his work will examine position at the expense of action, or unfold action while neglecting position to some degree. One may also have to allow that the historian, dealing with human affairs, will have greater difficulty in suppressing enthusiasm for or condemnation of the people and events being dealt with than his scientific counterpart. History, at most, is a social science, though for many it remains identified with philosophy and literature and the social accents can not be muted in deference to science. History, at least, by treating a biographical subject underlines the intensely human side of the past. "Read no history; nothing but biography," Disraeli once advised, "for that is life without theory." The hubris of Theodore Roosevelt, as it played itself out from 1909 to 1919, is an intensely human "object" to put to the test of the theory implicit in Heisenberg's Principle.

III

Given the experimental nature of this inquiry, deliberately separating Roosevelt's domestic outlook from his foreign policy attitudes during the post-presidential years is warranted by the analysis. Such a division is also happily consistent with Roosevelt's career after 1909 so that the requirements of the analysis place no particular strain on the facts.[5] In the discussion which follows, Roosevelt's altering position and the rise and fall and rise again of his momentum respecting national politics will be treated initially. Some consideration will then be given his attitudes and actions in international affairs.

At first, in 1909, Roosevelt's position on the state of the nation at home can be readily defined, for in departing from the presidency his political life had come to a virtual standstill. Lacking momentum, his position was clear. President Taft had been his personal choice to carry on the reform program of Republican Progressivism and he enjoyed Roosevelt's complete support. By purposefully removing himself from the domestic scene through the device of an Afro-European tour in 1909-1910 he was able to maintain this uncharacteristic posture of inaction. But much was occurring while the ex-President was out of the United States and virtually incommunicado which was likely to encourage a change in his support of the Taft administration. The President handled the tariff fight very badly and earned Roosevelt's scorn for his ineptitude. Taft's apparent willingness to protect some anti-conservationists in his cabinet Roosevelt read as betrayal. While in Africa and even after moving on to Europe he had an incomplete and jaundiced account of Taft's work in office, all of which eroded his support of the incumbent administration. Yet no sooner did Roosevelt begin to react to presidential policies than his position becomes increasingly difficult to define. The Heisenberg Principle, in other words, may be invoked. As Roosevelt at first preferred to go slowly and was reluctant to condemn his old friend, his position remained accurately definable for that long a time. Not only was he unwilling to attack Taft from Europe but he imposed his own sixty-day moratorium on any public pronouncements after he had returned to the United States. By the end of the summer, however, he had taken up a new position. His speech, "The New Nationalism," delivered at Osawatomie, Kansas, August 31, 1910, is proof of this. Yet how and why had he taken this new policy position? He had read Herbert Croly's *The Promise of American Life*, he brooded over Taft's apparent betrayal, he listened to many who urged him to return to active public life to serve and save the cause of reform under Republican auspices. All the while these various motivations and appeals were agitating him there were increasing signs that his next announcement would herald a new position. But there is no way to define that changing attitude on a day to day, week to week, or issue to issue, purpose to purpose basis. Indeed, the historian is anxious to assess the speed and significance of Roosevelt's views as they reach out for fresh statement in the Osawatomie speech. Is the historian not also discouraged from defining such alterations in position from mid-June to the end of August because he is intent on measuring the momentum (velocity and mass) of Roosevelt's thinking? It can be objected that during these same weeks change was what was historically relevant, but may this not also be thus because position measurement is precluded by ongoing momentum? By concentrating on momentum, position is sacrificed not only because it is unimportant but because it is not precisely measurable. Moreover, is it not unimportant exactly because it is not precisely measurable?[6]

The mid-term elections of 1910 which produced a stunning defeat for Congressional Republicans imposed a mood of gloomy silence on Roosevelt. His hubris was temporarily overmastered. Conservative Republicans in Congress had been defeated in large numbers, the Progressive wing had enhanced its party strength, but the party itself appeared more deeply divided than ever. Consequently Roosevelt's public position was susceptible to meaningful definition: a sullen and suspicious resentment of Taft as the President proceeded to deal with treaties for the arbitration of international disputes, the conservation of natural resources, and a decision to bring a suit against the United States Steel Corporation charging violation of the anti-trust laws. From such a set attitude of disdain for Taft's moves, Roosevelt was to generate fresh momentum. Taft's trust busting was opposed to the philosophy of the New Nationalism which looked upon bigness as the result of a natural, evolutionary growth, to be regulated by a powerful central government for the common good. The historian's use of Heisenberg's Principle may now be directly challenged. At this juncture in Roosevelt's career both position and momentum become the object of inquiry and the historian is bent on assessing both. But will he? Can he? Knowing in advance that Roosevelt's announcement for the presidency will challenge Taft and that his position will be one of radical Progressivism, the political steps taken to implement this decision demand attention. Fighting for votes in the primary elections as well as appealing for broad public support across the nation in anticipation of the Republican National Convention was the only way out of the political dilemma to which Roosevelt's hubris had led him. But why will the historian concentrate on the fight for political life? Because momentum makes it both impossible and unimportant to measure position. The momentum accelerated with Roosevelt's series of triumphs in the primaries and his rejection by the Republican Convention, whereupon he formed his own party, the Bull Moose Party, as history built to a climax. The fascination lies in Roosevelt's actions, his daring, his recklessness perhaps, but his position at a given time, even if measurable, would be of small matter to the historical outcome. Yet Roosevelt paused momentarily to define his own views. In his "Confession of Faith" before the Bull Moose convention he spelled out, even as he poured out, his convictions. Momentum was temporarily lost as definition became imperative in preparation for the moves to be next taken. Thereafter Roosevelt's speeches were frenzied until Taft tended to drop from the race. Roosevelt and Wilson then began to address themselves more and more to the issues. At this point, action again seems less appealing to the interested student than the opportunity to pause and consider critically the opposing philosophies of the New Nationalism and Wilson's New Freedom. Momentum fades in importance once the outlook of the opposing candidates can be contrasted and compared. This would appear to reaffirm the Heisenberg Principle, as would interpretative judgments placed on the outcome of the election itself. Certainly Roosevelt was already assessing the future of Progressivism in the wake of his defeat in November, 1912. His subsequent rejection of Progressivism seems to bear this out. Indeed, the historian, reflecting on the career of the Bull Moose, pays little heed to the gradual alterations in Roosevelt's attitude, concerned as he is to make some meaningful summary of the electoral outcomes of 1912.[7]

The coming of World War I had a profoundly disturbing impact on Theodore Roosevelt because it forced him to abandon one of the principles he cherished most as a public man. Roosevelt believed in race superiority. He further held such superiority to be acquired rather than innate insofar as the Western white race was concerned, though this qualification of his racism seems to have had as little effect on his policies as it has had on historians who have written about him. Roosevelt saw all modern history in terms of the spread of the superior European peoples across the world. This movement constituted progress, an overall upgrading of the level of civilization for the peoples involved—conqueror and conquered alike—and he therefore praised the dramatic resurgence of Western imperialism in the late nineteenth century. His "world movement" thesis, as he called this version of history since 1500, presupposed that the advanced nations would be wise enough to avoid a major conflict among themselves. At times, in fact, Roosevelt believed that the twentieth century would witness no great wars because the various Powers possessed weapons of destruction which had grown too terrible to use. A good deal of his diplomacy as president, well exemplified by his promotion of the Peace Treaty of Portsmouth ending the Russo-Japanese War and his role at the Algeciras Conference which defused an explosive confrontation between France and Germany in North Africa, was intended to reduce tensions between the Powers. Yet he continued to entertain misgivings about general treaties of arbitration down to 1914, a sure sign that the practical statesmanship in his outlook often took precedence over the historical theorist.[8]

Such particularization of Roosevelt's views only tends to stress that his position anent the international situation of the pre-1914 years was that much easier to measure because his world movement philosophy was fixed in his mind. Like the majority of his generation he did not foresee the deepening calamity of the Great War, just as his ongoing philosophy of history had no place for a war to the death among the superior nations. The expansive energies of these nations as expressed in their technological skills, their political stability, and their "fighting edge" had in the past promoted the welfare of mankind in Roosevelt's estimate; now these same energies were to clash on a darkling plain. The world movement in 1914 had indeed run on its own sword. Roosevelt's fixed position, in consequence, began to experience strong fluctuations, so violent in fact that the momentum engendered carried him rapidly away from internationalism and in the direction of a super-nationalism which characterized his outlook at the time of his death in 1919.[9]

When the myth of a world made necessarily better by the expansion of the great Western nations died, it died hard for Roosevelt. His initial reaction to the German march across Belgium in 1914 was that small countries might well be trampled on "when giants are engaged in a death struggle." This was his position in the late summer of 1914. Once the war settled down to the gruesome reality which was the Western Front, the ex-president moved gradually from being neutral to asserting that neutrality was not morally possible when the issue became one of justice. The immorality of the German thrust through Belgium contrasted sharply in his mind with the rectitude of Britain's decision to come to the aid of its ally, France, and to the side which espoused justice for Belgium. By early 1915 Roosevelt had come out openly against Germany. The sinking of the Lusitania in May of that year confirmed him in his judgment. In the practical order, being anti-German was tanta-mount to being pro-Ally, and in Roosevelt's case, being especially pro-British to all outward appearances. In essence, however, he had simply become an exaggerated nationalist, preferring American national interest to any other consideration, and secondarily, preferring the interests of those Powers friendly to the United States because they were less likely to collide with the interests of his own country. By 1918 Roosevelt could observe: "Nationalism is the key-note of my attitude. . . . I have never known an internationalist who was worth his salt." The effects of all this on Roosevelt's hubris were not entirely negative for he asserted his new beliefs with the same confidence as when in previous years he had spoken in tribute to the world movement.

How does Heisenberg's Principle apply to this side of Theodore Roosevelt's post-presidential career? The experiment, honestly conducted, reveals that the historian is able to measure both position and momentum, largely because Roosevelt moved deliberately from point to new point in his change of front. Is this not possible, in part at least, because one of the conditions present in his post-presidential Progressive role was not at all present in his attitude toward World War I? In the former instance, he was still very much politically alive and capable of exerting great influence on the outcome of events; in the latter, his star had clearly begun to set, especially after 1916. Because Roosevelt was not capable of wielding power in his later years he was free to move as he did from point to new point until he found a final fixed position, the 180° opposite of his world movement philosophy. What it may come down to is this. Both position and momentum can be measured, but with Roosevelt out of power the meaningfulness he possessed for history was reduced commensurately. This arises not because of the subjectivity of the observer but because of the phenomenon observed in the experiment. At this stage the historian of American affairs is rightly interested in Wilson, not Roosevelt. History imposes this on him.

IV

Like all theories which propose to explain history or account for historical interpretations, the Heisenberg Principle of Uncertainty would seem to fit some circumstances better than others. But suggestions as to the more appropriate circumstances are here clearly called for. The phenomena which historians usually study exhibit all the quantum propositions: position, velocity, and mass. The phenomena in question are worthy of serious consideration largely because they can be shown to be historically important. Example A: Roosevelt's attitude toward

Progressivism was vital to the whole movement; he was essential to it. Thus the focus is on what he influenced directly and substantially. Example B: Roosevelt's words and actions regarding World War I appear as trifles by comparison, and were in fact inconsequential by any fair judgment of the situation. In historical phenomena like Example A, therefore, the precise simultaneous measurement of position and momentum is not possible because the extraneous fact of historical value requires the student to concentrate on the worthwhile, be it position or momentum. In phenomena like Example B, the experiment may be successful in measuring position and momentum because neither is very important to the outcomes of history, as the historian realizes in approaching Theodore Roosevelt's post-presidential career. In historical studies, in other words, because they deal with human events an element may be said to be present which is missing in the experiment of the laboratory scientist. Perhaps this missing factor can be represented suggestively by the term "atmosphere," the atmosphere in which all historical experiment is conducted. Unlike a high vacuum laboratory system in which air can be controlled to reduce to negligibility its effects on the inquiry, the historian's world is not susceptible to a high vacuum equivalency. Paradoxically the outcomes of history which the historian has knowledge of renders Heisenberg's Principle applicable in Example A but tends to irrelevancy in cases akin to Example B. This consideration may help to explain why the historian, in dealing with matters of great moment, inclines to concentrate on position at the expense of momentum, or vice versa. His choice, while it will be in some sense a form of conventional subjectivity, will find itself re-enforced, confirmed, and made logically persuasive by the operation of the Heisenberg Principle of Uncertainty.

NOTES

1. Percy W. Bridgman in *Reflections of a Physicist* (New York: Philosophical Library, 1950) and *The Way Things Are* (Cambridge: Harvard University Press, 1959) discusses certain implications of Heisenberg's Principle for man in society.
2. The Roosevelt bibliography used in this essay concentrates on the major

scholarly biographies and special studies, including Henry F. Pringle, Theodore Roosevelt (New York: Harcourt Brace, 1931), W. H. Harbaugh, *The Life and Times of Theodore Roosevelt*, rev. ed. (New York: Collier, 1963), G.W. Chessman, *Theodore Roosevelt and the Politics of Power* (Boston: Little Brown, 1969), and George E. Mowry, *Theodore Roosevelt and the Progressive Movement* (Madison: University of Wisconsin Press, 1946).

3. Bridgman, *Reflections of a Physicist*, pp. 81–103.
4. This is not intended as a purely scientific statement but simply to indicate in a general way the nature of the scientific problem.
5. See for example, Harbaugh, in which he discusses Progressivism in Part Four (five chapters) and World War I in Part Five (four chapters); in Chessman's briefer study Chapter VII deals with Progressivism and Chapter VIII with World War I. Pringle, pp. 497–606, follows much the same pattern.
6. Chessman, pp. 159–169. This is what Harbaugh is concerned with as well, Harbaugh, pp. 355–401. Pringle does a better job of trying to keep a focus on both position and momentum, Pringle, especially pp. 540–571; even so, momentum tends to dominate his account. However, Mowry, pp. 188–200, 212–214, though his analysis is more concentrated, is more concerned with momentum; he pauses only occasionally to give attention to position.
7. Harbaugh, pp. 410–423; Chessman, pp. 184–186; Mowry, pp. 320ff. See as well John M. Blum, *The Republican Roosevelt*, rev. ed. (New York: Atheneum, 1969), pp. 142–161 for the historian's tendency to evaluate position. As Arthur Link has written in his account of Roosevelt and the Progressive Movement which underscores the problem of assessing momentum, "It is impossible to measure the influence of *The Promise of American Life* [by Herbert Croly] in Roosevelt's developing Progressivism." Link, *Woodrow Wilson and the Progressive Era* (New York: Harper and Row, 1954), pp. 19ff.
8. See my *Theodore Roosevelt Confident Imperalist* (Philadelphia: University of Pennsylvania Press, 1968), passim, for a discussion of the interplay of theory and practicality in Roosevelt's imperialism.
9. See especially Harbaugh, pp. 455–468; Mowry, pp. 367–381.

THEODORE ROOSEVELT

Few public men of his time, and his times were ripe with evolutionary thought, appeared more strikingly Darwinist than did Theodore Roosevelt. In his own remarkable physical transformation and achievement he seemed to embody the truth of "root, hog, or die." Survival itself for him on many occasions, whether the threat was a Dakota blizzard or gun-shot wounds as those received in the presidential campaign of 1912, had been due in no small degree to his bodily strength and stamina. Roosevelt's often expressed opinions on domestic and foreign issues continue the outline of a man influenced by the elementary propositions associated with natural selection; his speeches and writings bristle with the catch-phrases of this tough-mindedness. The policies of Theodore Roosevelt as a public man consequently were judged by many of his contemporaries and critics as Darwinist. Considering the place of evolution in American intellectual growth this estimate is neither surprising nor unwarranted. Publication of *The Origin of Species* (1859) and the birth of Roosevelt (1858) barely failed to coincide and throughout most of his lifetime the evolutionary thesis as applied to individuals, and later to groups, continued to enjoy a considerable vogue. The social milieu in which Roosevelt moved and with which he came to share convictions was permeated with Darwinism. At Harvard College in the 1870s perhaps such views did not go wholly unchallenged; nevertheless the curriculum young Roosevelt pursued there offered little criticism of the principle of progress through evolution. Later, under John W. Burgess, whose teaching of law and government at Columbia University Law School presupposed that only a few races were fit to rule, his Darwinism received a positive stimulus. And then the world as Roosevelt after-wards met it, in characteristic head-on fashion, included more than enough examples in economic and political pursuits to reassure him that competition was a natural and a potent force, perhaps even a decisive one, in individual and group achievement.

There is small question that Theodore Roosevelt was an evolutionist of some sort.[1] The label attaches easily because of his insistence that struggle was a means of progress, that there were superior and inferior peoples possessing differing responsibilities and privileges, that force was frequently needed to accomplish good among men as among nations; all these ideas and more, were usually rendered with dramatic, pungent confidence. The pertinent consideration is the kind of evolutionist he was and the persuasions which thus were wrought upon him and his policies. There is the temptation to ask how much the Rooseveltian temper was responsible for the evolutionary phrases he employed, how much his choice of language was an accurate index to an authentic attitude toward evolution as a rationale of history. The Darwinist label can be misleading, confirming the distortion to the popular image Roosevelt created of himself, and making difficult a serious effort to understand the influence of evolutionary ideas on his public policies. Of these policies none seemed more conventionally Darwinist in mood and purpose than his imperialism, and more specifically the rights and duties of conquering and conquered races. The imperialist situation of the late XIXth and early XXth centuries contained most of the ingredients likely to appeal to a mind sympathetic with the philosophy of natural selection, based as it was on force and involving competition in obvious form, contrasting superior and backward peoples, white and non-white, European and non-European, and producing what most western observers insisted was progress for mankind. Yet neither Roosevelt's policy of imperialism nor the explanation he chose to make of it mirror in life-like fashion the commonly conceived dimensions of social Darwinism. The evolutionary influence is present, but it is there in competition with other persuasive ideas. As his imperialism unfolded there appeared a continuous and critical modification of the evolutionary thesis: the ethical and political legacies bequeathed him by the Western tradition, an American sense of practicality, the Social Gospel of XIXth-century Protestantism, each offered its peculiar challenge.

In defining the kind of evolutionary principle Roosevelt subscribed to, the difficulty is not confined to the competition of ideas in what has been termed Roosevelt's "eclectic intellectual home."[2] There is also the problem of growth or change in the public man. Can the views espoused in 1895 be linked validly to the policies of 1905, for example; and if so, with what qualifications? Ordinarily the judgments of a statesman may be expected to alter, perhaps drastically, after years of exposure to political and diplomatic situations constantly in flux. Theodore Roosevelt was more of an exception to that rule than most men, and with regard to the place of Darwinism in his outlook, he was entirely exceptional. Writing in 1895 he noted that "the rivalry of natural selection is but one of the features of progress." Among others and by all odds the most important was what he spoke of as *character,* an attribute not affected by rivalry in nature.[3] In the Romanes Lecture for 1910, *character,* not force, was urged by him as the solution of national and international problems alike.[4] Recalling his Harvard days in his *Autobiography* which came out in 1913, Roosevelt was prompted to remark ruefully on the almost total absence of any teaching of the "need of collective action and collective responsibility."[5] One of his last essays, "The Origin and Evolution of Life," which appeared in *The Outlook* in 1918, contained a final rejection of unqualified evolution as a satisfying explanation of man in society.[6] If there was a change through the years in Roosevelt's appreciation of the place and purpose of evolution it was increasing certainty that it was inadequate when its laws were applied to social conditions.

Yet there is more in Roosevelt's reaction to the evolutionary thesis than simple rejection or complete surrender since he appears to have been both an advocate and an opponent of the application of Darwin's postulates to society. Behind appearances lies the reality of fundamental evolutionary propositions working, in competition with other principles to which he was committed, to give shape and direction to convictions on a myriad of issues. There were few things in the world of Theodore Roosevelt of which he was more convinced than the justice and the good fortune of world domination by the western races. In the apologia he offered for imperialism were mingled elements of the pragmatic and the moral, of history and Darwinism. Roosevelt presented himself as a statesman who insisted upon force to pacify the Philippines as required by the world situation and to police the Caribbean in the interests of his own country; at the same time he labored diligently for the welfare of backward races and the education of these people in the form and spirit of free government, calling upon the finest of his fellow Americans to assist him in this endeavor. If evolution in Roosevelt's imperialist thought is not its sole and underlying principle, it nonetheless is a singularly valuable guideline for understanding Roosevelt the Imperialist, whose confidence in the salutary effects of the world movement was predicated on the total of his intellectual heritage.[7]

Charles Darwin was to Theodore Roosevelt both a revolutionary and a seminal thinker. Darwin, along with Huxley, "succeeded in effecting a complete revolution in the thought of an age"[8] so that now "the acceptance of the fundamental truths of evolution are quite as necessary to sound scientific thought as the acceptance of the fundamental truths of the solar system."[9] Yet Roosevelt inclined to set Darwin and his work in an historical perspective. Writing to Oliver Wendell Holmes, Jr. in 1904, he allowed that Darwin was "the chief factor in working a tremendous revolution," but went on to express the opinion that in the future Darwin would be read "just as we read Lucretius now; that is, because of the interest attaching to his position in history, in spite of the fact that his own work will have been superseded by the work of the very men to whom he pointed out the way."[10] Roosevelt believed that Darwin had only opened a new era and that it would fall to others to exploit his contribution in succeeding generations. Thus he was exceedingly anxious to avoid revering Darwin as medieval schoolmen had accepted Aristotle; the consequences would be intellectual stagnation. Such a tendency, he found, already had come about with Darwin and Darwinists in some quarters and the extreme dogmatism resulting he deplored as non-scientific.[11]

Roosevelt's attitude toward Darwinism, however, was not simply that of the man of science who stood ready to reject Darwin or any part of his work should later investigations advance a stronger case. He was always prepared to tailor evolutionary modes of thought whenever they did not fit comfortably with the demands of his total and somewhat varied intellectual heritage. This dual position of scientific detachment and cultural involvement became evident in Roosevelt's first serious consideration of the meaning and implications of evolution for society, his review-essay of *Social Evolution* by Benjamin Kidd, which appeared in *The North American Review* for July 1895 under the title "Social Evolution."

Roosevelt centered his disagreement with Kidd's espousal of social Darwinism on the ground that it was faulty scientific method, reflecting a dangerously narrow orientation, for anyone to argue that the single postulate of natural selection could alone explain social progress. There were other factors, along with a notable body of contrary evidence, to be taken into account. With respect to the several factors which bear a direct influence on social progress Roosevelt took particular issue with Kidd's contention that there was no rational sanction in progress, that "it is a deliberate verdict that the conditions of life in advanced societies of today are without any sanction from reason for the masses of the people."[12] He was quick to object to this because it made out evolution to be materialist, and the sole principle of life as well. "Side by side with the selfish development in life," Roosevelt thought, "there has been almost from the beginning a certain amount of unselfish development too; and in the evolution of humanity the unselfish side has, on the whole, tended steadily to increase at the expense of the selfish, notably in the progressive communities."[13] This is not to deny that in the attainment of progress some individuals were not penalized. "The nations that make the most progress may do so at the expense of ten or fifteen individuals out of a hundred whereas the nations making the least progress or even going backward may sacrifice almost every man out of the hundred."[14] With this reply Roosevelt dismissed the contention that there was no rational sanction in progress. The sanction lay within the progressive community itself where ". . . the conflict between the interests of the individual and the organism of which he is a part . . . is at a minimum."[15] A second factor which he insisted upon for understanding man in society, but which had no place whatsoever in Kidd's discussion, was what he termed *character*. *Character* was a quality not to be confused or identified with reason though by no means was it inimical to reason. Rather than render a definition of *character* he chose to exemplify its meaning. *Character* was unselfishness, courage, devotion to duty, honesty, feelings which often occur "entirely independent of any religious considerations" of a denominational kind, feelings which were in keeping with the nature of man. *Character* was "the woman who watches over the sick child and the soldier who dies at his post."[16] Thus understood, *character* was vital to social progress and so much emphasis was Roosevelt willing to place upon it that he judged it more important than intellect to the person and to the race. "We need intellect," he concluded, "and there is no reason why we should not have it together with *character*; but if we must choose between the two, we choose *character* without a moment's hesitation."[17]

In addition to these considerations which worked to restrain him from adopting a one-dimensional evolutionary frame of reference, there was in Roosevelt's opinion a sizeable body of evidence to under-score how facile an evolutionary oversimplification was. For one thing he could not agree that if man were left to himself and presumably were guided by his reason "the average of each generation would continually tend to fall below the average of the generation which preceded it."[18] . . . [This] is undoubtedly true of the world, taken as a whole. It is in all probability entirely false of the highest sections of society. At any rate there are numerous instances where the law does not work. . . . ."[19] More concretely, the hypothesis that progress advanced farthest where competition or rivalry was keenest was not substantiated in his judgment by certain cultural facts. If this were so "the European peoples standing highest in the scale would be the south Italians, the Polish Jews, the people who live in the congested districts of Ireland. As a matter of fact, however, these are precisely the peoples who made the least progress when compared with the dominant strains among, for instance, the English and the Germans."[20] This was not a denial of the function of competition, but an indication that its value could be overstressed when taken as the only consideration, or if the competition were so severe as to wear out the race involved. Respecting the role of competition Roosevelt felt a further distinction had to be made between classes within the same nation or racial group. The leaders of society, philosophers, statesmen, judges, soldiers, successful businessmen, "all these come from the classes where the struggle for the bare means of subsistence is less severe . . . than in the class below. In civilized societies the rivalry of natural selection works against progress."[21] Progress was sustained in such communities because though the least fit survive "they and their children often tend to grow more fit" as they are taught by the superior if less numerous class above them.[22] Taking this argument from a different angle there comes into focus an additional factor militating against the theory of natural selection as the single law of social evolution. Since acquired attributes of *character*, as love, a sense of duty, courage, could be passed along through the efforts of individuals and institutions, through laws and ideals, men could learn from other men, with progress the likely result. Roosevelt had expressed this very conclusion just prior to "Social Evolution" in a review of *National Life and Character*.[23] "Even though the best people of society do not increase as fast as the others," Roosevelt had written, "society progresses, the improvement being due mainly to the transmission of acquired characteristics, a process which in every civilized society operates . . . [against] . . . the baleful law of natural selection. . . ."[24] He was to make use of the same Lamarckian reasoning in "Social Evolution," very plainly because it appealed to him as a way out of the cultural dilemma posed by an unqualified social Darwinism. It was a practical restriction of natural selection in keeping with his reading of history and his commitment to traditional Western morality.

"Social Evolution," written some years before Roosevelt assumed the presidential office, was at most a guarded endorsement of evolutionary principles. In fact, though the author saw no sense in questioning the fundamentals of evolution as scientific facts, he had large and critical reservations concerning the propriety of social applications. Such an approach was at once too simple and too much in conflict with other convictions Roosevelt firmly held. Yet as a practitioner of imperialism many of his policies took on, in his own mind at times and rather more often in the judgment of others, a Darwinist coloration. In the pursuit of empire Roosevelt had not abandoned the tempered philosophical attitude expressed in "Social Evolution," however. Quite the contrary, he was remarkably loyal to it, so much so that "Social Evolution" provides a sure if somewhat generalized guide to understanding the influence of evolution on Roosevelt's imperialist thought and action.

When Theodore Roosevelt brought out *The Winning of the West*, during the decade or so prior to "Social Evolution," he produced, in effect, a study of American imperialism as it had possessed much of the continental mainland. Knowledge of the dynamism of an expanding people gained from this considerable historical investigation enabled him to appreciate more readily the colonialist urge gripping the western world in his own era. Elements of the Darwinist ethic were common to his analysis of the westward moving frontier. Pre-eminent among them was the superior race argument as justification for military conquest and civilian occupation of the land. Roosevelt spoke of war against the savages as "the most ultimately righteous of all wars";[25] he refused to accord to native peoples the "same rules of international morality which obtained between stable and cultured communities."[26] Further, he defended the cruelty inflicted upon the Indians by the conquering race because of "the extraordinary conditions of life on the frontier,"[27] and gloried in the right of conquest itself.[28] The entire conception of his history of the frontier was predicated on the right and necessity of conquest,[29] and on occasion the author digressed to scold those of his readers who refused to acknowledge the applicability of his judgments to the imperialist conditions of the late XIXth century.[30]

Granting the evolutionary ingredients of *The Winning of the West*, the study also revealed the author's belief that expansion by a people must have a purpose outside the process itself, that the "con-quest and settlement by the whites of the Indian lands were necessary to the greatness of the race and to the well-being of civilized mankind."[31] There was involved here not some vague, romanticized notion of "civilization" but specifically the initiation of free government wherein men could learn to rule themselves.[32] This constituted progress in a tangible and worthy sense, for by the successful exercise of self-rule a people displayed *character*, the quality Roosevelt esteemed most highly in men as individuals or in a group. The cruelty, bloodshed or temporary injustice that had to be endured or countenanced to achieve conditions conducive to the growth of self-government, he believed, was worth it.[33] Though the means required might remain starkly brutal, suggestive of the unrelenting operation of the laws of natural selection, the purpose or outcome of the process as interpreted by Roosevelt marked a decided break with a logical social reduction of the tenets of evolution. The Anglo-Americans, after generations of struggle, had reached a level of civilization unequalled in human history because they had acquired the requisite ability for self-rule. In a word, they had come into possession of *character*. *Character* being artificial and not innate meant that western expansion had its justification in the spread of free government so that all might one day enjoy liberty as promised by the nature and history of man.[34]

The total lesson of the West had the same expression in one of Roosevelt's most famous and most widely quoted speeches, "The Strenuous Life" (1899). Perhaps no other single address early in his national career did so much to identify Roosevelt with Darwinism and its code. The speech fairly breathed the hard struggle from which alone progress resulted. Yet in "The Strenuous Life" Roosevelt observed that as the American Civil War was justified by the high purpose of saving the Union, the imperialism of his day was right, for it was "our part . . . in the great work of uplifting mankind," a responsibility America as a nation freely honored.[35]

Theodore Roosevelt was to make imperialist history much as he wrote it. Or perhaps it should be said that as he studied history with the purpose of setting down his judgments of the meaning of the past, he was led to construct a frame of reference which turned out to be a composite of the several faiths he gave his allegiance to. Consider the case of the Philippine Islands, the one great example of American imperialism, and in which Roosevelt took a dominant part. From first to last his way of thinking about the United States position in the Islands did not waver. Put directly, he believed the United States, as one of the superior nations, had an unquestioned right to possess the Philippines; this was an outgrowth of natural selection among races and nations. His view was stated unequivocally in "Expansion and Peace" (1899): "in the long run civilized man finds he can keep the peace only by subduing his barbarian neighbors; for the barbarian will yield only to force."[36] The conquest of the Philippines therefore was vital to world peace (and progress); and its corollary, the suppression of the Aguinaldan insurrection by a like use of force, was equally proper.[37] But associated with the right of conquest was the duty to civilize. "It is, I am sure," Roosevelt told a New York gathering in 1899, "the desire of every American that the people of each island, as rapidly as they show themselves fit for self-government, shall be endowed with a constantly larger measure of self-government."[38] Indeed, with regard to the future of the Philippines under American tutelage Roosevelt's mind sometimes ran to visions:

> . . . we can ultimately help our brethren of the Philippine Islands so far forward on the path of self-government and orderly liberty that that beautiful archipelago shall become a center of civilization for all eastern Asia and the Islands around about.[39]

There was one feature of evolutionary method in Roosevelt's projection of the Filipino movement toward self-government. Reflecting on the achievement of a genius for self-rule by the Anglo-Americans, he was at pains to emphasize that "our people are now successfully governing themselves because for more than a thousand years they have been slowly fitting themselves, sometimes consciously, sometimes unconsciously, toward this end."[40] A similar gradual unfolding of a capacity for self-government was to be expected in the Philippines, and Roosevelt while president would pledge himself on that account to no definite date for granting the Islands their independence.[41] Furthermore a failure by the United States to maintain a firm hold over the area might foster a regression to chaos and savagery.[42] Decline as well as growth was an evolutionary principle which must be respected in the affairs of men.

A more central theme in Roosevelt's consideration of United States involvement in the Philippine Islands was his concern for doing an effective job of preparing the Filipinos for eventual self-government, a purpose he derived from Anglo-American experience. Because he felt strongly that the Filipino people could not work out their own political salvation at that time the Americans were correct in staying in the Islands.[43] But "I would certainly try to prove to the islanders," he commented to one friend in 1900, "that we intend not merely to treat them well but to give them a constantly increasing measure of self-government, and we should be only too delighted when they are able to stand alone."[44] Roosevelt's contact with the realities of the situation was evident in his recognition that in the Philippines as elsewhere, the source and beginning of true self-government were to be found on the local level. There is where it must start, where it must be carefully nurtured, where it was to be tested and where it would ultimately succeed or fail.[45] The achievement of self-rule by the Filipinos, the acquisition of that quality of *character*, was Roosevelt's critical concern.[46] As he wrote pointedly to Charles W. Eliot in direct reference to the political difficulties in the Philippines ". . . freedom does not mean absence of all restraint. It merely means the substitution of self-restraint for external restraint."[47] The sincerity of this purpose can be gauged by Roosevelt's openly expressed pride and pleasure that the Filipino democratic experiment was going so well while he remained in the presidency. Not only did it compare favorably with what the English were doing in India and Egypt or with the French in North Africa[48] but there were reasons to hope that "within a generation the time will arrive when the Philippines can decide for themselves whether it is well for them to become independent."[49] If America adopted a paternal attitude it was a kindly paternalism[50] which in combination with her "spirit of genuine disinterestedness, of genuine and single-minded purpose to benefit the islanders" had enabled her to achieve considerable success in helping the Filipinos realize an increasing political maturity.[51]

One of the arresting qualities of Roosevelt's imperialist thought was that in spite of disparate sources which at times gave rise to conflicts, it had an integrated rationale discernible throughout. This was so because Roosevelt accepted as entirely consistent an attitude of race superiority and the responsibility of superior peoples for spreading civilization and acting generally in the interests of mankind.[52] Some races were, in his view, inferior and had to be treated thus.[53] This integrated rationale should not be taken to imply that Roosevelt was completely serene as an active imperialist, or that he never doubted the practicality of his philosophy, or that his doubts were easily dismissed. Particularly after he had had everyday experience with the implementation of his imperialist principles, misgivings arose and persisted.[54] An instructive example was Roosevelt's response to Egyptian nationalism with which he came face to face while on a visit to that country in 1910; it bore witness to the confusion possible when theory was applied to a live political situation. In his speeches there he encouraged Egyptians to become "men who will be able to shift for themselves, to help themselves and to help others, fully independent of all matters connected with the Government." At the same time he demanded that the British as the superior people ought either to govern effectively or to get out of Egypt. The antithesis was obvious enough to the Egyptians who heard him, but in Roosevelt's own mind his rationale remained intact; conflict arose because of the refusal of some men to accept his superior race thesis.[55]

In the Caribbean, where his policies had lasting effect as, with the world situation, a synthesis of Imperialism and Democracy, or Imperialism and Civilization, Roosevelt usually was able to manage. Thus though he favored the independence of Cuba before the outbreak of the Spanish War,[56] he came to understand that Cubans were not then prepared by their history or culture for a democracy, American style. But in remaining temporarily in Cuba as the United States did, following the end of hostilities, the purpose was only to "establish civil order" and "lay the foundations of self-government and prosperity"[57] with affairs so far as possible under existing conditions being conducted by the Cuban people themselves.[58] When self-rule proved to work poorly Roosevelt saw it as the clear duty of a superior people for the United States to provide protection and direction to the foundering Cubans,[59] though he "loathed the thought of assuming any control over the islands."[60] In like fashion the American acquisition of the Panama Canal rights evinced Roosevelt's willingness to take a tough line toward Colombia in the name of progress for mankind.[61]

The interplay of might and right was a prominent aspect generally of Big Stick Diplomacy and as such revealed both the Darwinist and the moral attributes of Roosevelt's policies. In 1904 in Santo Domingo, for example, he noted that "a hundred years of freedom so far from teaching the Santo Domingans how to enjoy freedom and turn it to good account, has resulted so badly that society is on the point of dissolution," and American intervention was required for the safety of Santo Domingo and the hemisphere.[62] Santo Domingans, Venezuelans, Colombians—it made no difference to Roosevelt,[63] who lumped them together with other backward peoples.[64] Regarding internal problems perennial in Haiti, some years after Roosevelt left the presidency, he pointed to the failure of self-rule there as typical of all backward races. The reason was simple and simply stated. Democracy was "much the highest ideal of government" and the Haitians were "preposterously unfit" to exercise it.[65]

The Romanes Lecture for 1910, which Lord Curzon, Chancellor of Oxford University, had invited Theodore Roosevelt to deliver, was entitled "Biological Analogies in History." For an awareness of evolution in Roosevelt's considered judgment of history and its influence on his imperialist philosophy the address is of unique value. Coming after the presidential years, the power years when he frequently acted like a Darwinist in imperial matters, years likely to affect his reflections on history, "Biological Analogies in History" nevertheless strictly qualified the role of evolution in human affairs.

Much of this lecture suggested a mind conversant with the phenomena of nature to be expected of an ardent and life-long naturalist, and of course one sympathetic with the general propositions of evolutionary science. As Roosevelt observed early in the address, "he who would fully treat of man must know at least something of biology . . . and especially of that science of evolution inseparably connected with the great name of Darwin."[66] The definition and use of terms as "new species," "extinction of species," "specialization" were in keeping with an organic notion of life, physical and social, between which there were certain parallels.

As in biology, so in human history, a new form may result from the specialization of a long existing and hitherto very slowly changing generalized or non-specialized form; as, for instance, occurs when a barbaric race from a variety of causes suddenly develops a more complex cultivation and civilization. This is what occurred, for instance, in western Europe during the centuries of the Teutonic and later the Scandinavian overflows from the north.[67]

Since this parallel applied to death as to life and growth, the analogy was, as it were, complete.[68] With regard to the death of a civilization Roosevelt recognized certain differences, which were also familiar to the biological order. Ancient Babylon and Nineveh as well as the New World Indians disappeared whereas the Roman way never became extinct in blood or culture because much of it was successfully transmitted to the barbarians and survived with them in an altered form.[69]

Despite this definite biological characteristic, Roosevelt agreed with both anthropologists and historians as to "how artificial most great nationalities are and how loose the terminology employed to describe them."[70] He went on to offer his own judgment that "most of the great civilizations which have developed a high civilization and have played a dominant part in the world have been, and are, artificial, not merely in social structure but in the sense of including totally different types. A great nation rarely belongs to any one race. . . ."[71] The existence and importance of race, "the half dozen great ethnic divisions of mankind,"[72] he was prepared to admit, though ethnic divisions as such had not normally remained unified and had not produced cultures. Again there is in evidence a tension, frequently encountered in Roosevelt's imperialism, provoked by the conflict between an evolutionary explanation of man and other meanings which history and tradition provided him. That Roosevelt acquitted evolution, standing alone, to be unconvincing is demonstrated by the concluding portions of "Biological Analogies in History." An emphasis on *character* significantly appeared again. For advice to the contemporary world he drew upon a lesson of the past that "free people can escape being mastered by others only by being able to master themselves. We Americans and you people of the British Isles alike need ever to keep in mind," he went on, "that among the many qualities indispensable to the success of a great democracy, and second only to a high and stern sense of duty, of moral obligation, are self-knowledge and self-mastery."[73] In personal and in national affairs "though intellect stands high, *character* stands higher."[74] It followed then that national problems must be approached in the "spirit of broad humanity, of brotherly kindness, of acceptance of responsibility."[75] Might is not right in the relationship of the conquering and conquered races. "In the long run there can be no justification for one race managing or controlling another unless . . . in the interests and for the benefit of that race."[76] This was the great rule of righteousness which Roosevelt asked the Anglo-Americans to continue to respect, as he felt he had done in his imperialist policies while president.[77]

The steadily more explicit character of Roosevelt's attitude toward evolution, in relationship to the other facets of his intellectual make-up, can be illustrated by contrasting aspects of "Social Evolution" (1895) and "Biological Analogies in History" (1910). In the earlier essay he had written that while the principle of natural selection was "undoubtedly true taken of the world as a whole . . . in all probability [it was] entirely false of the highest sections of society."[78] The implication was that in the physical universe, the realm of matter, evolution was a sound and acceptable theory, but with regard to the conscious world, the human condition, the principle and its corollaries were hardly applicable at all.

In "Biological Analogies in History" this distinction was presumed and treated as fundamental. Roosevelt wove into his discussion the essential difference between material and conscious; between pre-human and human history, between races with blood ties and nations which were artificial creations, between what he knew little of (the remote past) and history he had read in depth. Was his reliance on the evolutionary thesis, in other words, a substitute for knowledge, sincerely enough avowed, but all too likely to be limited and refined by history and tradition, by inherited mores and moral precepts? In both of his major excursions into the world of Darwin, "Social Evolution" and "Biological Analogies in History," Roosevelt assumed, loftily, the unquestionability of evolution as indisputable a fact as the solar system. Yet consistently, as he brought the theory to bear on the real human conditions which he was close to and striving to understand and master, particularly the problems of imperialism, evolution was less and less decisive, even less and less pertinent. It was still later, in his last review-essay, "The Origin and Evolution of Life," that he offered explicit and final reservations regarding the evolutionary hypothesis. Significantly he again dwelled on the fundamental distinction in nature as he interpreted it, the distinction between the conscious and the non-conscious or pre-conscious life forms. "The tracing of an unbroken line of descent from protozoan to Plato," he declared plainly, "does not in any way really explain Plato's consciousness, of which there is no vestige in the protozoan."[79]

Different conclusions can be derived from the refusal of Theodore Roosevelt to hew consistently to a social Darwinist line, given his evolutionary predisposition. It is perhaps worth suggesting that being a statesman he may have embraced some aspects of the doctrine of natural selection out of expediency because they justified actions he judged to be practically in order. This emphasis on business-like practicality is historically American and in many ways typical of Roosevelt.[80] Putting speculation aside, Roosevelt in many of his policies appears as an old-fashioned individualist, a character type well known before the tide of Darwinism began to run high. Darwinism in this light offers parallels more striking than causal. The difficulty with both of these conclusions is that they ignore Roosevelt's deep and continuous involvement with evolution as an historical principle to which his writings attest.

A final appraisal of the influence of Darwinism on Roosevelt and his imperialist philosophy might well settle upon the meaningful distinction drawn between evolution and social Darwinism. It was a distinction Roosevelt himself made and maintained.[81] Thus, in his last essay dealing with natural selection, he spoke of accepting "evolution as a natural law no more disputable than the law of gravity,"[82] and considered the universe as having gone through phases preparatory to the advent of man.[83] But Darwin and Darwinists hardly had all the answers; human consciousness, the creation of man, remained outside the evolutionary law.[84] The ultimate purpose of his imperialism likewise lay beyond the jurisdiction of Darwinism, in the welfare of mankind and the improvement of the lot of the individual. These made up the decisive if not always the most apparent quality of Theodore Roosevelt's imperialist thought and action.

NOTES

1. Only slight attention, and that indirectly, is given Roosevelt's evolutionary disposition in Henry F. Pringle, *Theodore Roosevelt* (New York, 1931) and Lord Charnwood, *Theodore Roosevelt* (Boston, 1923.). Carleton Putnam suggests it in terms of Roosevelt's urge to physical fitness in *Theodore Roosevelt—The Formative Years 1858–1886* (New York, 1958); 224–225; Howard K. Beale sees it largely as part of the race thesis, *Theodore Roosevelt and the Rise of America to World Power* (Baltimore, 1956), 72–74; 160–162; 181. A better characterization of his Darwinism as modified by other factors has been struck by John M. Blum in *The Republican Roosevelt* (Cambridge, Mass., 1954), 22–28; also his essay, "Theodore Roosevelt: Years of Decision," Appendix IV, vol. II, 1484–94, *The Letters of Theodore Roosevelt*, ed. by Elting B. Morison, *et al.* (Cambridge, Mass., 1951–54); hereafter cited as *Letters*. Blum's essay has influenced the recent full length study of Roosevelt, *Power and Responsibility: The Life and Times of Theodore Roosevelt* (New York, 1961) by William Harbaugh. Typical of general commentaries, Richard Hofstader, *Social Darwinism in American Thought 1860–1915* (Philadelphia, 1945) has pointed to Darwinism in Roosevelt's imperialism; see ch. 9, "Racism and Imperialism," 146–173; also Ralph H. Gabriel, *The Course of American Democratic Thought* (New York, 1940), 351–54.
2. Blum, "Theodore Roosevelt: Years of Decision," *loc. cit.*, 1491.
3. Roosevelt, "Social Evolution," *The Works of Theodore Roosevelt*, Memorial

Edition (New York, 1923–26), XIV, 109; 128; hereafter cited as *Works*.

4. "Biological Analogies in History," *Works*, XIV, 102; 104.
5. *Theodore Roosevelt, An Autobiography* (New York, 1913), 25.
6. "The Origin and Evolution of Life," *Works*, XIV, 33.
7. For an interpretation of Roosevelt's imperialism, stressing human values as a criterion for understanding it, see David H. Burton, "Theodore Roosevelt: Confident Imperialist," *Review of Politics* (July 1961), 356–377.
8. "History as Literature," *Works*, XIV, 9–10.
9. "The Foundations of the Nineteenth Century," *ibid.*, XIV, 198.
10. Roosevelt to Oliver Wendell Holmes, Jr., Oct. 21, 1904, Roosevelt *Mss*; to William Allen White, May 21, 1918, *ibid.*; Roosevelt, "The Origin and Evolution of Life," *loc. cit.*, 33.
11. Roosevelt to Francis H. Herrick, Jan. 15, 1912, Roosevelt *Mss*.
12. Benjamin Kidd, *Social Evolution* (New York, 1894), 78. The absence of a rational sanction for progress was the theme of chapter three.
13. Roosevelt, "Social Evolution," *loc. cit.*, 114.
14. *Ibid.*, 113.
15. *Ibid.*
16. *Ibid.*, 119 (italics added).
17. *Ibid.*, 128.
18. Kidd, *op. cit.*, 39.
19. Roosevelt, "Social Evolution," *loc. cit.*, 108.
20. *Ibid.*, 110.
21. *Ibid.*, 112.
22. *Ibid.*
23. This was a book-review of *National Life and Character: A Forecast* by Charles H. Pearson; it appeared in *The Sewanee Review* (August 1894).
24. "National Life and Character," *Works*, XIV, 248–249.
25. Roosevelt, *The Winning of the West* (Allegheny Edition), III, 45.
26. *Ibid.*, III, 45
27. *Ibid.*, II, 147; III, 190–191.
28. *Ibid.*, III, 1.
29. *Ibid.*, I, 1–5 *passim*.
30. *Ibid.*, III, 175–176. The orientation of *The Winning of the West* and some of the evidence offered to argue in favor of it, as well as added discussion, can be found in Roosevelt, *Thomas Hart Benton* (Boston, 1891); see especially, 1–4 *passim*; 51–2; 175–6. This book was first published in 1887.
31. Roosevelt, *The Winning of the West*, III, 175.
32. *Ibid.*, II, 381.
33. *Ibid.*, IV, 218 *passim*.
34. "Bodily vigor is good, and vigor of intellect is even better, but far above both is character; . . . in the long run in the great battle of life, no brilliancy of intellect, no perfection of bodily development, will count when weighed in the balance against that assemblage of virtues, active and passive, of moral qualities, which we group together under the name character." Roosevelt, "Character and Success," *Works*, XV, 496. For a further discussion of the West

in Roosevelt's thought, see David H. Burton, "The Influence of the American West on the Imperialist Philosophy of Theodore Roosevelt," *Arizona and the West* (Spring 1962), 5–26.

35. "The Strenuous Life," *Works*, XV, 267–281.
36. "Expansion and Peace," *ibid.*, XV, 286, 287–289, *passim;* see also "The Copperheads of 1900," *ibid.*, XVI, 499; "First Annual Message," *ibid.*, XVII, 133; Roosevelt to E.O. Wolcott, Sept. 15, 1900, *Letters*, II, 1405.
37. Roosevelt to Charles W. Eliot, Nov. 14, 1900, Roosevelt *Mss.*
38. "America's Part of the World's Work," *Works*, XVI, 475. Roosevelt to H. K. Love, Nov. 24, 1900, Roosevelt *Mss;* to Edward Everett Hale, Dec. 17, 1901, *ibid.*
39. Roosevelt to Raymond Reyes Lala, June 27, 1900, *ibid.*
40. "First Annual Message," *loc. cit.*, 128. "Think of the peoples of Europe stumbling upward through the Dark Ages, and doing much work in the wrong way, sometimes falling back, but ever coming forward again, forward, forward, forward, until our great civilization as we now know it was developed at last out of the struggles and failures and victories of millions of men who dared to do the world's work." Reported in *The New York Herald Tribune* (Oct. 10, 1910); quoted in Beale, *op. cit.*, 77–78; see also Roosevelt to David B. Schneder, June 9, 1905, Roosevelt *Mss;* to Charles D. Willard, April 28, 1911, *Letters*, VII, 250–256.
41. Roosevelt to H. K. Love, Nov. 24, 1900, Roosevelt *Mss;* to George F. Hoar, June 16, 1902, *ibid.;* "Third Annual Message," *Works*, XVII, 223.
42. Roosevelt to Raymond Reyes Lala, June 27, 1900, Roosevelt *Mss;* see also E. E. Garrison, *The Roosevelt Doctrine* (New York, 1904), 82.
43. Roosevelt to Federic R. Coudert, July 3, 1901, Roosevelt *Mss.*
44. Roosevelt to H. K. Love, Nov. 24, 1900, *ibid.*
45. Roosevelt, "First Annual Message," *loc. cit.*, 129.
46. For example, see Roosevelt to Joseph G. Cannon, Sept. 12, 1904, Roosevelt *Mss;* to Jacob G. Schurman, Aug. 26, 1904, *ibid.;* to Henry Cabot Lodge, April 6, 1906, *ibid.;* to Henry Cabot Lodge, April 30, 1906, *ibid.;* to Andrew Carnegie, April 5, 1907, *ibid.;* to Silas McBee, Aug. 27, 1907, *ibid.;* to Sidney Brooks, Nov. 20, 1908, *ibid.;* Roosevelt, "First Annual Message," *loc. cit.*, 129; Roosevelt, "Fourth Annual Message," *Works*, XVII, 306–307; Roosevelt, "Eighth Annual Message," *ibid.*, XVII, 633.
47. Roosevelt to Charles W. Eliot, April 4, 1904, Roosevelt *Mss.*
48. Roosevelt to Sidney Brooks, Nov. 20, 1908, *ibid.;* to Silas McBee, Aug. 27, 1907, *ibid.*
49. Roosevelt, "Eighth Annual Message," *loc. cit.*, 633.
50. Roosevelt to Joseph G. Cannon, March 2, 1907, Roosevelt *Mss.*
51. Roosevelt to Andrew Carnegie, April 5, 1907, *ibid.;* to Charles W. Eliot, June 20, 1904, *ibid.*
52. Roosevelt to Sir Percy Girouard, July 21, 1910, *ibid.;* also Roosevelt, "The Expansion of the White Race," *Works*, XVIII, 344.
53. Roosevelt to Charles D. Willard, April 28, 1911, *Letters*, VII, 250–256 *passim.*
54. Beale, *op. cit.*, 455.
55. For an examination of Roosevelt's reaction to Egyptian nationalism see David

H. Burton, "Theodore Roosevelt and Egyptian Nationalism," *Mid-America* (April 1959), 88–103.

56. Roosevelt to John Ellis, March 9, 1898, Roosevelt *Mss*; to Robert Bacon, April 8, 1898, *ibid.*

57. Roosevelt to Elihu Root, May 20, 1904, *Letters*, IV, 801.

58. Roosevelt to Elihu Root, Jan. 26, 1904, *ibid.*, IV, 711.

59. Roosevelt to Elihu Root, July 20, 1908, Roosevelt *Mss*.

60. Roosevelt to Sir George O. Trevelyan, Sept. 9, 1906, *ibid.*

61. For example, Roosevelt to Albert Shaw, Oct. 7, 1903, *Letters*, III, 626; to Kermit Roosevelt, Nov. 4, 1903, Roosevelt *Mss*; to Charles S. Osborn, Dec. 9, 1903, quoted in Joseph B. Bishop, *Theodore Roosevelt and His Time* (New York, 1920), I, 293; to Rev. D. D. Thompson, Dec. 22, 1903, *Letters*, III, 675; to S. W. Small, Dec. 29, 1903, *ibid.*, III, 685; to Sir Cecil Spring-Rice, Jan. 18, 1904, Roosevelt *Mss*. See also Roosevelt, *Autobiography*, 524; 525; "The Administration of Island Possessions," *Works*, XIII, 359; "Second Annual Message," *ibid.*, XVII, 176.

62. Roosevelt to Charles W. Eliot, April 4, 1904, Roosevelt *Mss*; to Elihu Root, April 30, 1906, *ibid.*

63. Roosevelt to Count Speck von Sternburg, July 12, 1901, *ibid.*; to William Bayard Hale, Dec. 3, 1908, *ibid.*

64. Among others the Chinese and the Koreans. See Roosevelt to T. E. Burton, Feb. 23, 1904, *ibid.*; to John Hay, Jan. 28, 1905, *ibid.*

65. Roosevelt to Winfred T. Denison, Aug. 3, 1914, *ibid.*; to Charles D. Willard, April 28, 1911, *Letters*, VII, 250–256, *passim*. Roosevelt's historical sense enabled him to appreciate that the superior races of his day had been the backward peoples two thousand years before. See Roosevelt, "National Life and Character," *loc. cit.*, 236; Roosevelt to David B. Schneder, June 19, 1905, Roosevelt *Mss*.

66. "Biological Analogies in History," *loc. cit.*, 69.

67. *Ibid.*, 78.

68. *Ibid.*, 82.

69. *Ibid.*, 82; 89–90.

70. *Ibid.*, 82.

71. *Ibid.*, 84.

72. *Ibid.*, 84.

73. *Ibid.*, 97.

74. *Ibid.*, 101 (italics added).

75. *Ibid.*, 102.

76. *Ibid.*, 104.

77. Roosevelt to Edmund R. O. von Mach, Nov. 7, 1914, Roosevelt *Mss*.

78. Roosevelt, "Social Evolution," *loc. cit.*, 108.

79. Roosevelt, "The Origin and Evolution of Life," *loc. cit.*, 36. "The claims of certain so-called scientific men as to 'science overthrowing religion' are as baseless as the fears of certain sincerely religious men on the same subject. The establishment of the doctrine of evolution in our time offers no more justification for upsetting religious beliefs than did the discovery of facts concerning the solar system a few centuries ago. Any faith sufficiently robust to stand the

surely very slight strain of admitting that the world is not flat and does move around the sun need have no apprehensions on the score of evolution, and the materialistic scientists who gleefully hail the discovery of the principle of evolution as establishing their dreary creed might with just as much propriety rest it upon the discovery of the principle of gravitation." Roosevelt, in *The Outlook* (Dec. 2, 1911), *Works*, XIV, 424; see also, Roosevelt, "Presidential Address," American Historical Association, Dec. 27, 1912, *ibid.*, XIV, 9–10; Roosevelt to William Allen White, May 2, 1918, Roosevelt *Mss.*

80. See, e.g., Howard C. Hill, *Roosevelt and the Caribbean* (Chicago, 1927), 198ff.; E. Wagenknecht, *The Seven Worlds of Theodore Roosevelt* (New York, 1958), 181ff.

81. Roosevelt cannot be considered seriously as a Reform Darwinist in view of the non-scientific qualifications he applied to evolution; neither did he favor economic interpretations of history, which were among the favorite analytical tools of the Reform Darwinists.

82. "The Origin and Evolution of Life," *loc. cit.*, 30.

83. *Ibid.*, 34.

84. *Ibid.*, 35.

IDEAS AND MEN

John Adams and Edwin Arlington Robinson were both men of their times. Adams personified the Age of Reason, Robinson reflected the Scientific Revolution. Born more than a century apart they were men of contrasting personalities. Adams was as intellectually keen as he was politically adroit. Robinson admired such men, wrote of them in his poetry, but was private to the point of reclusive in his lifestyle. But they were fellow New Englanders for all of that, at a time in the national experience when men of that part of the country commanded great respect, as much for how they thought as what they did. To link them together is at once artificial and artful. Artificial because the linkage appears to rely on the coincidence of birth, yet artful inasmuch as each of them intellectualized the spirit of an age. The mind of John Adams revealed few if any doubts about the right of political revolution and national Independence. The thinking of Robinson articulated the uncertainties of an America whose traditional values were being challenged by the methods of science. When their thinking is placed back to back, as it is here, intellectual history becomes a matter of men and ideas, the story of thought.

John Adams

John Adams, born in Braintree, Massachusetts, October 30, 1735, was of the fourth generation of his family in America. The first American Adams, named Henry, who was of yeoman stock and a copyholder of the manor of Baron St. David in Somerset, migrated from England about 1636 and settled at Mount Wallaston (Braintree). His descendents tended to remain in that locality, "virtuous, independent, New England farmers." Thus began the gestation phase in the growth of the famous Adams clan. Roots were put down, firm and deep. The Adamses partook of the New England experience, a nurturing necessary to achievement. Down to the generation of John Adams the history of the family was familiar enough to be commonplace. It took a remarkable individual, not a dramatic genetic mutation, to launch the Adams dynasty.

For all his talents John Adams owed something to his time and place. As the oldest of the family he was to have the privilege of a higher education, as had his Uncle Joseph, his father's older brother who graduated Harvard and became a schoolmaster and a clergyman. John might follow in Uncle Joseph's footsteps. It was a logical and a laudable prospect. Destined to be educated, John Adams related in his autobiography that his parents were "both fond of reading" and that he was "very early taught to read." Standing behind mother and father was Grandmother Bass, who was a "diligent reader" and an example to a favorite grandchild.

Reading and writing were but the tools. It mattered only what grew out of learning at a time when learning and religious belief were bound together. Derived from a strict Puritan family whose members were faithful in attendance at the First Church of Braintree, John Adams was not to have an untroubled religious boyhood. When he was about the age of ten Rev. Lemuel Briant, Arminian in his theology, became minister to the First Church. Typically Briant preached good works as an essential element in salvation, as opposed to the theory of the irresistible grace of God which saved men and against which no mortal might stand. Adams, naturally religious, heard Briant's preaching and came to know the pangs of inner spiritual turmoil. It was an intellectual confusion inasmuch as Puritan belief remained a religion which depended directly on learning. Briant's heterodoxy forced young Adams to ponder his religious convictions. The upshot, registered over many years, was that "moral sentiments and sacred principles" of behavior loomed more important than theological dictates.

The world in which John Adams was growing up was changing. Not only had Puritanism fragmented with half-way covenants and revivals, the Church of England had begun to proselytize in Braintree. The wars with the French in Canada, recurring as they did and growing more serious as the century advanced meant the local militia was a visible element in most New England towns. Adams was early impressed with the idea of the people armed. The French threat could never quite be put out of mind. New England had yielded its isolation from religious and political change. Adams himself lost the innocence of the rude farm boy as he went to school to Mrs. Belcher, to Mr. Cleverly, and then to Mr. Marsh, the latter to prepare him for the Harvard entrance examination. In all this he was smitten with a "growing curiosity" and an avid appetite for learning which he was to put to use at Harvard.

John Adams entered Harvard in 1751. The college had been founded more than a century before "to advance learning and to perpetuate it to posterity." The learning thus referred to was a knowledge of God through a knowledge of His creation. By mid-eighteenth century this idea had been somewhat secularized. In 1755 John Winthrop IV, Hollis Professor of Natural Philosophy, wrote his treatise on earthquakes, describing them as entirely natural phenomena and having nothing to do with God's displeasure toward sinful man. The Enlightenment spread its influence in various directions. It was felt even by the divines. Edward Wigglesworth, Professor of Divinity, instructed his students: "Believe in God, but remember it is man who makes doctrine. Think." While at Harvard Adams was drawn to mathematics and natural philosophy and studied with both Winthrop and Wigglesworth. Whether due to the lingering influence of Lemuel Briant or the intellectual tolerance of Harvard—tolerant at least by standards prevailing elsewhere in the community—or to something more highly personal such as a passion to become distinguished, Adams decided toward the close of his Harvard days that he would not be a clergyman after all. His traits of intellectual curiosity and wonder matched by a fine sense of candor were to make other careers attractive and suitable.

Harvard College provided John Adams a liberal education. By his second year he was reading Thucydides and Plutarch, albeit in translation, Shakespeare's plays, Newton and Boyle's scientific papers, Dryden, Pope's *Essay on Man*, Gravesande's (a Dutch disciple of Newton) *Natural Philosophy*, Locke's *Essay Concerning Human Understanding*. What were the effects of this growth in learning on the eager student? For one thing to think was to question, to question was to doubt, to doubt required the development of an intellectual self-confidence sufficient to resolve doubts in favor of principles of belief and behavior. In this way Harvard had a liberating effect. Yet the times were not ripe to translate theory into action. Colonial New England was at peace with itself in 1755 even as it was at war with the French. John Adams left Harvard with a mind open to change but prepared to accept the *status quo* for the moment. On the Commencement Day platform as a candidate for the degree of Bachelor of Arts, he responded to questioning of President Holyoke with the assertion that: "Political liberty does not consist in the absence of restraints. Law is necessary to government." Newton had said it about the universe; Adams believed him. He believed further that Newton's great principle of order under law was as germane to society as to the heavens. Though he became a leading man in the Revolution he continued to adhere to the dictum of rule under law. As author of the Massachusetts Constitution he offered singular proof of his attachment to this principle. Throughout his life Adams carried the stamp of Harvard. What Harvard had done was to enable him to confirm by learning his religious belief in a wise Creator, a benevolent universe, and the responsibility of man to understand and accept the laws of nature.

Having decided against the ministry John Adams drifted into the craft of schoolmaster. The town of Worcester needed a teacher, an offer was made, and by August of 1755 Adams was hard at work. He did not really enjoy the semi-isolation of Worcester, with but fifteen hundred inhabitants and too distant for his tastes from Boston with its window on the world. Though he taught but briefly and with no special success the move to Worcester was an important phase in his intellectual growth. He had arrived with Bolingbroke's *Idea of a Patriot King* in his saddlebag, betraying an interest in politics unusual in a schoolmaster. He might have remained a learned yet lonely teacher except for his friendship with James Putnam, the town's leading lawyer and under whom he commenced a study of law. Putnam, whose library of fifteen solid books on law included Coke's *Commentaries on Littleton* as well as his *Institutes,* was a man of genuine learning. Studying under him (Putnam set Adams the task of abridging the *Commentaries* section by section, for example), living in his household, and sharing his daily observations on the law and considerably more than the law. Adams's intellectual debt to his mentor was a heavy one. In the study of English law he learned English history, dealing with English history he came to see more clearly what were the rights of Englishmen and how they had been preserved through struggle. Knowingly, Putnam trained a lawyer; unknowingly he helped in the shaping of an American patriot.

In 1759 Adams returned to live in his father's house in Braintree and was admitted to the Suffolk County Bar. Practicing law by day he pursued his political education by night. He read and re-read the works of Coke, Bracton, Justinian and Vinnius on law, Edmund Burke's *Philosophical Enquiry,* and Adam Smith's *The Theory of Moral Sentiments,* the last of which influenced him profoundly. The years glided by quickly. His law practice was successful, he married Abigail Quincy Smith in

1764, children were born, and he wrote various articles of a Whiggish persuasion that appeared anonymously in Boston newspapers. In another sense, however, the years were not passing smoothly. French defeat in North America created almost as many problems as it solved, James Otis delivered the first legal salvo against the mother country in denouncing the writs of assistance, a new tax policy for the colonies loomed from across the sea as America's friends were harder and harder to find at Westminster. Soon the thunder would roll, occasioned at first by the Stamp Act. A long series of events was set in motion which culminated in American independence. Adams was to have his say in all of this, and to act in it as well.

John Adams answered the Stamp Act with a lengthy *Dissertation on the Canon and Feudal Law.* The piece was published in Boston and won notice in London where it was reprinted in the *London Chronicle.* What made this work distinctive if not distinguished was its in-depth historical argument. Examining the English background of canon and feudal law and asserting that the bad effects of both tyrannical systems still lingered in England, Adams was insistent on separating the American tradition from its English sources. New England, in particular, he contended, had been established to escape the evils of canonical and feudal interference with the sacred right of man's freedom.

> Let it be known that British Liberties are not the grants of princes or parliaments but original rights, conditions of original contracts, coequal with prerogative and coeval with government; that many of our rights are inherent and essential, agreed on as maxims and established as preliminaries even before a parliament existed. Let them search for the foundations of British laws and government in the frame of human nature, in the constitution of the intellectual and moral world.

Adams had been characteristically forthright. Years later he spoke of the Dissertation as a "lamentable bagatelle." For all its rhetorical splashes it was a learned analysis. It foreshadowed his later defense of political rights and revealed his deep feelings about tyranny.

In the years between 1765 and 1783 John Adams was an observer, a commentator, and a participant in the momentous happenings engulfing the American states. He moved surely from local matters to the great affairs of a nation. In 1765, for example, by means of a brief but informed statement he advised his fellow citizens of Braintree that the Stamp Act was contrary to the English constitution and "directly repugnant to the Great Charter itself." Once again he offered incisive legal arguments and indulged in colorful language, noting that "we have a clear knowledge and a just sense of our rights and liberties . . . we never can be slaves." Five years later he was elected to the General Court of Massachusetts for the town of Boston. Though he was not deeply involved in the Committees of Correspondence he was chosen as a delegate from Massachusetts to attend the First Continental Congress and became a respected participant in the deliberations of that body. A member of the draft committees for the Declaration of Independence Adams also served the Congress as minister to France for several months in 1778-1779. Returning home he took part in the Massachusetts Constitutional Convention and emerged as the "principal engineer" of the form of constitution which was finally approved by the voters. Shortly thereafter, in 1779, Adams was back in Europe to represent the States in France and Holland. At the close of the war, along with Franklin and Jay, he carried forward the peace negotiations with Britain and was appropriately one of the signers of the Peace of Paris of 1783. These years were crowded with events and Adams was in the thick of things. At the same time he set down some of his most significant political writings, the *Novanglus Letters, Thoughts on Government,* and the draft of the Constitution of Massachusetts.

The *Novanglus Letters* appeared in the *Boston Gazette* in 1774 and 1775. Their purpose was to refute the persistent Tory claim that the Parliament at Westminster represented and thus enjoyed the right to speak for the whole empire. Adams addressed these letters to the "inhabitants of the colony of Massachusetts Bay" and they should be considered a direct appeal to the people and not some finely spun argument by a scholar. Adams endeavored to use his words to persuade people to accept ideas and principles as a basis for action. In essence he advanced the proposition that Parliament was not supreme over the colonies but that the colonial assemblies were supreme. "I say we are not a part of the British empire. . . . Distinct states may be united under one king. And states may be further cemented and ruled together by a treaty of commerce. This is the case. We [the colonies] owe allegiance to the person of his majesty, King George III, whom God preserve." In the development of his thesis Adams went so far as to contend that the British Empire was not an empire because "an empire is a despotism." "The British Constitution is much more like a republic than an empire . . . and a republic [is] a government of laws and not of men. If the definition be just," he went on, "the British Constitution is nothing more or less than a republic in which the king is the first magistrate." As startling as this passage must have sounded, Adams's intention was not to shock but to advance a new conception of the political entity called the British Empire. It was a commonwealth of states (or nations) bound together by a common sovereign and Adams earned the reputation of a Britannic statesman.

If the *Novanglus Letters* uncovered in John Adams a gift of prophecy, *Thoughts on Government,* a brief essay dashed off as part of a letter to George Wythe of Virginia in January, 1776, demonstrated the spontaneity of his political thinking. Compacted in a few pages he set down the main outline and the concomitant justifications of a representative democratic government, division of political power between a bicameral legislature and a chief executive, and a strong and vital judiciary. "The principal difficulty lay," he thought, "in constituting the representative assembly. "It should think, feel, reason and act like the people. . . . equal interests among the people should have equal interest in it." Adams had broken new ground in so describing the character and composition of a modern republican legislature, yet he had done so in a letter to a fellow patriot in an almost casual fashion.

How well these and other principles were carried out in practice may be judged by examination of Adams's draft of the Constitution of

Massachusetts. It furnishes added evidence of how naturally thought and action mingled in his contribution to the cause of independence. As the Preamble bears out, Adams's mind was steeped in the English tradition of individual rights and liberties and quickened by the enlightened teachings of the philosophers. It read in part:

> The end of the institution, maintenance and administration of government is to secure the existence of the body politic, to protect it and to furnish the individuals who compose it with the power of enjoying in safety and in tranquility, their natural rights and the blessings of life and whenever these great objects are not obtained, the people have a right to alter the government and to take measures necessary for their safety, happiness and prosperity.
>
> The body politic is formed by a voluntary association of individuals. It is a social compact by which the whole people covenants with each citizen and each citizen with the whole people, that all shall be governed by certain laws for the common good. It is the duty of the people, therefore, in framing a Constitution of Government, to provide for an equitable mode of making laws, as well as for an impartial interpretation and a faithful execution of them, that every man may, at all times, find his security in them.

This Preamble and the Constitution it introduced were peculiarly the handiwork of John Adams. In promoting acceptance of the document as the frame of government for his state he acted as an intellectual broker for the voters, a middle man between the political philosophers and the plain people, poised at a historic moment when by their concerted action the theory of the social contract took on political reality. For Adams himself, his political thinking achieved maturity just as he came of age as a statesman.

Events often had an energizing effect on Adams's political writing. The Stamp Act had prompted his *Dissertation on the Canon and Feudal Law, Thoughts on Government* came about as a result of independence and thus the search for a form of government to provide for this new condition. It was a pattern of challenge and response which also obtained in the post-Revolutionary period. Between October, 1786 and December, 1787, while serving as minister to Great Britain, Adams undertook his most extensive work, *A Defense of the Constitutions of the United States*. It was written to refute the constitutional theories of Turgot. In a letter to the English radical political commentator, Dr. Price, Turgot contended that the American state constitutions were but imitations of the British model, too lacking in centralized authority with too much emphasis on a separation of powers. Adams was not intimidated by Turgot's reputation as a leading political theorist as his disagreement demonstrated. Apart from Turgot's strictures Adams was disturbed by Shays's Rebellion of 1786, the uprising of economic dissidents in central and western Massachusetts led by Captain Daniel Shays, late of the Continental Line. "The commotion in New England alarmed me," he wrote, "so much that I have thrown together some heavy speculations upon the subject of government." Adams feared centralized power as he feared the mob. Some Americans, Benjamin Franklin among them, appeared to favor certain centralizing features of government and Adams was impelled to make his position known. ". . . Power is always abused when unlimited or unbalanced," summed up his view simply but emphatically. Not untypically, it took him three volumes to say all that he felt needed saying on the subject. It is likely that his arguments in volume one, which was available in Philadelphia in 1787, influenced members of the Constitutional Convention. When the new government was launched John Adams was chosen vice-president, one of the host of first administration officials who were sympathetic to the cause of the young republic under the Constitution and whose ardor and ability helped to make it a success.

No sooner had the United States of America become a constitutional reality than that extraordinary train of events associated with the French

Revolution was placed in motion. At first Americans wished the revolutionaries well. "Liberty will have another feather in his cap," enthused the *Boston Gazette;* "the seraphic contagion was caught from Britain, it crossed the Atlantic to North America, from which the flame has been communicated to France." The *Gazette* had voiced the sentiments of most Americans because the revolution promised much by way of liberty and progress. When events moved in new and uncertain directions, however, Adams was one of the first to express his reservations about the ultimate objectives of the revolution. He set forth his views in *Discourses on Davila.* Written while he was vice-president and published in the *Gazette of the United States* in Philadelphia, *Discourses on Davila* was a protest against the too complete centralization of political power in the hands of the National Assembly in Paris. If in the *Discourses* Adams had done no more than protest this development, his thoughts would not have advanced much beyond the arguments he had stated in the *Defense of the Constitutions of the United States.* Much of the *Discourses,* on the contrary, involved Adams in an analysis of human nature, of man the political being, and the essentials of government. Writing as a political philosopher he showed himself more concerned with substance than with form and structure. The quality of his observations is no doubt lessened by the fact that he had borrowed heavily and without disguise from Adam Smith's *The Theory of Moral Sentiments.* But there is a great deal of Adams in the work, discernible in some little examination of the *Discourses.*

First of all, Adams brought attention to bear directly on man's nature, beginning with essential gregariousness of the human species in its primitive condition. Men "continue to be social, not only in every stage of civilization but in every possible situation in which they are placed." Of all the faculties with which nature endowed social man, faculties designed both for individual enjoyment and group welfare, none was "more essential or remarkable than the *passion for distinction.*" This was a generic faculty, thought Adams, and from it stem emulation, ambition, jealousy, envy, and vanity. To the passion for distinction he ascribed an indispensable part in the formation of human society and in

> . . . an insecure delight
> For man's prolonged abode,
> And the wrong thing for him to meet at night
> On a wrong road.

The danger inherent in this conception of liberty, Robinson went on to observe, was that it had no bounds, it derived its energy from legislation which of itself had no limitation. Instead, legislation was always ready for "the infliction of more liberty." The result, he thought, might be a liberty that would "moronize the millions for a few." In "Dionysus in Doubt" Robinson was in revolt against a middle-class tyranny that he looked upon as frightening in its effects and as all the more insidious than a totalitarian dictatorship because it was disguised as liberty.[27]

The most trenchant statement of his doubts about democracy Robinson presented in the last of his "Demos" pieces, "Demos and Dionysus." In this poem Demos was the social device that would make all men equal and happy, and thus equally happy, while Dionysus embodied man's immortal vision. The very idea of freedom Demos was seen to owe to Dionysus. Robinson again recorded the conflict that existed between equality and freedom and reproached man for having reduced everything to his own dimensions:

> . . . Reason and Equality, like strong Twins
> Will soon be brother giants, overseeing
> Incessantly the welfare of . . . all.

Equality issuing solely from reason was equality uninstructed by morality. Robinson once more was disturbed and fearful that an enforced standard of equality, without regard for Dionysus, would deceive men by the appearance of liberty. Reason and equality would reduce "the obedient selves of men to poor machines." In the end men would live a hive-life, where art would be a "thing remembered as a toy" and the "infirmity that you name love/ . . . subdued to a studious procreation. . . ." This denial of freedom to act—and for men a moral freedom to choose between right and wrong, between the spirit and sin—deleted the distinguishing characteristic of the traditional moral universe. With a sustained passion Robinson argued that the worst of all possible tyrannies could confront men in the name of Demos, with the Demos seeking to demonstrate that tradition had made "too much of the insurgent individual."[28]

That the hazards implicit in American democracy noted by Robinson in the 1920s might be part of the development or the decline of a civilization, he proposed in his last poem, "King Jasper." The malfunctioning of a capitalistic world, he insisted, was in the main brought about by the same cause that disturbed the private lives of men, that is, a contention between sin and the spirit. For Robinson, as for so many of his contemporaries, the coming of World War I portended the eclipse of their world which became a kind of "doomed Camelot." He was sorely disillusioned with the prospects for a peaceful society after the war. The continuation of economic greed among the nations which Robinson saw in a return to the old nationalistic tariff barriers worried him greatly, while the failure of the League of Nations, he imagined, would entail widespread social upheaval. In fact, the poet proved something of a political soothsayer in his distrust of Russia and in his speculations as to the future alignment of the Powers for World War II. His fear for the downfall of modern civilization stemmed from disillusionment and terror, though there was no panic in his diagnosis of the malady at work in the world. This was the subject of "King Jasper."

"King Jasper" took its primary significance from its symbolism of a world in decline rather than from its story of six unhappy mortals ensnared in a web of ignorance. Using characters as emblematic, Robinson enlarged on the effects of sin with a reminder that even in an evil system it was the sins of one man, or many men, that brought death to a society. What was important in the symbolism of the poem was not alone what the six characters represented but the fate which befell each of them. There was Jasper, who had built his kingdom on the straw of his personal ambition; there was Honoria, his wife, the sum of all that tradition held; and there was the elder Hebron, known only in Jasper's dream, whose initiative and genius had been sacrificed by Jasper in winning his domain. Of the second generation there was Jasper's son and namesake, heir to the kingdom and wise enough to know that it was not built soundly; there was young Hebron with his father's genius transformed into revenge; and finally there was Zoe, young Jasper's wife, the personification of man's spirit, "Beauty and truth and death" together.[29]

It is clear from Robinson's presentation that the sins of Jasper, greed and ambition, were fatal to his kingdom. Jasper admitted that it was his thirst for power that he recognized as his sin, though to an observing world it appeared to be lust for gold. Yet what in Jasper's conduct merited the destruction of his kingdom? Robinson, through Zoe, tells us that there is a God, an Intelligence, who makes life meaningful:

> . . . No God No Law, no Purpose, could have
> hatched for sport
> Out of warm water and slime, a war for life That
> was unnecessary, and far better Never have been—
> if man as we behold him
> Is all it means.[30]

It is precisely in the nature of Jasper's work in raising up his kingdom that he made other men a means of power. The roots of his kingdom went down to hell and this was the cause of his kingdom's end. Thus young Jasper said to the king:

> . . . But a king, father,
> Whose roses have long roots that find their way
> To regions where the gardeners are all devils
> May as well know there is a twilight coming
> When roses that were never so sweet before
> Will smell for what they are. . . .[31]

As young Jasper continued, the deeper tragedy of the kingdom's decline was that the king knew enough to save his crown. He realized much better than the "red rhetoric" of young Hebron that a kingdom must be built on integrity and a virtuous regard for men, yet he refused to acknowledge either duty or justice.[32] At the end of the poem all were dead save Zoë, the figure of art and honesty and noble aspiration, not "bound/Or tangled in the flimsy nets or threads/Of Church or state."[33] Thus closed Robinson's last lament for the larger tragedy of modern man.

The art of Edwin Arlington Robinson mirrored both the sources of the American mind of his generation and the growth nurtured by these sources. By the time of his death in 1935 the stamina of the ancient ethical code, attenuated to be sure but powerful still, was as evident as the maturation of scientific thought. Americans as a nation continually sought a composition of these divergent systems simply by acting as though there was no fundamental conflict between the two. Their action thus taken proceeded on the basic pragmatic supposition that if a workability between the two could be discovered and demonstrated, then the truth of the compatibility of faith and science was certified. In considerable measure the effort succeeded as new principles from life were adopted at one end and old ones, not yet absorbed or sloughed off, were retained at the other. For Robinson personally his thought achieved no such resolution. His failure cannot be lightly dismissed as the resulting paralysis of excessive reflection, however. It should serve, instead, as an annotation of the persistent uneasiness in American culture about its ultimate purpose. The unresolved conflict within the artist between what tradition held and science taught is evidence that he no longer accepted the collective myth of the American historical experience, that multifaceted jewel of "American mission." Both in theory and in fact, in the essential reservations he entertained concerning the nature of democracy, for example, and in his undisguised contempt for the imperialists of 1898, Robinson had come to doubt the national destiny. His own judgments amounted to little, perhaps, for he was obscure enough to be ignored; but his misgivings were symptomatic of a growing disenchantment of many American intellectuals with the old order, including national greatness and purpose. In the transition of American thought the erosion of the sense of mission, which had depended intrinsically on the old verities of tradition, provided the conditions proper to the life of an intellectual radicalism which Robinson's thought at least adumbrated. His deeply felt attachment to the past, his poetic temperament, the particular years of his life span all worked to confine his contribution to this new radicalism to that of allusion rather than definition. Increasing numbers of American intellectuals, however, would take the step that the poet for his part was unable and unwilling to: a considered rejection of the collective myth. As for Robinson, in the realm of his own mind, he stood face to face with an innate human desire for salvation, nirvana, fulfillment, and the scientific postulates in support of a purely biochemical humanity. Too firmly rooted in the past to renounce the old morality which called for the old God, too much a part of the present to discount the scientific doubts cast upon his mind, he left a legacy of anxious qualm as to the validity of the pragmatic solution. The American temper in the thirty years and more since E. A.Robinson's death has continued to display this disquiet, only partially obscured by the apparent success of faith and science yoked together for the common good as determined by a current majority.

NOTES

1. Of the several studies of Edwin Arlington Robinson the most recent, Where the Light Falls (New York, 1965), by Chard Powers Smith, is a sensitive portrait. Herman Hagedorn, Edwin Arlington Robinson (New York, 1939), remains useful. Estelle Kaplan, Philosophy in the Poetry of Edwin Arlington Robinson (New York, 1940), discriminates the various philosophical influences on the author. E.A. Fussell provides an in-depth discussion of his literary background in Edwin Arlington Robinson, The Literary Background of a Traditional Poet (Berkeley, 1954). Both Emery Neff, Edwin Arlington Robinson (Norwalk, Conn., 1948), and Yvor Winters, Edwin Arlington Robinson (New York, 1948), treat his poetry critically.
2. Collected Poems of Edwin Arlington Robinson (New York, 1948), p. 41. (Hereafter cited as Collected Poems.)
3. Ibid., pp. 582–591.
4. Ibid., pp. 921–957.
5. Ibid., pp. 961–1007.
6. Ibid., pp. 543–573.
7. Ibid., pp. 3–6.
8. Ibid., pp. 73–74.
9. Quoted in Hagedorn, op. cit., p. 286.
10. "Bewick Finzer," Collected Poems, p. 55.
11. Untriangulated Stars, Letters of Edwin Arlington Robinson to Harry deForest

Smith, 1890–1915, Denham Sutcliffe, editor (Cambridge, Mass., 1947), p. 4. (Hereafter cited as Untriangulated Stars.)

12. Lloyd Morris, The Poetry of Edwin Arlington Robinson (New York, 1923), p. 69; Kaplan, op. cit., pp. 47, 50, 52.
13. Selected Letters of Edwin Arlington Robinson, Ridgely Torrance, editor (New York, 1939), p. 13. (Hereafter cited as Selected Letters.)
14. Kaplan, op. cit., p. 11.
15. Untriangulated Stars, p. 263.
16. Winters, op. cit., pp. 17–18; 98–99; 119.
17. Untriangulated Stars, pp. 278–279.
18. Selected Letters, pp. 163–165.
19. Untriangulated Stars, p. 21.
20. Ibid., p. 298.
21. Ibid., p. 260.
22. Collected Poems, pp. 961–1007.
23. Ibid., pp. 460–461.
24. William J. Walsh, "Some Recollections of E.A. Robinson," Part II, The Catholic World (September, 1942), p. 711.
25. Alfred Kreymborg, Our Singing Strength (New York, 1929), p. 298.
26. Collected Poems, pp. 471–472.
27. pp. 859–870.
28. Ibid., pp. 904–918.
29. Ibid., p. 1457.
30. Ibid., p. 1471.
31. Ibid., p. 1429.
32. Ibid., p. 1460.
33. Ibid., p. 1402.

WHY PLUTARCH?

Plutarch, a Greek who lived in Rome in the first century of the Christian era, was a teacher by trade and an historian by instinct. He came to know a great deal about Rome and its leaders. As a Greek he was equally conversant with the great men of his native land. In his writings he approached Greco-Roman history through an extensive study of the parallel lives of eminent Greeks and Romans, accounts that have survived, if somewhat altered in form, for two thousand years. His purpose was confined to great public men, and the ideal he sought to celebrate was civic virtue. The device of parallel lives had several uses, including a contrasting of Greek and Roman civilizations in order better to understand the strengths and weaknesses of each. Plutarch's approach to history through parallel lives has obvious limitation. Greece and Rome were kindred civilizations between which there was a rare linkage. In modern Western history no two peoples appear more likely to yield to the Plutarchian formula than the British and the Americans, one the ever-acknowledged parent, the other the vibrant offspring, the two together consistently displaying a love-hate relationship. It would be a facile rule, and one not supported by the evidence, to apply the Greco-Roman model *mutatis mutandis* to the Anglo-American experience. A consideration of parallel lives of distinguished British and American public figures, nevertheless, may deepen one's appreciation of the separate cultures while noting the reciprocal influences of one upon the other. Paralleling the lives of Winston Churchill and Franklin Roosevelt as the history of the century played out offers a truly persuasive example of Plutarch's method, showing how these men helped to determine the fate of Western civilization.

WINSTON CHURCHILL

Winston Churchill was the great Englishman of his time. After a long and stormy but always fascinating career as a soldier, journalist, politician, senior administrator, historian-biographer, statesman, and prophet, in his sixty-sixth year he assumed the office of Prime Minister to stand forth as the captain of his island race. Soon thereafter, he was co-partner with Franklin Roosevelt in a personal kind of "special relationship," at the head of the Anglo-American alliance which helped to determine the fate of the world. Turned out of the premier's office in 1945 he again served as the chief minister of the Crown from 1951 to 1955. Meanwhile, continuing a writing career which had begun in the 1890s and which had included a biography of his father and a study of his famous ancestor, John Churchill, the first Duke of Marlborough, he began the publication of his six-volume account of the Second World War. Later, when in his eighties, he completed a history of the English-speaking peoples. In 1953 he was awarded the Nobel Prize for literature and oratory.

In the long view Churchill's most significant accomplishments came late in life, though his career had been distinguished almost from the first. Because of that, might not Plutarch himself have succumbed to the temptation to read events backward, by concentrating on the greater attainments. Reading biography backwards, as with history, is a bad habit. But in the case of Churchill it becomes a seductive proposition, especially if he is to be appreciated as the Anglo-American he was. Over the last two decades of his life he was staunchly pro-American without sacrificing the best interests of his own country.

Invited to address the Congress of the United States in December, 1941, Churchill good-naturedly remarked: "I cannot help reflecting that if my father had been American and my mother British, instead of the other way around, I might have gotten here on my own." And there is every prospect that he would have done so. As it turned out, he was a true House of Commons man. It was a body whose protocol was appropriate to his talents. He often described himself as a "child of the House of Commons," not simply because his father had been a distinguished House member, however powerful an example this was for him, but because it was his natural habitat. To become Prime Minister was therefore the sublime achievement, and to gain that office at a time of utmost peril to the nation suited his sense of history and his sense of purpose. Few leaders have made history with quite the same success as did Winston Churchill beginning in May of 1940, and fewer still have written about it in so memorable a fashion. The Churchill of "blood, sweat, and tears," of "V" for victory, and of the Iron Curtain speech is most easily and best remembered. But as the child is father to the man it may be wiser after all to address the early years in order to understand better those ingredients which led to his greatness. It was a career whose ultimate success was by no means ordained.

The place of his birth and his lineage might suggest otherwise. Winston Leonard Spencer Churchill was born in 1874 at Blenheim Palace, the residence of one of the great ducal families of England. He was the first son of the second son of the 7th Duke of Marlborough. His parents were Jennie (née Jerome) and Randolph Churchill. Jennie was American, the daughter of Leonard and Clara Hall Jerome. Leonard Jerome was a successful New York businessman at a time favorable to "adventurers." He is well described as a sportsman millionaire. Jennie was one of four daughters and through her mother she had inherited Iroquois blood. Thoroughly American Clara Jerome nonetheless took her children to France when she separated from her husband, who continued to pay the bills for his brood abroad. Jennie was thirteen at the time. Wealth and good connections combined to place the Jeromes within the orbit of the fashionable society of the Second Empire. With the fall of Louis

Napoleon the family moved to London and gained entry to society there. Randolph, by contrast, needed no such entry: it was his by birth. Educated at Eton and at Oxford, where he narrowly missed winning a first in history and law, Lord Randolph quite naturally followed in his father's footsteps when he chose to enter politics. He enjoyed some success in Parliament and in the cabinet but due to a combination of stubbornness and haughty self-righteousness, fell well short of realizing his potential. He was also, for a long time, a sick man, which no doubt limited his career. Winston Churchill was, then, by birth an Anglo-American, by heritage an aristocrat, and by example a likely public man.

The bright promise of his life was dimmed almost from the beginning. His father was soon gravely ill and over the next twenty years was reduced by a wasting disease from which he died in 1895. Owing partly to his condition and partly to the conventions of the aristocracy, Winston, the boy, saw little of his father, though he admired him from afar. In twenty years they had perhaps four or five serious conversations, yet often in the future, after he had entered public life, he expressed himself as consciously imitating his father's conduct of affairs, as though to convince people and himself first of all, that he was a worthy scion of Lord Randolph. Winston would, of course, totally eclipse him. Jennie, who enjoyed the life of a society beauty to the hilt, barely took time enough to give instructions to the boy's nanny, Mrs. Everest, who was the dearest companion of his youth. Winston was educated at Harrow where he was anything but a scholar and something of a hellion. His occasional brilliant flashes at school were overshadowed by a daily performance which ranged from dull to rebellious. His father decided that he should attend neither Oxford nor Cambridge, to which universities it is not certain he would have been admitted. Instead he was entered as a cadet at the Royal Military College, Sandhurst, where he had to have a second try at the entrance examination. Winston's was to be an army career. What he would make of it his father did not know or very much care for by that time Lord Randolph's health had deteriorated badly. If he worried about his first son's future at all he could be reassured that at least he would have a profession.

As it happened Sandhurst and his short stay in the army suited Churchill just fine. The former liberated him from the shackles of Greek and Latin exercises, the latter gave full scope to his exuberant spirit. He passed out of Sandhurst eighth in a class of one hundred fifty, not a bad record at all for someone who had trouble with the entrance examination and whose father had about despaired of his son's future. His army years revealed in Churchill an unquenchable thirst for adventure as well as a considerable ability at self-advertising. Nor was he above a little influence peddling, often through his mother, in order to push himself forward. No sooner out of Sandhurst and awaiting assignment he travelled to Cuba to report on the insurrection for the *Daily Graphic*. His life of adventure and his work as a writer were thus simultaneously launched. The next year, 1897, his regiment, the Fourth Hussars, was posted to India, a part of the Empire Churchill would prize all his days. There he played polo—very well—read voraciously—Plato, Aristotle, Schopenhauer, Macaulay, Lecky, Gibbon, Shakespeare—and saw action on the northwest frontier—mentioned in dispatches. Churchill also had arranged to do some articles for *The Daily Telegraph*, and wrote his first book, *The Story of the Malakind Field Force*. In it he was critical of the generals but saw this as no reason not to send off copies to Lord Salisbury, the Prime Minister, and to the Prince of Wales. When people in London asked: "What is Randolph's son like?" the answer might well have been "pushy," an attitude he shared with his American mother who now began to take a serious interest in his career and often opened doors on her son's behalf.

After some months in India Churchill obtained leave and hurried back to London. His time there included a visit to No. 10 Downing Street as he pursued his intention of joining the Kitchener expedition which was preparing to go to the Sudan. The Sudanese were again in rebellion, the same tribes which had defeated the British at Khartoum in 1883 and put General Gordon to death. Solely through connections in Whitehall Churchill was able to arrange an assignment to the twenty-first Lancers and he took part in the campaign which followed. With his appetite for action he, predictably, was in the grand cavalry charge which was the feature of the battle of Omdurman. The defeat of the tribesmen by Kitchener's forces was complete and the vengeance wreaked upon the conquered foes was nothing less than barbaric. In Churchill's book length account of the conflict, *The River War*, he was outspokenly critical of the British Command, the sort of criticism to which senior military officers do not take kindly when delivered by a free-lancing lieutenant. Churchill was insouciant; he never envisioned his long-range future to be in the army and was to resign his commission in 1900. One thing was for sure, young Winston was making a name for himself which one day, as he had been planning all along, would serve him well when he entered politics.

Fresh adventures awaited him in South Africa. The long-simmering dispute between the Boers and the Britons had flared into open warfare in 1899. Churchill was determined to go there to see for himself. Still on leave from his regiment he arranged to do some articles for the *Morning Post* to help defray his expenses. While reporting on an attempt to relieve the garrison at Ladysmith he was captured by Boer militiamen and placed in prison in Pretoria. After three weeks in jail he made his escape. The Boers had put a price on his head of £25 but Churchill made sure no one collected it. His feats of derring-do made him a hero in England and his political prospects advanced accordingly. After another six months of service with the South African Light Horse he was back in London by the summer of 1900 and in September began electioneering for a place in the House of Commons by seeking one of the two seats for Oldham. A Conservative, he ran second in a field of four, edging out the Liberal, Walter Runciman. For the next half century Winston Churchill, whether as prime minister, cabinet officer, or back bencher was a presence in the House of Commons.

It was well understood that Churchill would enter parliament as a Conservative in keeping with family tradition and his father's party affiliation. He himself seemed to fit the mold. In his maiden speech of April 18, 1901, he addressed issues raised by the Boer War, of which he was able to claim some personal knowledge. He defended British imperialism and insisted that the war be fought to a successful conclusion, yet he expressed the hope that in defeat the Boers would become cooperative and valuable members of the Empire. He urged them "not to remain deaf to the voice of reason and blind to the hand of friendship." The first speech was hailed as a great success, the promise of future accomplishment, and a properly imperial appeal to the British and the Boers alike.

The same imperialism which Churchill so boldly championed in this and other matters would soon create a set of circumstances which drove him from the Conservative Party and branded him a traitor to his class. The issue was free trade versus imperial preference. If the British were to retain their economic power and their Empire in the face of severe competition from Germany, the United States, and Japan now seeking world markets, the Conservative leadership under the sway of Joseph Chamberlain counseled a move away from free trade. The inroads made on the British economy were already considerable by the start of the new century, had economic facts which supported Churchill's rhetoric. In time a majority of the Conservatives in the House of Commons believed the era of free trade had passed. Churchill would have none of it and opposed the preference proposal inside and outside parliament. This was a dangerous tactic once party leadership had endorsed Chamberlain's basic idea and it imperiled his future. The moment of truth came on March 29, 1904, when as Churchill was about to speak Prime Minister Balfour left the House, followed by his cabinet and a majority of the Conservative members. Had Winston committed political suicide by his insistence on free trade in the teeth of announced party policy? Had he, like his father before him, overplayed his hand? Not so; the son was more flexible than his father.

Churchill's entry into the Liberal Party was confirmed in 1905 when he was chosen that party's candidate for North-West Manchester. To the chagrin of the Conservatives not only did the traitor Churchill win but the Liberals had gained a majority in the House as a result of the general election. The new Prime Minister, Henry Campbell-Bannerman, named Churchill Under Secretary of State for Colonies. For the next sixteen years he served in various cabinet posts, and for the next half century he was an officer in successive governments for all but fifteen years. Churchill was to be a presence in the administration of government as well as in the House of Commons. His genius, as it developed, lay not merely in winning elections and electrifying parliament and the nation with his speeches; it included an ability to govern, which must be the final purpose of any political system. In Great Britain, at home, and abroad, there was, in 1905, much governing to do.

At the Colonial Office Churchill served under Lord Elgin, a person of considerable administrative experience which included five years as Viceroy of India. The two main problems faced by the Colonial Office were the constitution of the Transvaal and the abuses visited upon the Chinese contract laborers in South Africa. As the Government spokesman for the administration of the Transvaal Churchill learned to walk a narrow line between conceding to local prejudice and maintaining imperial interest. The constitution which gave the Transvaal local self-government was approved by the House of Commons 316 to 83 and the Under Secretary had an important part in guiding the legislation successfully through the Commons. The second matter was equally taxing, the exploitation of some 50,000 Chinese workers, the so-called "coolie problem." In debate Churchill described their condition as "sufficiently unhealthy, unwholesome, and unnatural . . . to seal the fate of Chinese labor" in South Africa. By 1907 the Transvaal government began a system of repatriation whereby the coolies were able to go home as their labor contracts expired. In so doing it demonstrated that local government, when properly constituted, could act in the interests of the Empire.

The task of governing well at home, in the British Isles, loomed far more formidable, once Churchill moved from the Colonial Office to the Presidency of the Board of Trade. In the transition he changed from being an administrator who was liberal to a Liberal reformer. If the change was not abrupt in light of his well-defined sense of justice and fair play, it nonetheless constituted a drastic alteration in his activities as a cabinet minister. The conditions of industrial workers in Britain were bad, as they were for all members of the "lower classes." The nation was well behind its chief European rival, Germany, in providing some form of social security for its large body of workers. Born an aristocrat Churchill had slowly come to understand and sympathize with the British poor. He read Seebohm Roundtree's *Poverty: A Study of Town Life*, which he confessed "fairly made my hair stand on end." Nor did he have any difficulty verifying by observation of the industrial towns he visited that Roundtree's book was an accurate rendering of the situation. Churchill, the patriot, and Churchill, the humanitarian, were moved to action because he realized that a nation poor in health and disgruntled by working and living conditions was vulnerable from within and without.

With the death of Campbell-Bannerman Herbert H. Asquith became the Liberal Prime Minister and David Lloyd George his Chancellor of the Exchequer. Lloyd George's origins were as humble— raised in the coal fields of Wales—as Churchill's were aristocratic. They made an excellent team as the Liberal Party set its sights on social reform at home. Unlike the Colonial Office where he had been actively in charge Churchill was to be a second, but a powerful second, to Lloyd George in pushing for laws which provided for workmen's compensation, unemployment benefits, and health services. To one Manchester gathering Churchill announced: "If I had my way I would write the word 'Insure' over the doorway of every cottage and upon the blotting book of every public man." Such reforms were to cost much money and Lloyd George's budget proposals sought heavy taxes on the rich to relieve the heavier burdens of the poor. The Welsh Wizard was the first object of Conservative scorn for leading and winning the battle of the budget in 1911 and Winston Churchill, still a traitor to his class, was a close second. In 1910 Churchill had been named Home Secretary in which capacity he had to deal with industrial disturbances. One such incident was a labor dispute at Tonypandy in Wales. He refused to allow troops to be used to control the tense situation, instead sending a contingent of unarmed London policemen. Loss of life was thus avoided and quiet was restored. As Home Secretary Churchill strongly supported the Mines Act aimed at improving safety conditions for underground workers. His efforts at prison reform while laudable proved to be ineffectual in light of the statistics on recidivists. As he rotated from office to office this youngest of cabinet ministers gained a variety of administrative experience as at the same time he deepened his knowledge of Britain and its problems.

From 1911 to 1915 Winston Churchill served as First Lord of the Admiralty. It was a post wonderfully suited to his bias in favor of the Empire to which an all-powerful navy was essential, to his patriotism at a time when imperial Germany had arisen to challenge British sea power, and to his energy, a requisite for a position of such scope and responsibility. In addition to making key personnel changes, such as naming Prince Louis of Battenberg the First Sea Lord, Churchill established a Naval War Staff whose purpose it was to achieve and maintain a state of battle readiness. In improving the armor and firepower on capital ships and in ordering the shift from coal to oil as the standard navy fuel he was taking steps to modernize the fleets. He also pushed hard for the acquisition of the Middle Eastern oil fields. When the war broke out in 1914 it was clear that Churchill had done his job well; the Royal Navy was ready.

For some men in the public eye wars are an opportunity to add to their laurels, for others to know the pain of defeat. Churchill's star had risen steadily—almost spectacularly—from the time he entered public life. He appeared to have a golden touch, an instinct for the sure thing. World War I spelled trouble for his success story, yet he emerged from the conflict a more seasoned administrator and perhaps a more wary adventurer. As a senior cabinet official Churchill was fully justified in thinking about the war in terms of grand strategy and devising means for carrying out strategic initiatives. By 1915 it was becoming increasingly obvious that czarist Russia would be unable to remain effectively in the war against the Central Powers. Defeated in battle, disorganized on the home front, beset by political opponents of all stripes Nicholas II appeared to be the last of the Romanovs. Were Russia to lay down arms vast numbers of German troops would be released for duty on the Western front, with perhaps disastrous effects for the Anglo-French armies there. But if the Straits of the Dardanelles could be forced by virtue of the weakness of the Ottoman Empire then the Allies might be able to supply the Russian armies sufficiently to encourage them to remain in the fight. In addition, a third front, in the Balkans might be established by taking advantage of the dissident peoples of the Austro-Hungarian Empire. Churchill proposed rushing the Straits by means of a naval force. Admiral Cardon drew up the battle plan, the First Lord approved it, and it was endorsed by the cabinet and the War Council. The flaw in the plan, there at the beginning, was that it was not conceived as a combined operation of naval and land forces. General Kitchener thought little of the idea and supported it accordingly. The Navy was reluctant to move ahead without an army working with it once it had suffered some heavy losses and by the time troops could be assembled in large numbers the element of surprise succumbed to the ineptness of leadership to bring on a catastrophe.

Rightly or wrongly Churchill was blamed for Gallipoli and driven from the cabinet. He served briefly in France, first as a major in the Grenadier Guards, and then as a colonel with the Royal Scots Fusiliers, before Lloyd George, who had taken over leadership of the cabinet from Asquith, brought him back in the cabinet as Minister of Munitions in 1917. His talents would better serve the war in Whitehall. By building on the efforts of his predecessor Churchill was able to increase productivity by some 20 percent at the same time streamlining the ministry's organization and methods. And once again his ability to get things done was demonstrated when as Minister of War and the Air Force, his next assignment, he handled the delicate matter of demobilization without mishap. But Gallipoli would haunt Churchill for years to come. As he was not a man inclined to look back this did less to undermine his confidence in himself than it did to mar his reputation with many of his old enemies in and out of government.

The Lloyd George Coalition government fell in 1922 the victim, in part, of a postwar backlash. Britain had not become a land fit for heroes and those who had fatuously promised a bright future were made to pay by the electorate. Churchill was out of office and out of parliament until 1924 when, *mirabile dictu,* he returned to the House of Commons as a Conservative. In reality he had no other place to go than the Conservative fold. The Liberal Party was breaking up on the shoals of change and the Labourites would hardly have welcomed him. The question remains: why did the Conservatives accept him at all? The simple answer is that Winston Churchill was Winston Churchill, a force to reckon. A fuller explanation points to slack leadership within the Conservative Party. Stanley Baldwin's remark upon becoming Prime Minister, that it was safer to have Winston in the cabinet than outside it, is evidence enough. But such a judgment hardly justifies Churchill's appointment to the key post of Chancellor of the Exchequer, for which he was ill prepared. His work as Chancellor has been termed his least successful ministry. By restoring the value of the pound to $4.87 his policy helped the rich and by making British goods more expensive abroad contributed to rising industrial unemployment as sales sagged. In tune with this Churchill was one of the leading opponents of the 1926 General Strike. Through his management of *The British Gazette* he went so far as to suppress the news that the Archbishops of Canterbury and York had urged upon the coal mine operators a restoration of the wage cuts, the issue which had precipitated the strike. By the time Churchill left the Treasury in 1929 he had earned the reputation as the worst Chancellor of the Exchequer in history, an estimate which, he said, "I am inclined to agree with."

Though he continued to sit in parliament for the next decade Winston Churchill was much reduced in political importance, a Conservative back bencher, excluded from the ministry even with the return of Stanley Baldwin as Prime Minister in 1935. He had talked of retirement, of "clearing out," but such a move would have betrayed his ambition quite as much as his sense of public duty. As might be expected of one so well supplied with energy Churchill put his time away from Whitehall to work in other familiar fields. He lectured and published widely, both articles and books, including his monumental study, *Marlborough, His Life and Times.* At home at Chartwell, his country place in Kent, he painted his pictures, pruned his roses, and practiced the art of bricklaying. There too he enjoyed the company of his wife and family, taking a keen interest in the careers his son and daughters were pursuing. He also spent his time in worry, as he peered out on a world given increasingly to international violence. The Japanese were driving deeper into China, the Italians were slaking their neo-imperialist thirst in Ethiopia, and most ominously of all, the Germans were preparing to redraw the map of Europe, while Russia continued an enigmatic but perpetual menace to parliamentary democracy and individual freedom. Churchill's knowledge of the world and its history was immense and his power of penetrating analysis was unsurpassed, but his warnings about the impending doom of Europe were out of step with both official and popular British opinion, and worst of all, his political influence was negligible.

Long an outspoken opponent of Russian communism which in 1919 he advised the victorious Allies to strangle in its cradle, Churchill turned the full force of his invective on the fresh menace, Nazi Germany, because Germany was on the move. As early as November, 1932, he cautioned the House of Commons that the Germans were not looking for "equal qualitative status" but for weapons. And he went on, "When they have their weapons they will ask for the return of their lost territories and colonies and when that demand is made it cannot fail to shake and possibly shatter to their foundations the nations of Europe." Such was Churchill's gift of prophecy, a prophecy disdained by His Majesty's Government.

German rearmament which began shortly after Hitler's accession to power in 1933, as it progressed intruded a new note of urgency into Churchill's warnings. Could Great Britain afford not to rebuild its own forces in the face of the rising German threat? Churchill's formula for the future was simple: to preserve peace, prepare for war. It was not a message which Britain, France, or all of Europe wanted to hear. Such are the historical ironies that Churchill was, at times, dismissed as a warmonger and he was "politically very much alone." To borrow his own phrase, he was "one of the few" who in this case argued that indifference to National Socialism in Germany, or to the appeasement of its leader, Hitler, was a breach of the nation's security. He spoke his mind shortly after the Munich Agreement:

The partition of Czechoslovakia under pressure from England and France amounts to a complete surrender of the Western Democracies to the Nazi threat of force. Such a collapse will bring peace or security neither to England nor France.

It is not Czechoslovakia alone which is menaced, but also the freedom and democracy of all nations. This belief that security can be obtained by throwing a small State to the wolves is a fatal delusion.

In these same days Churchill, who was working on his history of the English-speaking peoples, in his uncanny way of prophecy, spoke of the Anglo-Americans as "the authors, then the trustees, and now they must become the armed champions" of "the rights of the individual and of the subordination of the State to the fundamental and moral conceptions of an ever-comprehending community." The contrasts between democracy as it was embedded in the British and American systems of government and the methods and purposes of totalitarian dictatorship, so well exemplified by Hitler's Germany, confirmed the common bond linking Britain and America. Was Churchill not implying that the shared intellectual and historical values of the English-speaking peoples should have, and might have to have, a concrete, contemporary expression?

Churchill was brought back into the cabinet as First Lord of the Admiralty with the outbreak of war in September of 1939. It was an obvious choice by Neville Chamberlain and one of his happier decisions. The appointment meant that the Royal Navy, which was crucial to the defense of the British Isles, would be guaranteed a state of readiness. It also brought Churchill into the War Cabinet where his knowledge of major policy matters would assist his transition to the prime ministry the next year. Apart from the destruction of Poland and a considerable loss of merchant tonnage in the Atlantic the months from the autumn of 1939 to the spring of 1940 were rightly termed "the phony war." Beginning in March events became all too real. Denmark,

Norway, Holland, Belgium, and France fell like ripe fruit into the German basket. In the midst of this ongoing debacle Churchill was called upon by the King to form a new ministry. On May 10, Winston was back. Three days later he addressed the House of Commons for the first time as Prime Minister. It was a rousing speech.

> You ask, what is our policy? I will tell you: It is to wage war by sea, by land and air with all our might, and with all our strength which God gives us: wage war against a monstrous tyranny, never surpassed in the dark, lamentable catalogue of human crime. What is our aim . . . Victory, victory, at all cost victory, in spite of terror, victory however long and hard the road may be, for without victory there is no survival, let it be realized, no survival for the British Empire, for the urge and the impulse of the ages that mankind will move forward its goal.

> But I take up my task with buoyancy and hope. I feel sure that our cause will not be suffered to fail among men. At this time I feel entitled to claim the aid of all, and I say, 'Come, then, let us go forward together with our united strength.'

Was such confidence in fact misplaced? With the fall of France in June Britain stood alone. Victory in the Battle of Britain, however inspiring, might prove no more than a brief respite should Germany march against England. Even Hitler's decision to attack Russia in June, 1941, was no guarantee of British safety as the Soviet armies reeled under the massive German assault. For all its sacrifices, and they were monumental, the Soviet Union was not the answer to Churchill's prayer. If Britain was to deliver herself from defeat it must rely on a more powerful and a more kindred ally, it must look to the United States.

Churchill was prepared to do as much. As early as 1898 young Winston had asserted, "As a representative of both countries—the idea of an Anglo-American *rapprochement* is very pleasant. One of the principles of my politics will always be to promote a good understanding between English-speaking communities." Shortly thereafter he wrote an article for the *North American Review* in which he spoke of the "great community with whom we are united by a sympathy of a single language and the consciousness of a common aim." The United States was viewed by him as "the Great Republic." In a 1903 speech Churchill made the point that England would do well to cultivate the friendship of the United States because in any future major war American agriculture could supply the basic food requirements of the British people. In a similar vein by supporting Home Rule for Ireland he sought to influence important segments of the American electorate. As First Lord of the Admiralty Churchill was eager to have the United States enter the war in 1914 on the Allied side. In his book, *World Crisis,* published in the 1920s he celebrated the fact that the two Atlantic powers had carried on the war in common. Between the wars the idea of some sort of Anglo-American union occupied much of Churchill's thinking as he contemplated the future. On a visit to the Unites States in 1927 he was struck by the single civilization which the two people enjoyed, despite obvious differences between them. At times he even dreamed of an Anglo-American "covenant of the English-speaking Association," carrying with it a common citizenship. It was in the late 1930s that he devoted much reading and writing to the *History of the English-Speaking Peoples* so that the prospect of Anglo-American cooperation in peace and in war was a present expectation. At the start of World War II England's needs coincided with Churchill's long maturing view of the historical future, that is, a world dominated by the Anglo-Americans, once the war had been won. But first the United States had to become an active military partner.

Except for the Japanese attack on Pearl Harbor—as distinct from Japan's aggression in Southeast Asia—it is difficult to imagine how America could have been prompted to go to war as early as 1941. Quite possibly the shipment of war material to Britain would have provoked incidents between the United States and Nazi Germany which could have built up to the flash point of a declared war. But it is just as likely that Roosevelt and Hitler would both have backed off from such a declaration, though obviously for unlike reasons. The flow of Lend-Lease material had increased appreciably after March, 1941, and incidents in the North Atlantic were sure to multiply. But if that was the road Americans would travel on the way to war it appeared at least in Britain to be a long and an uncertain one. The August, 1941, meeting of Churchill and Roosevelt off the Newfoundland Banks the Germans chose not to interpret as a reason for war with the United States, just as they had swallowed hard at the time of the destroyers for bases deal and the passage of Lend-Lease.

The key to victory was, therefore, the heavy American defeat at Pearl Harbor. In one sense the Germans were the victims of reckless adventuring on the part of their Japanese ally. Prime Minister Churchill seized on the meaning of all this at once. In the pages of *The Grand Alliance* he recalled his thoughts at that time. "So we had won after all . . . we had won the war . . . England would live. . . . Britain would live . . ." His satisfaction with the turn of events at Pearl Harbor was complete, as he wrote, "saturated and satiated with emotion and sensation" he "went to bed and slept the sleep of the saved and thankful." His dreams of Anglo-American unity had become a reality.

"War," Edmund Burke once observed, "never leaves a nation where it found it." Much the same statement might be expressed regarding alliances and the leaders who form them. Shortly after the entry of the United States into World War II Churchill took the initiative by travelling to Washington to convince the Roosevelt administration that the defeat of Germany and not vengeance upon Japan should be the first order of business for the Alliance. Once this was agreed upon it was further decided that there should be a Combined Chiefs of Staff Committee to preside over the conduct of the war. Churchill was no doubt better prepared than Franklin Roosevelt to assume direction of the Anglo-American common cause, which the two men had dramatically spelled out in the 1941 Atlantic Charter. The Prime Minister's experience in such matters was to his advantage while British military and naval forces, admittedly none too successfully, had engaged the enemy for over two years. In laying down strategy Churchill pushed hard for control of the

Mediterranean area as a first requirement for the liberation of Europe, and accordingly American troops landed in North Africa in November, 1942, prepared to link up with the British Eighth Army. But counter tides had already begun to rise and to run strongly. High-ranking Americans including Generals Eisenhower and Arnold favored a direct assault on German strength on the continent instead of nibbling away at the enemy's flanks. The issue of a second front in France in 1942 proved a sore spot in Anglo-American planning. Churchill believed a cross-channel invasion imprudent, a venture sure to fail, with the Americans blithely disagreeing. Stalin was calling for a second front to relieve pressure on Soviet forces in the east; without it some observers thought Russia might be forced out of the war. The fact is Churchill appears correct in his assessment of the disaster awaiting a cross-channel invasion in 1942 in light of the failure of the reconnaissance in force raid at Dieppe and the truly massive buildup needed for the successful 1944 invasion.

As the United States was drawn deeper and deeper into the European war, first in North Africa, then Sicily, Italy, Normandy, southern France, the success of the Anglo-American advance depended more and more on American numbers and American productivity. As a consequence Churchill was able to have less and less influence on events. For example, after the 1943 Casablanca Conference Roosevelt proclaimed unconditional surrender as the only terms acceptable to the Allies for an end to the war, even though Churchill expressed grave reservations about so inflexible a policy. In 1944 the Prime Minister was still voicing doubts about a massive invasion of the continent, preferring a series of smaller strikes along the coast to keep the German General Staff befuddled and large enemy forces pinned down. In the end an opposing strategy, the D-Day invasion—the brainchild of the American Chief of Staff, General Marshall—was launched. Yet as late as February, 1945, at the Yalta meetings Churchill was able to hold his own in discussions with Roosevelt and Stalin.

It is impossible and hardly necessary to fix with precision the date when the balance of power finally shifted away from Churchill and Britain and to Roosevelt and the United States. Evidence accumulated that such was the case and the climax came when FDR's successor, President Truman, made the unilateral decision to use the atomic bomb, not once but twice. In the meantime another kind of bomb had exploded over the political landscape in Great Britain. In July of 1945 Churchill was turned out of the prime ministry as the result of a general election. Americans more so than his countrymen stood in disbelief, if not horror, but he bore the defeat gamely. That he was out of government but not on the shelf Churchill demonstrated by once again mobilizing the English language, this time to do service in the Cold War. The "Iron Curtain" speech which he delivered in March of 1946 at Westminster College, Fulton, Missouri, as President Truman and the world listened, signalled the start of chilly confrontation fed by icy suspicions between the United States and Soviet Union. Britain's great wartime leader felt no satisfaction in pointing out that what he had warned and feared would happen, the loss of Eastern Europe to parliamentary democracy "from Stettin in the Baltic to Trieste in the Adriatic" due to the presence of the Red Army, had happened. It is fitting that he delivered his remarks in America, in the nation's heartland, to an American audience. Before long the theory of containment would be Administration policy. Military aid to Greece and Turkey, the European Economic Recovery Program, and the North Atlantic Treaty Organization followed swiftly upon Churchill's warning. The torch of Anglo-American leadership had passed to the United States. Had not Churchill said, in his own way and time, that the United States remained the "world's last, best hope?"

During his declining years rare honors awaited Churchill. In 1953 Queen Elizabeth II raised him to the Rank of Knight of the Garter, a tribute reserved for those most distinguished in British life. Ten years later he was named an Honorary Citizen of the United States, which he shared exclusively with the Marquis de Lafayette, because it was given only to America's staunchest friends. He accepted both honors as his birthright. At age ninety Winston Churchill died and was buried in the parish churchyard at Bladon, not far from Blenheim Palace, where it all began.

Franklin Roosevelt

For a number of American presidents the office has appeared larger than life and some men, so disposed, have worked hard to measure up to its responsibilities. But Franklin Roosevelt emerged to become larger than the office itself, as had Washington and Lincoln before him, so that his personality—his persona—tended to dominate the America of the New Deal and of World War II. It was William Allen White, the sage of Emporia, Kansas, and as fine a midwestern Republican as there was, who may well have encapsulated the magic of Roosevelt when he gamely conceded, "We who hate your gaudy guts, salute you!" There was something compelling about "that man," even to his enemies, who did hate him with a passion, but who recognized his power if not his greatness. It was left to the mass of Americans of the 1930s and 1940s to love him . . . with a passion . . . because he stood for dignity without indifference to the unfortunate, for warmth but with purpose, and for vision in the face of grim reality. Roosevelt was the first president to use the word "love" in his public utterance and he did so without a trace of self-consciousness. The fireside chats were a mixture of charm, concern, and respect for the intelligence of the average American voter. On the hustings when FDR was in top form—as he was down to 1944— he was quite simply "the champ." The electorate was rarely far from his consideration while he was president, not in the vote-grubbing sense but more by way of calm recognition that to stay in power he had to remain very much in touch with the people. Roosevelt found that congenial. He loved to campaign. Friendly crowds exhilarated him, and the occasional unfriendly audience he accepted as a challenge. Mostly he liked people.

If you treat folks right, they will treat you right, ninety percent of the time, he liked to argue. Having been elected four times to serve them as their president there seems little doubt that FDR achieved a remarkable rapport with the American people.

The life of Franklin Roosevelt has a storybook quality, yet one at odds with the log cabin tradition of the American success story, whether in politics, business, or the professions. He was born—in 1882—into a life of ease and security, the only child of James and Sarah Delano Roosevelt, wealthy Hudson Valley landowners. His father was all of fifty-five years when he was born of a mother twenty-five years his junior. The couple showered their boy with care and affection. Though raised in affluence his father saw to it that he learned to ride, swim, sail, and to race iceboats, one of James Roosevelt's favorite winter diversions, on the Hudson. Sarah Delano was more the doting mother, reluctant to let go of her son when, at the age of fourteen, he was sent to Groton School. Groton was a newly founded prep school, socially exclusive, as much interested in shaping character as in honing minds. At Groton, as at Harrow, the playing fields were important. The headmaster, Reverend Endicott Peabody, described Franklin as an "intelligent and faithful scholar and a good boy," no doubt what his parents wanted of him and what they expected to hear. It was also an honest appraisal of Roosevelt's Groton days.

FDR entered Harvard with the class of '04, and he appears to have enjoyed college life immensely. Though he was content to graduate with a "gentleman's C" he worked hard to become editor of the *Crimson* and thus a notable person on the Harvard scene. Writing to his mother in January, 1904—his father had died in 1900—he appears to have summed things up rather neatly and not altogether with tongue in cheek. "I have been up every night to all hours, but am doing a little studying, a little writing, and few party calls. It is dreadfully hard to be a student, a society whirler, a 'prominent and democratic fellow' and a fiancé—all at the same time." Such a college experience was typical of young men of Roosevelt's station. Harvard was a place to grow up, to get some idea of what career to pursue, and to learn enough from books to help make it all happen. FDR's son, James, once offered a stinging comment on his father's life down to 1904. "To me," he wrote, "the miracle is that Father was strong enough in later life to rise above his Hyde Park-parental-Groton-Harvard background and to become such a warm, sympathetic, understanding individual." To an important if not easily calculable degree credit for this triumph belonged to his wife, Eleanor.

During his senior year at Harvard Franklin became engaged to his distant cousin, Anna Eleanor, the niece of the president of the United States. Eleanor was the daughter of Elliott Roosevelt, TR's younger brother. Hers had been an unhappy childhood. Born in 1884 of well-to-do parents she was orphaned by the age of ten when her father, whom she adored, died of complications arising from alcoholism. The circumstances of his passing, with her mother already dead two years, made Eleanor a lonely and timid child. Thereafter she was raised by her maternal grandmother. Something of an awkward girl she grew up quite plain but plainly intelligent too. In her early teens she was sent off to boarding school near London where she came under the influence of the strong-minded, liberated French woman, Mlle. Souvestre. Returning home she was presented to society in 1902. Eleanor had known Franklin from childhood; now, in 1903, the friendship ripened into romance. Sarah Delano was not keen on the prospect of losing her son but Franklin won her over. Uncle Ted came up from Washington to New York to give the bride away and he and his wife, Edith Kermit Roosevelt, were the official witnesses to the marriage of Eleanor and Franklin—a remarkable foursome. As for Eleanor her place in her husband's public career could hardly have been imagined at the time, and in fact only slowly did she assume that critical role she was eventually to enjoy.

Between 1904 and 1913 Roosevelt's life was busy but not particularly promising. He studied law at Columbia and practiced with the well-regarded firm of Carter, Ledyard and Milburn. Like many other successful politicians he thought legal practice less than satisfying. By 1911 he had turned to politics, becoming the first Democrat to be elected to the New York senate from his Hudson Valley district in more then half a century. During his campaign and while in Albany he was to show his colors as a reformer as at the same time he displayed finesse as a politician. Though he established no notable record in his brief tenure as a legislator Roosevelt was clearly a progressive. In one 1913 speech he noted that as individual liberty had been secured to a large extent it was now time to work for the "liberty of the community." The best interests of the state and the nation required guidance "in the evolution of a new theory of the liberty of the community," President Wilson named him Assistant Navy Secretary (to Josephus Daniels) in 1913. The position gave him considerable administrative experience, brought him closer to one of his two political role models, Woodrow Wilson (the other was Uncle Ted), and enabled him to gain a clear, more definite identity within the ranks of the Democratic Party. During these years Roosevelt also experienced defeats. In 1914 he ran unsuccessfully for the United States Senate and again in 1920 was on the losing presidential ticket of Cox and Roosevelt. He had a promising career, nonetheless. After only ten years in active politics he had won considerable notice, a rising star within his party. Roosevelt was young, vigorous, articulate, handsome, wealthy, and eager to succeed to office. The ultimate prize in American politics had frequently gone to less gifted and less fortunate men.

Two powerful influences affected the political career of Franklin Roosevelt in a fashion meaningful enough to be termed decisive. One was the steadying presence of his wife which threads its way in and out of his presidential years, especially during the days of the New Deal. The other was Roosevelt's tragic illness. In 1921 he contracted infantile paralysis which crippled him for life physically but which worked to reveal in his character resources of courage and optimism, and of under-standing and sympathy for others overtaken by disaster, which otherwise would quite possibly not have been part of his outlook. Because this has been a much written about episode in the life of Franklin Roosevelt and because the story has what is basically a happy ending—FDR rising phoenix-like—there is a tendency to take the whole affair as something which was sure to work out in favor of the president. In the event he did overcome the effects of this cruel blow of fate, and he might not have been elected president except that his sickness put him, a Democrat, out of action during a period of Republican ascendancy. This meant avoiding the occasion of defeat. Yet recognition that FDR fended off the "cruel blow" by something best described as "guts," perhaps even gaudy guts, must never be lost sight of. Roosevelt was forced to make gutsy decisions in the future, decisions which cost many people their lives, but none was more courageous than his determination to come back, to reenter politics, and to prove to others as well as to himself that he had the right stuff. It is only fair to compare the decision of TR to "make his body" with that of FDR to "remake his body." The Roosevelts could be tough, but surely Franklin comes away the more heroic.

It is then slightly ironic that his wife by reason of her steady companionship began more noticeably to influence her husband's future. There was a time in 1918 when the marriage appeared headed for the divorce court. Roosevelt had become involved with Lucy Mercer, a part-time social secretary to his wife and a young woman of distinguished ancestry though decidedly without great means. Eleanor was prepared to go through with a divorce but Sarah Delano, who still controlled the purse strings of the family fortune and who had not quite let go of Franklin, was unalterably opposed. By that time there were five children to consider and, if one cares to be cynical, a political career in the bargain. It was not clear for that matter if Lucy Mercer would have married Franklin once he was free because her religious convictions were heavily weighted against it. The break in the Roosevelt marriage was consequently mended though a sense of intimacy had been lost. With her husband stricken in 1921 Eleanor rallied to his needs. She and Louis Howe, a close friend of Franklin and Eleanor, both held out the prospect that he could and would one day return to the political arena. As Eleanor was later to write of the significance of Franklin's struggle to regain his health: "I have since come to realize and to appreciate that a strength of character was built during these years which made him able to give complete confidence to the people of the nation when they needed it, so that when he said: 'The only thing we have to fear is fear itself' they knew he held that conviction. He had lived through fear and had come out successfully." The cosmetic touches are surely apparent in such a summation but they cannot hide the basic truth of Franklin Roosevelt's will to win.

If the dark clouds hovering over Roosevelt's political future parted suddenly the occurrence was due to FDR himself. In what has been termed "the most crucial decision of his mature political life" he allowed himself to be drafted for the 1928 race for governorship of New York. Most observers agreed that 1928 would be a Republican year nationally and more than one governor would coattail into office. Roosevelt simply decided to defy the odds. Against the advice of most of his political confidants, including the highly influential Louis Howe, he chose to throw the dice—it was that kind of gamble. Roosevelt won the election, of course, and he was reelected for a second term in 1930. Few would question his political instincts thereafter.

Like Herbert Hoover in the White House, Governor Roosevelt faced the brunt of the depression as it affected New York, at the time the most important state in the Union. It was to be a trying apprenticeship. But that is only one way to see Roosevelt's tenure in the state house. It is also important to bear in mind that he was building on four years of progressive reform which had been carried forward by Governor Smith. In housing, education, budgeting, welfare legislation, and water-power he attempted to further the work undertaken initially by Smith. Roosevelt, in response to the socioeconomic calamity of the Great Depression, went beyond the reforms of his predecessor however. The farmers of New York no less than those of the Great Plains were experiencing a depression on top of a depression and Roosevelt advocated legislation to raise farmer income and farm buying power. He kept an eye out for the plight of the industrial worker by means of welfare programs. Less successful was his attempt to promote cheap electricity by generating power from public-owned water sources. Yet in no way was Roosevelt an enemy of the free enterprise system, save in the eyes of the most extreme advocates of *laissez-faire*. Exercising dynamic leadership Roosevelt demonstrated his growing awareness that the old order was passing and that it was essential to the building of a new order to be flexible in conception and pragmatic in implementation. In this way the Albany apprenticeship truly foreshadowed the New Deal.

During his presidency Roosevelt gave a number of notable addresses, including his two Inaugurals, the 1937 Quarantine of Aggressors speech, and his message to Congress on December 8, 1941. The Commonwealth Club Address of 1932, at the beginning of his campaign for the White House, deserves to be ranked among his most important public statements. In essence it was both an analysis of why the nation must change and a challenge that the old order would give way to a new deal. Praising the accomplishments of the past—"So great were our natural resources that we could offer relief not only to our own people but to the distressed of all the world"; "In the middle of the nineteenth century a new force was released and a new dream, created. The force . . . the industrial revolution"; "During the period of expansion there was equality of opportunity"—Roosevelt announced that the conditions brought about by success called for a "reappraisal of values." The day of freewheeling capitalism was over. "The day of enlightened administration has come." The task of government therefore was to assist the development of "an economic declaration of rights, of an economic constitutional order." Conflict between government and business must give way to cooperation, based on mutual need and trust. What the first New Deal became Roosevelt had broadly described in the Commonwealth Club Address. By implication the task of bringing a new day about rested with the president. The "crucible years" as they have been termed were over for FDR. When the election returns were in he had become the thirty-third president of the United States. Destiny and the depression stared him full in the face.

The 1929 stock market crash and the Great Depression which followed were, apart from the Civil War, the most trying episode in American domestic history, if not in the whole life of the Republic. The United States had become the model of both a highly prosperous capitalistic economy and a continually successful constitutional polity. Capitalism and constitutionalism were the twin pillars upon which American society rested. As capitalism experienced shock wave after shock wave beginning in 1929, the constitutional underpinnings were correspondingly threatened. Not that the basic stability of the United States government was immediately at risk; but a downward economic spiral if left unchecked could produce dire political results. Inasmuch as Americans had always prided themselves on their sturdy constitution its intimate association with failing capitalism might well lead to a questioning of some of the assumptions upon which American civilization rested.

As the depression deepened and then stagnated more than one critic doubted whether capitalism was worth salvaging, unless it were drastically modified. The country was on a political razor's edge when in 1933 Franklin Roosevelt assumed presidential power; what could happen under his administration of the government and how he would restyle the relationship of government and the private economic order could well determine the long-term future of both the constitutional and capitalistic systems. FDR himself understood this as well as any of his contemporaries, which was reason enough for him to proceed with bold caution, that is, to appear to promote far-reaching reforms of institutions in order to retain a place for them in American society. One of the first moves of the president was thus to protect the privately owned banks from some kind of nation-alization. In saving the banks he wanted to put them within an updated framework, and one which would be in keeping with a fresh emphasis on socially responsible capitalism. Both bankers and reformers had reason to be grateful for New Deal banking policy and legislation.

Few historians claim that Franklin Roosevelt solved the economic problems associated with the Great Depression. Troubles remained until business made a strong comeback in response to war orders emanating from preparations for World War II. The reason for Roosevelt's failure is not hard to identify: general recovery was beyond the ability of any one man or any one scheme of reform. Too many factors which gave rise to the depression were outside the control either of individuals or institu-tions. As for the president he possessed only limited economic knowledgeability though he had gained some under-standing of banks, real estate, insurance, taxes, and stocks and bonds as a result of his law practice and the conduct of family business. On the other hand he had gained impressive political experience in relating governmental policy to economic problems during his two terms as New York governor. His campaign for the presidency found him calling for a balanced budget. He told one audience in Pittsburgh in October, 1932, balancing had become a top priority in his thinking. In this respect FDR differed little from Hoover.

The New Deal never achieved a balanced budget and deficit spending became a hallmark of the Roosevelt administrations. Once in office the pragmatist in the president came quickly to the fore. A balanced budget should not be an end in itself but a means of promoting recovery. Using the Keynesian argument that deficit spending was an acceptable alternative if the large socioeconomic objectives of recovery were to be achieved Roosevelt urged the proposition that the end justified the means, adding that if the end did not justify the means, what did? This may appear as a glib rationalization at a distance of fifty years; at the time it made a lot more sense than Hoover's standpattism which gave the appearance that the nation was too frightened to act.

Friendly and hostile critics agree that what FDR did was to defeat the depression psychology by insisting that there was nothing to fear but fear itself, which he coupled with his stirring challenge: "This generation of Americans has a rendezvous with destiny." Sometimes he used words alone and more often words designed to explain deeds and excite hope—everything from the bank holiday of 1933 to the 1937 Second Inauguration in which he said: "I see one-third of the nation ill housed, ill clad, and ill nourished. It is not in despair that I paint you that picture. I paint it in hope because the Nation, seeing and understanding the injustice in it proposes to paint it out"—Roosevelt spurred and challenged his fellow citizens. Harsh economic conditions became more tolerable because of ongoing efforts to overcome them and because of steadying reassurances on the part of the president whose words were balm for a bruised and suffering people.

Did Roosevelt achieve this psychological breakthrough in a single-handed fashion? At times it must have seemed that way for he relished the role of exponent of the New Deal quite as much as he did that of facilitator of diverse philosophies within his administration and among his advisers. FDR as president has been variously portrayed: heir to progressivism, broker of disparate ideas, manipulator of public opinion, party chieftain, democratic dictator, last of the patrician presidents, among others. None of these characterizations represents him as a leader possessed of economic sophistication or expertise. His abilities lay in other directions. For example, he took his grave physical disability and turned it into a great humanitarian—and incidentally a great political— asset, The March of Dimes. Roosevelt almost always managed to appear on what was popularly deemed the side of the angels. His 1935 revenue proposal was termed "soak the rich"; his opponents were "economic royalists"; when he was called a "traitor to his class" it came across more as a compliment than insult. The president's name had a magical quality. Union leaders, endeavoring to organize workers in the iron, steel, automotive, and other industries whispered: "The President wants you to join" and that struck many as reason enough to do so.

The businessman's New Deal of 1933 gave way to the second New Deal which stressed reform more than recovery, in some measure because Roosevelt was under heavy fire from the conservatives and from the radical reformers. The president personally resented what he considered the ingratitude of the business community which by 1934 was saying that it was time for the government to back away from its various schemes to prime the economic pump and allow the nation's economy to self-adjust in the best Adam Smith fashion. Roosevelt was not convinced that the meager momentum thus far achieved would be able to propel the economy sufficiently to put millions of unemployed back to work. The business proposition was to him selfish and callous and he struck back by denouncing so shortsighted and self-centered an attitude. Meanwhile his critics on the left were busy attacking the New Deal, saying it was token reform at best. According to Dr. Francis Townsend nothing had been done for the old folks. Father Charles Coughlin in a style reminiscent of Populism accused Roosevelt of being in collusion with the Wall Street bankers therefore necessarily neglecting the interests of the common man. Huey Long, the kingfish of Louisiana politics and a redneck capable of depriving Roosevelt of the support of the Solid South, announced that the only way to bring the country out of the depression was "to redistribute the wealth," a euphemism for heavy personal and corporate income taxes. Roosevelt was too moderate a reformer to embrace the extreme views of these left-of-center spokesmen but he was too astute a politician to ignore the fact that Townsend-Coughlin-Long were able to generate mass appeal by their demands.

Roosevelt tended to take many of these strictures of the right and left rather more personally than most politicians. Because his ambition inclined to a second term he launched the second New Deal in 1935, thereby turning his back on the business community to seek votes from among the great mass of Americans still disaffected, but less so because the president had undertaken significant if moderate steps, supporting Social Security legislation, pro-labor laws, new restrictions on public utility holding companies, and the banks—laws generally identified with the public interest. In all this the president was prepared to put his political future on the line. It was the president who would or would not be reelected. And as the presidency went, so also the New Deal.

The 1936 Roosevelt landslide magnified FDR's sense of his own power and led him to his one stunning political defeat while in the White House, the proposal to reorganize the Supreme Court. After some initial decisions which favored the New Deal the Court reversed itself in 1935 by striking down certain legislation, including the National Industrial Recovery Act and the Agricultural Adjustment Act, centerpieces of the recovery program. Very quickly the Court was perceived by the president as a stumbling block to measures he thought vital to the welfare of the people. He dismissed the membership of the Court as "the nine old men" and contended that not only were they out of touch with the times but that their age made it impossible for them to keep abreast of the cases on the docket. Immediately after the 1936 election Roosevelt, in close and highly confidential consultation with his Attorney General, Homer Cummings, developed a plan to bring the court into line with administration thinking. The bill which was submitted to Congress in January proposed that if a justice did not retire at the age of seventy—there was a majority of sitting judges at or approaching that age at the time—the president might nominate an additional justice up to a total number of fifteen. Once again Roosevelt had interpreted the position of the Court as a personal affront which must be revenged, and he believed, as it turned out incorrectly, that his power and prestige were great enough to force the Court to answer his call. It was a rare display of bad political judgment on Roosevelt's part. The nation's newspapers were almost unanimous in denouncing the bill and many a New Deal legislator deserted the president on this one. Once the dust had settled, was the Court reorganization proposal nothing more than Rooseveltian ploy? Did the president act simply to throw a scare into the Court, to put it on notice that the people had spoken and the Court must now listen? After all in 1937 the "nine old men" declared constitutional the Social Security Act, the Wagner Labor Relations Act, and other important pieces of legislation from the Second, or classic, New Deal. Admittedly the decisions were rendered by a five to four vote, winning approval by the narrowest of margins, but the results were the same: the New Deal had become legitimatized almost at the same time as it had been approved by the people. The president was pragmatist enough to be satisfied with losing the battle while winning the war.

President Roosevelt took only a limited interest in the conduct of American diplomacy during his first four years in office. Domestic problems relating to recovery and reform were too pressing to allow diversions in that direction, so that Secretary of State Cordell Hull was in charge of what foreign policy activity there was down to 1937. While the world was greatly troubled from the mid-thirties on Hull took no important initiative. In the Far East the United States denounced the Japanese drive into Manchuria and north central China; the administration supported but did not extend the scope of the Stimson Doctrine. The Clark Memorandum which in Hoover's administration had proclaimed the end of the Roosevelt Corollary to the Monroe Doctrine the president would reenforce with his Good Neighbor Policy. But as

Latin America was not a hot spot at the time Roosevelt's journey to address a Pan-American Conference in Argentina in 1936 was mostly a friendly gesture. As for Europe, despite the rise of dictators intent on scrapping the Versailles Treaty the president went along with the neutrality laws passed by the Congress after 1934. Designed to prevent the outbreak of World War II, as has been suggested by many authorities, Roosevelt was apparently content with these neutrality laws.

It is best to remember, however, that FDR was an old Wilsonian internationalist who retained a good bit of the ex-president's idealism as part of his outlook. By 1937 it was increasingly apparent to many observers, including the president, that a major European power political realignment was in the offing, whether by means of concession-diplomacy or by war. Germany under Adolph Hitler was rearming openly, Italy had invaded and conquered Ethiopia, the Berlin-Rome Axis alliance was aborning, and three major powers, Germany, Italy, and the Soviet Union, were involved in the Spanish Civil War. What the president had to bear in mind was how such developments would affect the vital interests of the United States. As early as October, 1937, he announced at a huge gathering in Chicago that the United States proposed to "quarantine aggressors," not only in Europe but in the Far East. If the Chicago address was intended to intimidate any of the aggressor powers it failed utterly; if it was intended as a means of sounding out American public opinion in support of an active, interventionist policy its seeds were cast on sterile ground. Nonetheless from the Quarantine of Aggressors speech can be dated a notable shift both in American foreign policy and in the conduct of that policy; Secretary Hull was replaced by President Roosevelt as the officer in charge, a position he had fully consolidated by the time he took the unprecedented step of running for a third term in 1940.

Although the European War broke out in September, 1939, it took the fall of France in June, 1940, to arouse the nation to some realization of the menace of Nazi Germany to American national interest. The president was well ahead of public and Congressional opinion, however. The year 1940 was also a presidential election year. The fragile international situation—only Britain of the major powers had been able to defy Hitler—prompted FDR to seek a third term. At the time he was openly in favor of all possible aid to Great Britain short of war. The Republicans had an unexampled opportunity to give the electorate a clear choice by nominating one of any number of prominent isolationists. Instead Wendell Willkie, who tended to sound like imitation Roosevelt in foreign policy while excoriating the New Deal, was chosen. Meanwhile the president decided to make the destroyers for bases deal with the British, a move which was readily interpreted in Berlin as well as at home as a hostile act. Coming as it did in September Roosevelt seemed to be saying to the isolationists, do your damnedest, but I'm not playing politics with American security. The president, nonetheless, sometimes voiced what people who were afraid of war wanted to hear. In Boston just a few days before the election he declared: "I shall say it again, and again, and again. Your boys are not going to be sent into any foreign wars." Perhaps the electorate failed to distinguish between the president's words and his actions. After his election triumph Roosevelt proceeded to move resolutely in the direction of armed conflict. The United States must become "the great arsenal of democracy" he told the American people in a Christmastime fireside chat. In his usual message to Congress in January he called for the passage of a Lend-lease act to provide military aid to any country whose defense was deemed vital to American interests. The Congress responded quickly, passing the law in March, but at a time when only Great Britain was Germany's enemy.

With the German invasion of Russia in June, 1941, Roosevelt's foreign policy stood at a crossroads. The "arsenal of democracy" idea was totally incongruous if American supplies were to be shipped to a totalitarian state like the Soviet Union. On the other hand Lend-lease aid might have to be extended to the Russians to keep them in the war. Russia was tying down huge numbers of German troops and inflicting heavy casualties on them, even in retreat. Roosevelt's pragmatism prevailed: the enemy of my enemy is my friend. But there remained in FDR much of the idealist. In August, 1941, he met with Prime Minister Churchill off the Newfoundland Banks and there the two men jointly announced the principles of the Atlantic Charter. A document which protested that men must everywhere be free, it was the kind of sentiment which Woodrow Wilson would have gladly endorsed. This combination of Rooseveltian pragmatism and idealism was, nonetheless, exposing the country to a possible war. By October United States destroyers were engaging German submarines in the waters of the North Atlantic and suffering casualties in such encounters. To some at least it seemed only a matter of time and place.

December 7, 1941, was the time and Pearl Harbor the place. Japan, a nation friendly to Germany, launched its devastating attack on major components of the U.S. Pacific fleet. The American response was instantaneous and unambiguous: the enemies of the nation must be beaten into unconditional surrender. Within hours the United States was at war with Germany, Italy, and Japan, and allied with Great Britain and the Soviet Union. If the argument can be advanced that the United States would have been under the gun with the triumph of the Axis powers Roosevelt's management of American foreign policy vis-a-vis the aggressor states was anything but sinister. As it was Japan which chose to attack the United States initially, there necessarily arises the question relative to presidential scheming at the time of Pearl Harbor. Yet Roosevelt might well have been justified in believing that the Japanese would not strike at American sovereign territory in the Hawaiian Islands. There were sound reasons against such a move. It was quite simply reckless. It was the Japanese who blundered at Pearl Harbor arousing the American people as no other act perpetrated against them had ever done. Certainly the president's task of leading the nation in defense of its vital interests was made easier.

Roosevelt's wartime leadership encompassed both military and diplomatic affairs. It was FDR who decided that Hitler was the greater menace and that the United States should put primary emphasis on the war in Europe, and it was he who made the fateful decision to construct the atom bomb. But his ongoing concern was diplomacy. The great wartime conferences at Casablanca, Teheran, and Yalta were remarkable opportunities for personal diplomacy, but the results were not always to

America's advantage. This was especially true of the meetings held at Yalta in February, 1945. Indeed Yalta is a word not unlike Munich in that it connotes to some a surrender to Russian demands for hegemony in eastern Europe. In as far as this was the case the burden of responsibility was largely Roosevelt's. Stalin's refusal to allow for the development of free governments within the Soviet sphere of influence has haunted statesmen since the end of World War II. In dealing with "Uncle Joe" Roosevelt's highly touted "personal touch" was ineffective. There were mitigating circumstances which help to explain this. FDR was a sick man, in fact a dying man, in February of 1945; he lacked the strength and determination to play the game of diplomatic chess. The Red Army was in full occupation of eastern Europe at a time when Japan was still in the war. Perhaps Russian aid would be crucial in that last great battle. The atom bomb remained a secret weapon but it was an unproved weapon as well. Taking all these factors into account Roosevelt did as well as might be expected of him though a younger, tougher man—and Truman's performance at the July Potsdam Conference comes to mind at once—might have done considerably better.

Franklin Delano Roosevelt died April 12, 1945. He left much work unfinished, yet his accomplishments were of the first magnitude. The war in Europe was all but over, Japan was on the ropes militarily while stubbornly refusing to recognize it, the United Nations organization—a mix of idealism and pragmatism—was about to be born. Beyond these considerations FDR had taken up the glorious burden of the presidency in 1933 with the nation dispirited and confused. And he had turned the country around by giving Americans something to believe in and work for. His critics were harsh and not always wrong. His followers were legion and sometimes blind. By unifying the opposition as well as galvanizing the country Franklin Roosevelt stood at the center of American public life for the twelve most crucial years of twentieth century history. Only recently has the shadow that he cast on the presidency and the nation begun to fade.

Ideas and Women

Clara Barton and Mary Ritter Beard were women of high ideals, and that was the provenance of their ideas which had such a powerful impact on America. A common regard for the welfare of mankind, and especially those men and women who found themselves in dire circumstances, motivated both Barton and Ritter to think and to act. In a word they were activists, activists of a different strain to be sure, the difference in some ways brought about by the times in which they lived. The Civil War had a shaping effect on Barton with its shattered bodies of men dead or dying, whereas Beard was moved to action by the suffering imposed on innocent men and women due to the excesses of the Industrial Revolution. Barton went on to institutionalize her ideas with the founding and management of the American Red Cross. For her part Beard through female suffragist activities and her writing of the history of women helped win recognition and acceptance of this life force and therefore the vital place of women in history no less than in today's society. For both Barton and Beard the ideal gave birth to the ideas on which they acted for the everyday good of humankind.

CLARA BARTON

Clara Barton was born on Christmas Day, 1821, and died on Good Friday, April 12, 1912, prompting the biographer and reader alike to ponder the meaning of her remarkable life of service and whatever message it might convey with the passing years. It would be artificial, however, to make too much of the model intimated by her birth and death days, even though for her burial she asked that the old-time hymn, *Jesus, Lover of My Soul,* be among the songs her friends would remember her by. Raised a Universalist, Clara Barton did not hold much with the churches. Toward the end of her life she was attracted to Christian Science and came to regard Mary Baker Eddy as "our greatest living woman." But she never joined her church. The world was too much with Clara Barton to encourage reliance on divine grace or divine science.

Is Clara Barton then better understood as a version of Florence Nightingale, whose feats of caring for the wounded during the Crimean War were legendary in America almost as quickly as in England? She looked after the wounded in the American Civil War and like her English counterpart was to struggle with bureaucrats and politicians and she too triumphed. Less than ten years after Florence Nightingale performed her miracle at Scutari Clara Barton was serenaded by Union soldiers as the "Florence Nightingale of America" and it was to be a recurring tribute to her in the years to come. Again similarities, often no more than coincidences uniting these two nineteenth century heroines, may work to obscure rather than to reveal the stature of this great woman whose reputation as the "Angel of the Battlefield" was a preliminary to her far more lasting accomplishment as a founder of the American Red Cross.

Clarissa Harlowe Barton, as she was named by her parents, was the fifth and last child of a typical New England family. Her brothers and sisters were many years older than she. The baby of the family, Clara was to a degree coddled, a factor helping to shape her character. As she was sometimes a willful child, so she was a willful adult whenever she was in pursuit of her life's work?service to others.

She grew up in awe of her father, Captain Stephen Barton, a man important in the town of Oxford, Massachusetts, where the family lived. Captain Barton had fought alongside Mad Anthony Wayne and had been present at the death of Tecumseh. When other little girls listened to fairy tales Clara sat spellbound as her "soldier-father" recounted stories of his part in the great drama of wresting land from savage Indians. If her taste for war was not innate, it was early a secure part of her outlook. Other aspects of her childhood were more conventional: she learned to sew a dress, milk a cow, cook a meal, ride her horse, all skills she put to good use in the years to come when she roamed the world from Texas to Turkey to aid people in distress. As a youngster Clara studied hard, began a scrapbook, kept a daily journal. Meanwhile she perforce became the nurse of her brother, David, who was badly injured in a farm accident. For two years Clara was David's constant companion, responsible for his medicine and his morale. No doubt she helped to keep her brother alive and got to know firsthand the psychology of the sickroom, all the while being made aware of her deepest impulse, to be of help to others.

Her parents were advised to make a schoolteacher of Clara, not only to give her an occupation but also a purpose since throughout her teens she was restless and unsettled. Schoolteaching was the most common calling a Yankee girl of eighteen might answer but it proved to offer too little of the satisfaction from work and sacrifice that Clara expected and needed. She was to have a variety of teaching positions, first in the local school district of North Oxford, then as a teacher of the children of the factory hands employed in her brother's mill. She entered the Liberal Institute at Clinton, New York in 1850. With its advanced instruction in any number of school subjects the Institute did much to add to her self-confidence and to expand her knowledge. She also met one or more eligible bachelors at the Institute though by this time Clara?she had just turned thirty?appears to have put aside any thoughts of marriage. The death of her mother combined with provision by the family for her father enabled her to cut ties with home. She next took employment in a school at Highstown, New Jersey, and within a short time decided to open her own school?probably the first free school in New Jersey?in nearby Bordentown. This venture was an overnight success, in part no doubt because she agreed to work for no salary until the town was convinced of the worth of her efforts. Before long the school enrolled six hundred boys and girls. The town decided that so large a responsibility required the presence of a man, and when one was appointed principal Clara resigned immediately. Throughout her long life of service to others she always found it irksome and often impossible to work under someone else. This attitude was a source of much of what she was able to accomplish but it also helped to explain why, at last, she was forced to retire from the leadership of the American Red Cross which she had founded and fostered for so many years.

From schoolteaching Clara Barton went on to be a federal government employee, arriving in Washington in 1854, and fully intent on supporting herself. At first she worked as a copyist in the Patent Office at a rate of pay of ten cents per hundred words. Within three months, largely because of her unstinting and meticulous performance, she was named confidential secretary to Judge Charles Mason, Commissioner of Patents. Clara was beginning to take on the profile of a liberated woman, best dramatized perhaps by her salary of fourteen hundred dollars per year. The very novelty of her achievement soon brought disappointment. Secretary of Interior Robert McClelland disapproved of women in government service working alongside men and she was forced to revert to copyist with loss of both pay and status. Because she had always lived frugally and in fact enjoyed the benefit of some independent means Clara soon thereafter returned to Massachusetts to visit her family and she remained largely unoccupied for the last years of the 1850s. Her physical health, which tended to fluctuate between a robustness uncommon to a woman of her slight build and a state of collapse, had much to do with the lassitude of these years. For that matter her mental health followed the same pattern, alternating between fits of near total euphoria and absolute depression, even to the point, on occasion, of contemplating suicide. It is unclear whether her loss of physical stamina produced her psychological difficulties or whether the reverse was true.

With the close of the decade the nation was moving closer and closer to civil war. Clara Barton had relocated in Washington by that time and through her family connections, which she was never reluctant to exploit, she met Henry Wilson, Senator from Massachusetts and Chairman of the Senate Committee on Military Affairs. He was to be her most constant and powerful political friend as long as he lived. When the time came for Clara Barton to launch her great war work the backing of Wilson was nothing less than essential.

Modern warfare with its high casualty rate received an early expression in the American Civil War. Not since the great campaigns of Napoleon did troops in such numbers engage in battle. The scale of carnage rose sharply because of advances in weaponry while a fratricidal warfare has a way of bringing about rare acts of valor and brutality. Lincoln proved able to match Southern determination to defend a homeland with an equal Northern determination to preserve the Union. Heavy losses were the result; yet neither of the armies was well prepared to deal with battle casualties. The Union government created the Sanitary Commission, the official agency charged with the myriad details of caring for the sick, wounded, and dying?hospitals, doctors, medicines, nurses, bandages, food, shelter. But such was the magnitude of the soldiers' needs that there was room, ample room as it turned out, for Clara Barton's free-lance efforts.

She was drawn into the business of ministering to Union troops when the Sixth Massachusetts Regiment, ordered to Washington in April of 1861, had to fight its way through Baltimore, a city with pronounced Confederate sympathies. News swept the capital that the Massachusetts boys had arrived in Washington "ragged, bloody, and draggled." Clara Barton felt impelled to act at once in their behalf. The few items which she could gather up to offset the loss of baggage by the regiment were hardly sufficient. Through the columns of the *Worcester Daily Spy* she appealed to the people back home to send supplies. Before long all New England was ready to pitch in. Clara Barton had become a kind of quartermaster. The amount of goods received swelled to such proportions?everything from shirts and socks to candy and jellies?that a warehouse soon had to be rented.

For the next several years Clara Barton continued to expand her "war work." Like Captain Stephen Barton, she proposed to go onto the battlefield. To enter a war zone required permission of the army, however. The idea was so novel that despite the direct intercession of Governor Andrews of Massachusetts the army was unwilling at first to provide the necessary permissions to pass. After much importuning General D.H. Rucker, Assistant Quartermaster General, finally yielded. He provided not only permission but wagons as well. Soon army transport was a matter of routine. The fact is the Sanitary Commission was understaffed and could not possibly have satisfied all the demands of the battlefield. Clara Barton stood ready to supplement where required and to initiate aid where there was no other and she soon won the respect of important Union generals, Burnside and Butler among them.

The stories about Clara Barton, the "Angel of the Battlefield," were soon common coin of the private soldier's realm. She was known to have cradled the dying soldier boy in her arms, pretending to be the sister he longed to see. She supervised the loading of Union wounded on hospital trains within earshot of Confederate troops. She met President Lincoln and rubbed elbows with generals, cabinet officers, and members of Congress, always with her work foremost in the conversations she had with the men who ran the war. The legend was born?there was nothing that Clara Barton was not able to do to ease the pain of those who were prepared to fight and die for their country.

Generally Clara Barton's efforts were directed at assisting in the collection and distribution of hospital supplies and all similar necessities, blankets, clothing, tobacco, sundries. Her forte was not nursing as such. There were occasions, however, as at the battle of Fredericksburg, when she went directly into hospital to help the operating surgeon as he tried to save life and limb. And in the aftermath of Fredericksburg, one of the bloodiest battles of the entire conflict, she dressed the wounds of Confederate and Union soldiers alike.

The end of the Civil War in April, 1865, meant that Clara Barton had to redirect her "war work." In March she obtained permission from President Lincoln to commence the grim task of determining the fate of those missing in action. She had already received a number of letters from families who had turned to her for assistance. Senator Wilson as usual had lent his helping hand by placing Clara in touch with the President. Lincoln's laconic note authorizing her to act deserves quotation. "To The Friends Of Missing Persons: Miss Clara Barton has kindly offered to search for missing prisoners of war. Please address her at Annapolis, giving her the name, regiment, and company. [Signed] A. Lincoln." But she did not confine her searches to missing prisoners of war. Any missing soldier, whose family supplied the details, she assumed responsibility in accounting for. Once again she was undertaking a task which might be thought as properly belonging to the army, and once again this invasion of an official domain caused friction. The situation was made worse when she and her staff turned up numerous errors on the part of the army, especially respecting graves. The particular difficulty was the misidentification of graves at Andersonville, the notorious Confederate prison. She clashed directly with the officer in charge only to discover that influential friends in Washington were unable to convince the Secretary of War to support her. Such petty quarrels should not be allowed to detract from Barton's accomplishments. In the search for missing men she supervised the exchange of over one hundred thousand letters of inquiry and information, often meeting the running expenses of such work from her own funds. The "Angel of the Battlefield" did not leave her post until taps could be finally sounded for the three hundred sixty thousand Union soldiers who had died in the fighting.

Bouts of illness which recurred throughout her lifetime were especially frequent and prolonged in the years following the Civil War. She was very much in demand as a speaker and people flocked to hear her, or simply to be able to say that they had seen her, whether she was in Brooklyn, New York or Des Moines, Iowa. Yet it may have been more than the strain of travel across the country which produced a major collapse in 1869. Was it that without war to provide the victims who needed aid, Clara Barton discovered insufficient purpose in life? If so, it is a cruel paradox but not an altogether fanciful one.

Upon the advice of her doctor Barton left for Europe in late 1869 where it was believed she would be completely free from the distractions derived from her fame. As Picasso once said: "Fame is the castigation of the genius by God." Clara would remain in Europe for nearly four years. Instead of the rest she sought she was soon in the middle of another war, that between Prussia and its German allies and France. She was to perform the same acts of heroism which had distinguished her during the American Civil War. At the same time Clara Barton was made aware of the relatively new International Red Cross which aimed to do in organized fashion but in an entirely neutral manner what she had done for her country. Clara Barton had always been glad enough to care for wounded Confederate soldiers on an individual basis but an international organization which counted wounded soldiers as neither friend nor foe was a different matter.

Staying first with friends in Geneva Clara Barton met Dr. Louis Appia who was eager to see the American Nightingale. Appia spoke at length about the Red Cross, going over its ten principles as stated in the Geneva Convention of 1864, its enabling document. Already two dozen nations had signed the agreement but, she was informed by Dr. Appia, the United States was not among them. The fact is the United States had been invited to become a signatory but had refused. Both Secretaries of State Seward and Fish advanced the argument that such a move would violate the Monroe Doctrine as it would be a first step in entangling the nation in the affairs of Europe. Clara Barton confessed that she had known nothing of the organization much less that her country had spurned membership.

When the Franco-Prussian War broke out in 1870 Barton, whose health had shown no marked improvement since her arrival in Europe, quite spontaneously assumed her familiar role on the battlefield. She may have lacked the strength and stamina exhibited during the Civil War but a brief account of her activities demonstrates that the opportunity to aid men and women in distress in the wake of war (and at later times due to all manner of man-made and natural catastrophes) worked as a tonic to her spirit no less than to her physical prowess. As it turned out she did most of her work behind the German lines and became a lifelong friend of the Duchess of Baden who herself was an ardent supporter of the Red Cross. The fall of Strasbourg?to the troops of the Duke of Baden?was Clara's golden opportunity to put her organizational skills and experience to work on behalf of soldiers and civilians who were desperate in the aftermath of battle. As supplies came pouring in from Baden she oversaw their distribution, acting very much on her own initiative. She was not in any way an official of the Red Cross, only a stranger in a strange and tormented city. Her sense of purpose and her skill at organization easily transcended these considerations. From Strasbourg she moved to Metz, and from Metz to Paris where she undertook to distribute the various supplies which had arrived there from America and which had been held back by the United States minister, Eli Washburne. In all these activities Barton was protected by the flag, arm band, and markings of the Red Cross, which spoke her neutrality and guaranteed her freedom of action, Fully impressed by the concept of the Red Cross as well as how it worked in the field it is hardly unexpected that when Clara Barton returned to the United States in 1873 she undertook a campaign to win American adherence to the Geneva Convention.

On March 16, 1882 the Senate confirmed the Geneva Treaty and the United States became a party to the Convention. Of the event Clara Barton wrote simply and somewhat sadly: "So it is done . . . I had worked so long and got so weak and broken I could not even feel glad." She had indeed waged an uphill and uncertain battle to convince the American government that it was honor bound and duty bound to be associated with other civilized nations in the work of human relief. There were real reasons why Barton could claim this most important triumph only after years of setback and delay, reasons having to do with the lady herself and with the posture of the United States government. Clara was no sooner back home than she faced a double tragedy. Her sister Sally's death hit her hard. Soon thereafter her old friend, upon whom she had been counting to help her in the fight for American approval of the Geneva Convention, Henry Wilson?he had become Vice President Wilson?also died. Clara's faltering health required that she enter a sanitarium. It was 1877 before she was again able to live on her own.

When well enough to assume the task, Barton decided to promote the Red Cross on two fronts. By recognizing that the public knew little or nothing of the Red Cross she prepared a brochure: *The Red Cross of the Geneva Convention: What It Is* for circulation among influential people inside and outside of government. With the blessing of officials in Geneva who accorded her formal recognition as their American spokeswoman she began to lay siege to key officers in the Hayes administration. Her health remained fragile, but her spirit grew more determined.

Determination, even of the magnitude of Clara Barton, could not guarantee results. As Seward and Fish had opposed America's place in the International Red Cross, Secretary of State William H. Evarts was of the same mind and for the same reason, the Monroe Doctrine. Nor was President Hayes of much help. With the election of James A. Garfield in 1880 prospects brightened. He was well disposed toward the treaty and his Secretary of State, James G. Blaine, was enthusiastic. He dismissed the bugbear of the Monroe Doctrine, insisting that it "was not made to ward off humanity." Secretary of War Robert Todd Lincoln was also favorable. Meanwhile Barton had widened her campaign to secure backing from important people and set about to establish a formal chapter of the Red Cross in Washington. Once the public better appreciated what the Red Cross was and could do in peacetime as well as during war chances for acceptance by the Garfield administration would be enhanced. The death by assassination of the president in the late summer of 1881 delayed but did not defeat Clara Barton's purpose. The new president, Chester A. Arthur, looked kindly on such a treaty and Clara rallied old friends, among them Generals Grant, Sheridan, Burnside, and Butler, to her side. The new Secretary of State, Frederick T. Frelinghuyson, was sympathetic. No enemy now stood in the way, no door was now closed. President Arthur signed the Geneva Treaty on March 1, 1882 and two weeks later, with Senate ratification, it became the law of the land. Clara Barton was in her sixty-second year and those who knew her slightly, or not at all, might well have assumed that she would now gracefully retire.

Clara Barton still had thirty years to live and she lived them to the full. By ceaseless activity in confronting human misery arising from flood, fire, and earthquake as well as by war and massacres she became the embodiment of the American Red Cross. As its longtime president she chose to be in the field rather than behind a desk whenever possible, at the site of trouble, ordering, organizing, soothing as only she could. Whether it was a forest fire in Michigan, floods along the Mississippi or at Johnstown, a Carolina hurricane, or a tidal wave at Galveston Clara Barton was there in person. She understood better than most that after the initial relief had been provided plans had to be made and funded to help bring about recovery. This also, she came to believe and to practice, was the work of the Red Cross.

The massacres in Armenia and the attendant sickness and starvation along with the Spanish-American War, both coming at the close of the nineteenth century, afforded Clara Barton further opportunity to add to her international reputation. In 1896 she went to Constantinople, the very place where Florence Nightingale had served, to establish a bridgehead for access to the remote provinces. She was received by the Turkish government and allowed to begin the flow of supplies to Armenia. Especially did the Red Cross make available seed and simple tools so that the survivors might begin the task of feeding themselves. Food stations along with hospitals were set up and the fight against typhus and cholera begun. How this little old lady of seventy-five was able to endure the hardships and escape fatal illness is hard to explain. Even so there were signs, because of the scope of the operation, that certain of her staff had reason to question some of her decisions. These were the first clouds on the horizon, warnings of a storm to follow.

There were more than enough disasters to keep Clara Barton busy.

The Spanish-American War found her back in action. She went to Cuba before hostilities commenced to see what could be done for the *reconcentrados*, whose plight was exploited in the American Press, and was in Havana when the *Maine* was sunk in February, 1898. She stayed on, under the flag of the Red Cross, when war followed. Instinctively she wanted to be of service to American soldiers but friction quickly developed between her and the army. The army thought she would be be in the way and she wanted to be with the wounded. Much of what the Red Cross supplied in Cuba was of help to the rebels fighting the Spanish. They had no medical support and the Red Cross was a singular blessing. Not that the Army Medical Corps had things fully in hand for the American soldiers. Barton told of visiting one hospital near Santiago which brought back some of the worst of her Civil War memories. In a flash she was in the cook house supervising food preparation and searching the surrounding area for supplies. But it was the spirit of the Red Cross which was ever uppermost with her. When Colonel Roosevelt approached her to inquire if he might buy some medicine and bandages for his wounded Rough Riders, she told him "not for a million dollars," but "you can have them for the asking." The legend of Clara Barton continued to grow. The war ended but not before the *State of Texas*, a ship loaded with supplies, entered Santiago harbor in July, Clara Barton in control if not in command. With the war there were renewed complaints, however, about Barton's freewheeling conduct of Red Cross affairs in Cuba. The storm clouds were thickening, nearer now and more ominous.

In June, 1900, the American Red Cross received a federal charter by act of Congress. President McKinley signed the bill into law and presented Clara Barton with the ceremonial pen. It was an event the founder had looked forward to, yet ironically the incorporation speeded her downfall as head of the organization. By terms of the charter there was required a strict accountability by means of a War Department audit of all funds raised. Careful bookkeeping had not had much appeal to Clara who firmly believed that money raised be money spent as needed. That several thousand dollars gathered to meet one emergency was actually expended on another did not trouble her in the least. She had suffering people in mind, not neatly balanced ledgers. Had they chosen to, her enemies inside and outside the Red Cross could really have accused her, not of malfeasance, but of unsupervised expenditures which broke the law. Such charges were eventually leveled at her, if only to precipitate her resignation as Red Cross president. For several years she resisted pressure brought by an array of important people, including President Theodore Roosevelt, the heiress Mabel Boardman, and Episcopal Bishop Potter of New York. The fact is, the kind of philanthropy practiced by Clara Barton had become outmoded. In her eighty-fourth year, the "Angel of the Battlefield" had become obsolete. At last she gave way to new, more organization-conscious leadership. Clara Barton lived another eight years, bittersweet years suffused with the glow of great accomplishment and scarred by the wounds of rejection. These last events in her life make an uncomfortable chapter in the story of a lady who had endured much for the comfort of others.

MARY RITTER BEARD

The entry in *Current Biography* for 1941 reads: "Beard, Charles A. and Beard, Mary." At the time the Beards were well known for their joint authorship of a number of volumes dealing with the history of the United States, especially *The Rise of American Civilization,* highly regarded for its candid appraisal of the American experience. Yet throughout her lifetime Mary Beard sought to achieve a personal identity on the basis of her own accomplishments and their worth. Her husband had always favored his wife's professional independence but he, no less than she, was fighting a mind-set which viewed women as helpmates rather than equal partners in life, and of necessity therefore in the writing of books, Charles Beard was justly famous as a historian, Mary Beard was unjustly famous as his wife and assistant. To be fair, part of the mingling of reputations flowed from the fact that the Beards thought much alike on social issues, on political activism, on the role of the intellect in human affairs, and on the writing of history. Their early marriage with its shared experiences as social workers, their common intellectualism and literary accomplishments, their happy life together?all this encouraged the conclusion that Mary Beard was indeed her husband's *alter ego.* But she had an ego very much of her own which does a great deal to explain her successes and her failures?or were they only stalemates? The richness and variety of her work made her an important American who happened to be a woman, revealing the complexity of the women's movement, a historical fact which needs to be stressed again and again.

Mary Ritter Beard fits no stereotype of the feminine activist or suffragist. Her life as with all lives was unique. She was born in the late

Victorian era when restrictions on women in society were as severe in America as they were in England and she lived well past the midpoint of the twentieth century by which time women had begun to show some real progress in their determination to gain status. How did Mary Beard see women in history and in society? "If there is in all history any primordial force, that force is woman," she argued. Woman is "continuer, protector, preserver of life, instinctive, active, thoughtful, ever bringing thought back from sterile speculation to the center of life and work." This is the central proposition in Beard's feminist rationale. The support which she lent to specific causes, including the suffrage movement, was only an expression of a more profound commitment. To grasp her significance is to accept as a premise that she was first and foremost an intellectual and what she undertook as an activist followed directly from that premise.

Mary Ritter Beard's inheritance was mainstream American. She was born in Indianapolis, Indiana, in 1876. The Ritters and her mother's family, the Lockwoods, derived from old American stock, firmly Protestant in religious persuasion. She was raised a strict Methodist. Both the Ritters and the Lockwoods included churchmen and educators, prosperous farmers, lawyers, and businessmen. Mary's father, Eli Ritter, was an attorney in Indianapolis, a reformer, a leader in the temperance movement, and an advocate of clean government. Seriousness of purpose, devotion to ideals, and a taste for translating principles into practice were elements in a public philosophy which Eli Ritter passed on to his six children.

The Indiana of the 1890s was educationally progressive. Several of the major Protestant denominations had established worthwhile colleges in the state. The Methodist institution was DePauw, located at Greencastle; it had been a coeducational school since the late 1860s. The security and the ideals which Mary Ritter experienced at home were replicated at DePauw where the faculty, administration, and student body were Methodists. Religion appeared to exist comfortably alongside learning at DePauw. When Mary Ritter graduated in 1897 she had done some serious study of history, political science, philosophy, science, mathematics as well as English, Greek, Latin, and foreign languages. She was well and liberally educated according to the standards of the day. But at DePauw she also came to know for the first time the reality of the "male bastion" and the male feeling of superiority. If there were fraternities, there had to be sororities, if there were debate clubs for men there had to be a female counterpart. Mary accepted the situation as she encountered it, but it began to make her somewhat uneasy.

If men in groups were baffling at times Mary Ritter thought one man in particular was decidedly to her liking. Charles A. Beard began his studies at DePauw in 1895 and quickly established a reputation as a promising student of history and politics. He had the same seriousness of purpose as Mary Ritter but he was very much the extrovert who liked to talk and who liked to do things. Their romance ripened. Beard finished his degree requirements in three years and while there seems to have been an implied promise to wed Mary he nonetheless went to England in 1898 for further study. He returned to America the next year and in 1900 Mary Ritter and Charles Beard became life partners. They left for England at once.

The two years in England which Mary Beard spent with her husband were critical to her development. They have been termed "the most vital years in the life of the Beards" and given the range of their activities there and the multiplicity of their contacts with the people as well as with the leaders of English radicalism this is not an overblown judgment. Mary and Charles Beard were friendly with Kier Hardie, James Sexton, Ben Tillett, John Burns, and Ramsay MacDonald. At the same time their work for the extension service of Ruskin Hall, the college at Oxford for working-class men which Charles Beard had had part in founding in 1898, took them to Birmingham, London, Liverpool as well as Manchester where they had rented living quarters. These excursions brought them into close contact with the people of the industrial class, miners, railway men, textile operatives, dockworkers. Mary Beard also came to know Emmeline Pankhurst and her daughters. Christobel Pankhurst in particular she was to recall with affection as she had been "so hospitable" and "we loved her so much at the time." For Mary the

English sojourn had a lasting effect. The plight of the working class in general had come as a shock to the young American so long sheltered from the world's grim realities. The struggle of the suffragists, or rather their failures in the first years of the century, were an added source of concern and anger. The more Mary saw of the world the more she realized she had to do something to try to set things right.

The Beards returned home in 1902 in part because they preferred that their year-old daughter who had been born in England grow up in America and in part because they wanted to further their education. They were both keen to study "why the United States with its wealth and wisdom had not fulfilled the American dream of equal opportunity and abundance for all." Due to her exposure to English social life Mary came to reject the principles of *laissez-faire* capitalism and its Social Darwinism accompaniment and accordingly had embraced the concepts of the general welfare state equipped with broad powers of regulation in the name of the public good. In the sense that she had no desire to see capitalism toppled she remained a moderate reformer but she became a radical in her expectation that drastic changes were required in the distribution of the profits of the capitalistic system.

Both Mary and Charles Beard enrolled in the Graduate School of Columbia University in New York once they were back in the United States, she to study sociology and he to pursue history. He was awarded a Ph.D. in 1904 and was invited to join the Columbia faculty. Mary soon dropped out of school, however. Perhaps Columbia was too stale and courses in sociology too far removed from the actualities of life to strike her as pertinent. Perhaps she resented a fresh exposure to the male bastion with its air of masculine superiority. Whatever the case, after 1904 Mary Beard turned her back on academe, preferring instead an active role with the opportunity to write and speak out in the name of social justice.

The year 1902 marked the beginning of the Progressive Era in which improvements in the economic and social sides of American life were expected to be accomplished by a reinvigorated democratic process. Under the leadership of presidents, governors, and mayors the people would now have a meaningful voice in determining their own affairs. All across the nation, from the newspapers and magazines which provided outlets for the work of the muckrakers to university political science departments experimenting with new ideas and offering new applications of governmental power, the nation was awakening to an era of popular government. The aspirations of the Progressives were the aspirations of Mary Beard. Not simply the use of new political devices but a new democratic spirit was essential to move the nation forward. Included in this neo-democracy was the vote for women. Female suffrage was in Beard's judgment neither an abstract right nor a special privilege. It was a tool to be utilized in concert with other means to bring about a better society for men as well as for women. Once in places of political power and influence women could focus on the evils of prostitution, of exploited child and women labor, of inadequate milk inspection, of exorbitant consumer prices, of overcrowded schoolrooms; these were issues to which women would be particularly attracted. But Beard wanted to root out these social sins as part of building a better overall society. There was to be a general awakening by government to its responsibilities to help the people and women could not and should not remain indifferent to Progressive purposes. The ballot was a weapon with which to fight for reform and an instrument to undertake its implementation. It was for such broad reform objectives that Mary Beard became a suffragist.

According to Harriet Stanton Blatch, one of the leading American suffragists of the era, "The suffragist movement was completely in a rut in New York State at the opening of the twentieth century. It bored its adherents and repelled its opponents." The fact is the whole of the suffrage movement was sputtering because its leaders could not fully and finally decide whether enfranchisement should be sought in a state-by-state fashion or whether it was better to push for a federal amendment. In the judgment of those who favored the vote as guaranteed by the states New York would be an important victory, while to those who supported a Constitutional amendment this method could not succeed unless the women of New York had achieved the vote. The Empire State had become pivotal in the quest for women's suffrage. It was about this time, 1910, that Mary Beard actively entered the suffragist movement. She worked as an organizer and served as an editor of the monthly magazine, *Woman Voter,* published by the Woman Suffrage Party of New York. In 1913 when the American Woman Suffrage Association decided to bring pressure to bear for a national amendment Beard became a member of its Congressional Committee. In this capacity she spent much time in Washington in early 1913 helping with the arrangements for the suffrage parade which was to take place the day before the inauguration of Woodrow Wilson as president. The riot which resulted was one of those confrontations which Beard and her associates deemed useful for dramatizing the cause of suffrage. Indeed, she developed into a tireless organizer and spokeswoman. Her appearance before the House Rules Committee in 1914 created a deep impression on the Committee because Beard displayed "such a knowledge of politics as they [members of the committee] never had met in a woman." By this time she had become a militant. She refused to attend a meeting of the Congressional Union (successor to the Congressional Committee) at Marble House, the mansion of Mrs. O.H.P. Belmont of Newport, Rhode Island. To Beard "Newport and money stand in popular mind for one and the same thing," and she wanted no part of it. She remained active in the Union and in the New York Woman Suffrage Party despite her objections to some of the tactics being pursued. To her it had become immaterial which way women gained the right to vote, so long as it was won, because only when women voted would they come into political power by reason of which the evils of society could be alleviated and then effaced. She was looking beyond the franchise to the purposes of reform. A confrontation with President Wilson in 1917 is some indication of both her courage and her convictions. One of the three suffragists invited to address the president at the Waldorf-Astoria her position was that it was up to the Democrats who controlled the national legislature and the executive to deliver a constitutional amendment guaranteeing women the right to vote. In response Wilson indicated that he preferred state action, as the sounder method of proceeding. At that Mary Beard retorted, to the discomfort of the president who was unused to being addressed so directly, that the Clayton Anti-Trust Act devised to help workers had not been gained by state action but by Democratic administration and congress. Clearly Beard was frustrated by lack of success because without the ballot women could not exert the leverage needed to bring about social reforms.

After 1919 Mary Beard was less the activist and more a critic, turning her energies to the writing of articles and books. Women's suffrage had become a reality and as a follow-up certain militant feminists began to demand an Equal Rights Amendment, advancing it as a necessary complement to voting rights. This agitation Beard dismissed as "trash." To appreciate the reasons for her rejection of an ERA stress again must be placed on her system of social values. She was devoted to the achievement of a better world. In the world as it existed she saw the industrial workers as the worst off, female and male alike. Her English experience had scarred her memory and had brought her to see how in America also the workers were badly treated. This was especially true of women and children who found themselves in the factories and the mines working scandalously long hours for a pittance wage. She had long been in support of legislation to favor women workers because they were vulnerable and because their place and function in society were special. To support an ERA would be tantamount to throwing away what gains had been made in the name of women workers and to give up the fight for further concessions. Such a turn of events was to Mary Beard nothing less than retrogressive. Some of her friends in the women's movement agreed with her but others were strongly pro ERA with the result that their ranks divided over the issue and they lost some strength in consequence. It would be incorrect, however, to conclude that Beard withdrew from feminist activities because of the ERA muddle. In assuming the status of author and critic, and especially of a historian of women, she was following her natural bent as a scholar whose writings might contribute to the improved place of women in society.

Mary Ritter Beard had already written a number of useful studies before this change of emphasis in her career. *Woman's Work in*

Municipalities was published in 1915, a *Short History of the American Labor Movement* in 1920; in addition she had coauthored with her husband *American Citizenship* (1914) and a *History of the United States* (1912), as well as having done a number of articles on her own. During the 1920s she and her husband would work closely together on what is still a notable account of American history, the two volumes entitled *The Rise of American Civilization*, a telling combination of scholarship and muckraking, the best such combination in American historiography. But Mary Beard was eager to speak in her own behalf and to advance the proposition fundamental to her life's work, namely, the centrality of women in the human experience. This thesis and its supporting evidence she first stated fully in 1931 in *On Understanding Women*. "Looking backward toward the horizon of dawning society, what do we see standing clearly against the sky?" she asked. "Woman?assuming chief responsibility for the continuance and the care of life. We are in the presence," she continued, "of a force so vital and so powerful that anthropologists can devise no meter to register it and the legislator no reason strong enough to defeat it." This was both a novel and a provocative way of interpreting history. Its novelty led many to question its value if not to dismiss it out of hand while at the same time it provoked controversy among feminists themselves. In writing as she had Mary Beard granted that she may have exaggerated the power of "eternal feminism" but deemed it entirely appropriate in order to counter the effects of centuries of neglect regarding the proper place of women in history.

The twin purpose of *On Understanding Women* was to set the record straight and to use history to justify the lives of women for the future. That women will always be central to life, of that there was no doubt. The future should be made distinct and separate from the past by the fact that their contributions would now be noticed and respected as women made their way into business, the professions, and public office. In the rationale of Mary Beard an awareness of the fundamental role of women in history was like winning the right to vote. Its value did not reside in the fact but from what might be accomplished for society in the future by taking that fact in account.

One critical weakness of *On Understanding Women* was its lack of documentation. The book was not intended as a scholarly enterprise complete with citations from an endless list of authorities, but it did expect to be taken seriously by those who probed the past. In writing the book Beard came to realize how precariously little written evidence in support of her thesis was extant. If her studies and those who sympathized with her were to go forward time must be taken to assemble the appropriate materials. Thus was launched in 1936 the World Center for Women's Archives. Established in New York City it began to solicit and receive some material almost at once but the trickle never became a flow. Many feminists, for example, noted the idea of an archives devoted only to women as running counter to a desire to men and women integrated in all activities. Beard herself thought of the task as one with a definite time limit, made necessary by the past and the continuing neglect by established archives of documents germane to women in history. The WCWA was similar to the admitted exaggerations in *On Understanding Women*, that is, an expedient designed to rectify age-old abuse.

A noble prospect, the World Center for Women's Archives was difficult to translate into reality. There were two problems in particular, one to be anticipated, namely a need of funds, and the other somewhat surprising, a lack of interest in the project. The proposed budget of $12,000 a year to pay a staff of six represented a sum which the Center was unable to raise in any single year of its five-year existence. Contributions in amounts of five dollars to one hundred dollars met about half of the projected budget. Even more discouraging was the reception the Center received. There was a very limited interest in women's history in the 1930s. The activism of earlier years was muted both by the winning of voting rights and the impact of the Great Depression. There simply was no "women's history" at the time, no university faculty, no courses, and few books on the subject. The Center did receive any number of valuable items, including forty-four bound volumes of *The Women's Journal*, the original maps and charts of Amelia Earhart's last flight, and much material on the history of women in Japan. This latter cache of documents constituted the basis of Mary

Beard's 1953 study, *The Force of Women in Japanese History*. The Center did more than collect materials, however. Under Beard's leadership?she had been named the Director and served without pay?plans were laid to study "Women in Science," "Women in Music," "Women in Diplomacy," and "Working Women." Such categorizing tended to emphasize once again a division of the sexes and offended some forward-looking women as a consequence. Correspondence between Beard and women of this persuasion underscores the basic differences between them. What Beard saw as positive others interpreted as negative. Lack of funds, lack of interest, and lack of unity on the part of women activists spelled an end to the WCWA in the late summer of 1940. By that time the old, familiar Europe was in ruins and America's entry into the war seemed more likely with each passing month. The World Center for Women's Archives had become a victim not only of its limitations but of a changing national mood.

It was well that Mary Ritter Beard was a self-directed person who was able to sustain her spirits by turning to writing books of her own as well as continuing her fruitful literary collaboration with her husband. The failure of the WCWA was matched by unsuccessful efforts to overcome the neglect and misunderstanding of women in history discoverable in the world of encyclopedias. Mary Beard had been one who had felt the need for an "encyclopedia of women." She had often protested in writing to the editors of the *Encyclopedia Britannica* of their unsatisfactory treatment of women and women-related subjects. In the spring of 1941 Walter Yust, the Editor-in-chief of Britannica invited Beard to help correct the deficiencies of which she had complained. As the *Encyclopedia Britannica* was the most widely used and frequently quoted authority of its kind this appeared to be a rare opportunity to promote the Beardian thesis of women as a force in history. At the direction of Yust she and three associates combed the pages of the Britannica to identify areas requiring reworking and submitted their report to Yust who expressed great satisfaction with the results. The critique listed entries which were acceptable to Beard *et al*, items which needed redoing (some badly so), and finally suggestions for additional entries. Yet little or nothing came from the report. Certainly there were no discernible changes in the next edition of the Britannica, and Mary Beard felt cheated by what had happened.

Equally discouraging were Beard's later efforts to promote women's studies in colleges and universities. Such studies were for her appropriate no less for men than for women. She had contact and some encouragement from the heads of several of prestige women's colleges, Smith, Radcliffe, Bryn Mawr, and Vassar, telling Sarah Blanding, president of the last named institution, "I do venture to make the suggestion that you launch at Vassar the project of studying women in long history." Such courses would be a good opportunity for breaking down the prevalent notion that women's history somehow began with agitation for reforms in the nineteenth century. The approach Beard had in mind would examine and evaluate not only feminists but queens and courtesans, not in any sensational way but as matters of historical fact Though most of the projects she touched flowered only long after her involvement with them she exercised some influence on the establishment of the Radcliffe Center for the Study of Women, the Smith College Laboratory Plan, as well as a women's studies program at Syracuse University.

Meanwhile Mary Beard had written an important and challenging book, *Woman as a Force in History: A Study in Traditions and Realities.* When it was published in 1946 the author was seventy years of age. It is a volume rich in learning and in insight, it is bold but never reckless, devoid of emotion yet full of Mary Beard's passionate desire to have others understand women as a force in history. In the preface she set forth her objectives: to study the "tradition that women were members of a subject sex throughout history . . . a tradition which has exercised an almost tyrannical power over thinking about the relations of men and women for more than a hundred years." Secondly, "The idea of subjection is tested by reference to historical realities?legal, religious, economic, social, intellectual, military, political, and moral or philosophical." Finally, "The origin, nature, and application of the idea of equality as a perfect guide to women in their search for escape from subjection are brought to the inquest." Beard's book became especially notable for its attacks on those who had misinterpreted passages from Blackstone's *Commentaries on the Law of England,* published in 1765. She charged that nineteenth century feminists had misread Blackstone, that he spoke only metaphorically when he observed that women were civilly dead upon entering marriage, and that by misrepresenting the position of Blackstone, an authority of enormous influence, the feminists had provided their enemies with invaluable weapons. In Mary Beard's presentation of this basic historical error the feminist and scholar never showed to better advantage. *Women as a Force in History* along with *The Force of Women in Japanese History* established the septuagenarian Beard as the outstanding feminist scholar of the early post-war years. It was a reputation unchallenged at her death in 1958.

HISTORIC FRIENDSHIPS
OLIVER WENDELL HOLMES AND
PATRICK AUGUSTINE SHEEHAN

From the time of Lytton Strachey's Eminent Victorians it is probably impossible and certainly unlikely to encounter serious, fully limned biography of any significant figure lacking a psychological dimension. So persuasive have psychological interpretations, whether Freudian or Jungian, become. The "definitive life" will nonetheless incline to concentrate on other historical methods, more conventional no doubt, but with a better prospect of yielding trustworthy results. No one will deny psychoanalysis is a useful tool for today's biographer. In his *The Nature of Biography* Robert Gittings has observed, "We do not write as we might have done before Freud." In historical biography, however, the psychobiographer's couch is no substitute for the written record. To wit, the correspondence of Oliver Wendell Holmes and Canon Sheehan is a small but telling part of the historical record of the mind and faith of the justice. Holmes was an inveterate letter writer exchanging ideas with some of the best minds of his day. His friendship with Sir Frederick Pollock was based on a juridical comradeship. It was Sir Frederick who spoke of Our Lady of the Common Law. A second English friend of a younger generation, Harold Laski, helped keep Holmes's mind *au courant* with the thinking of a new century. The written record shows that Sheehan brought out an enduring traditionalism in Holmes's thought; Pollock offered fresh insights for him to ponder; Laski prodded the aged justice to make his peace with a new era as he continued to study the place of law in war and peace, in prosperity and depressions. With all these men it is the written record which spells out their friendships, adding to our understanding of the history of their times and place.

The writings of Canon Sheehan—Patrick Augustine Sheehan—attained a considerable appreciation and something of a vogue among American Catholics in the early years of the twentieth century. His novels, *My New Curate* and *The Blindness of Dr. Gray,* were particularly popular with people interested in the inner ways and the inner life of the Roman Catholic priesthood. Although Sheehan's settings were almost always Ireland, he explored human situations with sufficient psychological awareness to liberate his characters from their surroundings, thus generalizing their appeal. Such was his popularity that his novels were translated into various languages and were highly regarded on the Continent as well as in the British Isles. In America Sheehan came into print with the help of Rev. Herman J. Heuser, editor of *The Ecclesiastical Review.* Heuser published *My New Curate* in installments, starting with the May 1898 issue of *The Ecclesiastical Review.* From the first Heuser had, in his own words, "a hit."[1] Canon Sheehan's later writings were read enthusiastically in America over the course of the next ten years.[2] His collection of reflections, *Under the Cedars and the Stars,* earned him a reputation as a writer of learning and insight. Not surprisingly, he acquired a wide circle of American friends, perhaps the most distinguished of whom was the jurist, Oliver Wendell Holmes, Jr.[3]

Holmes was an unlikely intimate of Canon Sheehan. Born in Boston in 1841, the elder son of Dr. Oliver Wendell Holmes, "the autocrat of the breakfast table," his name and background were distinctively New England American.[4] While studying at Harvard in the late1860s he was a member, along with William James, Charles Peirce, and Chauncey Wright, of the "Metaphysical Club." These young intellectuals had a fondness for empiricism which combined with an enthusiasm for science to help them develop American pragmatism. Trained in the law, Holmes first became noted for his treatise, *The Common Law,* a scholarly investigation into the origins and the nature of Anglo-American legal principles. The study amounted to a broad-gauged attack on all *a priori* notions in the law, a premise Holmes proceeded to apply to life as well as to the law. In 1902, after some years on the bench in his native Massachusetts, he was appointed an Associate Justice of the Supreme

Court of the United States by Theodore Roosevelt. In that position over a span of some thirty years—Holmes lived to the age of 94—he became renowned for his highly practical and always flexible interpretations of the Constitution and the laws of the United States. To the end of his career as a judge he remained skeptical of any final version of the supreme law of the land. He once styled himself a "bettabilitarian," or one who thinks "you can bet about" the formula of the universe, but you can never be sure of it, for any such formula is only "a spontaneity taking an irrational pleasure in a moment of rational sequence."[5] Enjoying a reputation as a "great dissenter" in his judicial opinions while on the Supreme Court, Holmes also questioned many of the traditional assumptions of American society.

Canon Sheehan's world of moral certitudes marked him off from that of Holmes by a deep and seemingly unbridgeable chasm. Sheehan was a priest of touching piety and strict devotion. Born in the parish of Mallow near Cloyne, he was baptized on St. Patrick's Day, 1852. Educated at the local National School and at St. Colman's College, Fermoy, he entered the Seminary at Maynooth in 1869. Ordination was followed by some years on the English Mission (at Plymouth and Exeter) before a return to Ireland. In 1895 he became parish priest at Doneraile, a poor living in a small town in County Cork. Although it was at Doneraile that Sheehan, the man of letters, came into prominence, he continued in his role as shepherd of souls even while he wrote his books. As he had lived, so also did he die, a man of simple faith, obedient to the Church to the end. His biographer, Heuser, relates that he passed away, rosary in hand, fortified for his last journey by the ancient rites of the Church.[6]

From the first meeting of Holmes, the "bettabilitarian," and Sheehan, with "the faith of a Breton peasant's wife,"[7] the chemistry of a common love for things of the mind drew the two men, if not their worlds, together. They came to know each other in the early autumn of 1903. Justice Holmes had been vacationing in England and had gone over to Ireland at the invitation of his friends, Lord and Lady Castletown of Upper Ossory, who lived at Doneraile Court. Whenever Lord Castletown had a guest of distinction he introduced him to Sheehan for the Canon's reputation as a priest and as an author stood high with him. In this way Sheehan made Holmes's acquaintance. Sheehan has recorded his impressions of his new friend. "He was a most interesting man," he wrote Fr. Heuser, and "when we got on philosophical topics he talked well."[8] Their discussion of "philosophical topics" in subsequent visits and especially in numerous letters became the foundation of an abiding friendship. Holmes was an avid correspondent, fond of learned gossip and serious dialogue with notable men as different as Sir Frederick E. Pollock and Harold Laski. Canon Sheehan, because of the demands of his parish duties and his devotion to his literary pursuits, found this kind of literary conversation much to his liking. In Doneraile his life of the mind was understandably meager. Holmes not merely symbolized the larger world of the philosopher and the erudite man of affairs to which Sheehan was drawn; he was, in fact, a living part of that world. As Sheehan later was to tell Holmes: "The great want of my life is lack of intellectual intercourse; and your letters are a stimulus that drives me from the superficialities of daily life into depths of thought where I have no temptation otherwise to plunge."[9] In a letter to Holmes shortly after those first encounters, Sheehan spoke of looking forward to his return "for your little morning visits to me were gleams of sunshine across a grey and monotonous life."[10] In short, Holmes brought him face to face with an original thinker "on subjects that were of the deepest interest" to him.[11]

Sheehan's concern with matters beyond the ken of the typical Irish cleric of his time manifested itself before his years of training at Maynooth. He entered the Seminary with a high ideal of the priesthood, to which he remained steadfast. Excellent preparation at St. Colman's College fused with a native intellectual curiosity to enable Sheehan to take courses in philosophy at once, passing over rhetoric and humanities. By temperament he was unsympathetic to scholastic philosophy as it was then taught. He was already well read in Carlyle whose theories, ethical, religious, and political, attracted him. Wordsworth, Shakespeare, Goethe, Swinburne, "the incomparable Dante" were congenial minds. Among philosophers, Kant, Fichte, Schelling all advanced speculations which he became convinced no serious-minded person could dismiss lightly. At Maynooth Sheehan was well on his way toward becoming a modern learned Catholic. In those years when the *Syllabus of Errors* seemed to condemn the spirit and the letter of modernism, while at the same time the claims of the new scientific materialism were no less dogmatic, such an intellectual accomplishment was, in some sense, *a tour de force*. In Ireland it could be exceedingly controversial as well. Many years after he left Maynooth he returned to the Seminary to deliver a paper on Spinoza which, he was told by one friendly cleric, sounded "as a voice from unknown worlds."[12] Such was Sheehan's intellectual breadth that he could find in Pascal, for example, not merely a skeptic, but a "bold enquirer." "When the *Provincial Letters* are forgotten or neglected as splenetic sarcasm, and have passed away like the Junius and Drapier Letters," he wrote in *Under the Cedars and the Stars*, Pascal's *Pensées* "will remain, broken fragments of an incomplete, but immortal work."[13] In commenting on this and other passages in the book Holmes enthused: "I simply want to tell you more emphatically than before now that I have finished your book that I owe you my admiration and thanks."[14] The judge had discovered a kindred spirit in the priest.

Holmes's intellectual profile is no more conventional in outline than Sheehan's. His strongly pragmatic and scientific inclinations were tempered by experience and reflection. Wounded three times while serving as an officer in the Union Army during the Civil War, he came to know suffering and to believe in the nobility of sacrifice. Taking no stock in abstract rights, an assertion he often proclaimed, he worked long and diligently while a judge to protect workers, children, women, and other vulnerable groups in American society. As he declared in the famous dissent in *Lochner* vs. *New York* (1905), "the Fourteenth Amendment does not enact Mr. Herbert Spencer's Social Statics." By way of contrast, he once wrote Harold Laski: "Little as I believe in [freedom of speech] as a theory I hope I would die for it and I go as far as anyone whom I regard as competent to form an opinion, in favor of it."[15] Holmes remained a mixture of traditional values and scientific imperatives. Insistent that men aspire to noble ideals, the kind of faith in God typified by Canon

Sheehan was nonetheless "devoid alike of historical and rational foundations." He could not believe in God, but only admit to a semi-shudder when he thought of millions of intelligent men who would hold him to be barred from the face of God unless he confessed a faith of some kind.[16] With Madame de Staël, Holmes was fond of saying that while he did not believe in hell, he was afraid of it. Fully appreciative of the frailty of man and the effects of cosmic fear, he once exclaimed to Sheehan: "What a refuge your religion is from the terrors of the universe. I could not believe it except by a total collapse—but it must be a joy and warm up the interstellar spaces."[17] Canon Sheehan's orthodoxy—to his keen delight—exhibited ideas "very stimulating in the way that many things are that one doesn't believe."[18]

If particular authors ever could be said to suggest the boundaries of Canon Sheehan's mind, and thus of his interaction with Justice Holmes, they might well have been Dante in literature and Suárez in philosophy.[19] In any case, Sheehan drew copies of *The Divine Comedy* and *De Legibus* from his personal library to present to Holmes as gifts. In each instance he sought to remind Holmes of the inescapable tradition within which Sheehan believed they both consciously should move. "I am taking a liberty in sending you . . . my own copy of 'Dante'—the companion of my holidays," he wrote Holmes in 1911. "I have unfortunately made pencil marks here and there; but they will only amuse you."[20] Sheehan's thoughtfulness in part was inspired by a comment Holmes had offered the year previous. "I read [Dante] through," he related, "the great poem that is—and had the greatest literary sensation of my life—much to my surprise . . . the intensity of his spiritual rapture expressed in divine song moved me through and through."[21] Holmes had little time or patience, it will be recalled, with what he once described to Sheehan as "Newman's suggestion that a man may be high minded, honorable, etc., and yet find himself classed among the enemies of God." Thus he was "powerfully moved by the opposite view as Dante shows it."[22] Such comments as these struck at the heart of the Canon's orthodoxy and no doubt were deeply felt because of the ongoing war within Sheehan himself between the priest and the artist.[23] Holmes was not unmindful of this and often closed his letters with an apology for entering into sensitive and debatable areas. But he was confident enough of their friendship and perhaps insufficiently aware of Sheehan's personal dilemma to want to continue to explore such topics. Holmes closed one letter in characteristic fashion. "I send this with some fear that parts of it may strike you as better omitted, but I will take the risk."[24]

In contrast to Dante, there was little Holmes deemed likely to be worthwhile in Suárez. On his last visit to Doneraile in the summer of 1913—when Canon Sheehan was conscious of being a dying man though still full of cheerful conversation—his host asked Holmes to choose a book from his library as a memento. Their talk, as usual, had swung round to philosophy.[25] From among his books by Suárez, Sheehan urged *De Legibus* on his friend. To Sheehan, Suárez was the *"ne plus ultra* of original philosophy."[26] No doubt he believed that Suárez's systematic exposition of the law in which the voluntary element was so greatly stressed would have a built-in appeal. Holmes never brought himself to read *De Legibus,* however. He was skeptical of Sheehan's estimate of Suárez at the time the gift was made; and as late as 1929 he wrote Laski that although he thought of reading *De Legibus* one summer, he chose not to do so because he "didn't quite trust" Canon Sheehan's judgment.[27] The fact is that old philosophers were not necessarily the best philosophers for Holmes, and in some sense, might even be the worst. On this ground he had explicitly rejected an earlier suggestion by Sheehan to read Suárez. "You will not quite share my point of view," he explained, "but I regard pretty much everything, and especially the greatest things, in the way of books, as dead in fifty, nowadays in twenty years. The seeds of thought germinate and produce later seeds. The old structures are remodeled and have electric lights put in. One of the proofs that a word contains living thoughts is that it kills itself. So, I know, a priori, that no one who wrote in the 16th, 17th, or 18th century will say the poignant thing I want. He will not have the historic sense, he will not have the *philosophy* that seems to me vital."[28] For Holmes, Suárez was rooted too deeply in a bygone era to be relevant, yet Dante had somehow transcended the barriers of time.

If philosophy was the subject to which Holmes and Sheehan invariably reverted in their letters and conversations, the range of their common interests was varied nevertheless, and their exchanges marked by insight and passion. One issue raised in their letters, unexpectedly perhaps, was the contemporary argument about socialism *vs.* capitalism. Holmes was first to air his mind. "It makes me a little sad to be led to believe that the hatred of Capital is widespread with us. All the natural laws seem to be set down to the discredit of the rich and people who would not dare to blaspheme are ready enough to damn Rockefeller or Morgan. Meantime I incline to believe . . . that before our clamorers for 8 hours (with which clamor I rather sympathize) know it, the Chinese with their endless gluttony for work, their honesty and their imperturbable patience will cut the white races out in the markets of the world."[29] Somewhat later, Holmes returned to this theme, telling his friend of the remarks he made at Williams College when he was given an honorary degree. "I took the chance to fire off some of my economic opinions—that most people think dramatically not quantitatively." "It is not popular," he admitted, "to tell the crowd that they now have substantially all there is, and that the war upon capital is the fight of the striking group against all the other producers for a larger share of the annual product that is divided among them."[30] Sheehan responded: "Your remarks . . . as to the attitude of the working man towards the capitalist, viewing life spectacularly, and not rationally, have often occurred to me. . . . If ever the masses come to understand that money is the meanest and most powerless factor in creating human happiness; and that all the great and good things of life are unpurchasable, things might swing round to an equilibrium." But Sheehan was as pessimistic as Holmes. The judge had warned of the danger in contrasting the palace of the employer and the hovel of the worker and Sheehan echoed his sentiments: "the brownstone mansion seems such a contrast to the tenement house that reason has no place there."[31] Though Holmes was thinking in terms of an economic theory and Sheehan stating his convictions based on Christian antimaterialism, their kindred conclusions may be taken as a sign of a deeper unity in their outlooks.

America was often discussed by the two friends, partly because the Canon was saddened to think of the corrosive effects of the materialism of American life on so many of the sons and daughters of old Eire who had migrated there. Consequently he put great faith in the future of the Catholic Church in the United States. In commenting on an article by Fr. Hugh Benson in the *Atlantic Monthly* which interpreted the signs of the time as showing the future favored the Church in America, Sheehan wrote: "Whether America is yet in its adolescence, or whether it be the result of climatic conditions, there is a certain buoyancy and delightful optimism in the character of the nation that is very much akin to the Catholic spirit. And there is also depth of feeling and generosity which the older nations have long since cast aside in favour of the 'critical spirit'."[32] Holmes could only respond obliquely. He said he would not be puzzled at this prospect "if I knew that the opposing force would be not Protestantism but unbelief. . . ."[33]

Sheehan was resentful of the condescension which many English critics displayed toward American literature, insisting that "everything American [was] very 'young' and immature." "Only quite lately in the 'Times' literary supplement, some letters of Swinburne's were published," he pointed out, in which the critic "speaks in a very patronising manner of your Emerson; and again, quite lately, I have been reading the letters of Coventry Patmore in which he ridicules the idea that Longfellow could ever be considered a poet." All this was preliminary to his congratulations to Holmes upon his honorary degree from Oxford. "When, therefore, Oxford found *you* out, I am beginning to respect the English intellect a little," he added playfully.[34] Nor was Holmes above a humorous shaft now and again. "I forget to say that I am with you down to the ground about Tennyson. I call it stall-fed poetry—and when I want to be unpleasant to Britons I airily advert to persons as at the Tennysonian stage of culture."[35]

As good friends will, Holmes and Sheehan gossiped, each about his work, his friends, his surroundings, and his frustrations. For example, Holmes took occasion to comment on reaction to his dissent in the *Northern Securities Case* of 1904, "which caused me some pain at the moment, as I was compelled to express an opinion contrary to what the President ardently desired. The newspapers were full of stories of his wrath, etc., but he is all right and the incident is closed."[36] He shared with Sheehan some of his most intimate memories. "On the 17th [of September] I drank a glass of wine . . . to the living and the dead, it being the anniversary of Antietam, where, 1862–1908—46 years ago(!) I was shot through the neck."[37] And he spoke with fondness of his retreat at Beverly Farms. "I am afraid you idealize Beverly Farms," he cautioned. "My little acre has some rocks in it of which I am proud, and which I love—for the Beverly rocks are my first recollections of country."[38] For his part Sheehan, removed from the traffic of large affairs, told of the "French compliment" paid him by some priests in Australia who had registered a desire to have him appointed their bishop. "Of course," he mused, "Rome is too wise to listen to such a suggestion."[39] When he came out of the hospital in 1912, his final sickness having been diagnosed, his parishioners gave him a public demonstration of their esteem. "Poor people! They insisted on it," he related, "and it would [have been] churlish to refuse any little testimony of their affections."[40] And he wept over Ireland, calling it "an unhappy and distracted country; and the one thing which hitherto saved it—a certain kind of Celtic idealism—has now given way before the advance of materialism."[41] But more often, Sheehan was brighter, with tales of the Castletowns or the pleasures of his library and garden.[42]

Because "philosophical topics" had been the consistent reference point in their conversations since that first meeting in 1903, was there, strange as it may seem, an ultimate unity in the diverse philosophies of Justice Holmes and Canon Sheehan? And is this, in turn, the clue to the nature of their enduring friendship? In a lengthy letter, dated August 26th, 1910, Sheehan undertook a justification of the intellectual content of the Roman faith, and by implication the intellectual defensibility of the concept of God. He launched his argument by stressing the place of reason in the divine scheme and condemning "emotionalism" or "intuitionalism" as a sole motive of belief. For him reason was the "solid foundation on which Faith rests." Inasmuch as reason has its own limitations in a quest for truth, Sheehan continued, reason needs faith. He was troubled, however, by those who support reason as the one way to truth. Whose reason? he asked. Aristotle's or Bacon's, or the reason of the man in the street? He underscored his objection by showing how in his autobiography Herbert Spencer "modified, at the age of 60 or 70, half his dogmatic teachings as a young man." In other words, reliance on reason alone rendered truth relative. "This won't do!" he exclaimed. "The Absolute Mind alone can discern absolute Truth. The moment you speak of limitations, or say 'we cannot know,' you admit that. Therefore, what we can know about the Universe is just what our Reason verifies and what Absolute Truth has *chosen* to reveal." This plea for the syllogistic methodology was altogether unpalatable to Holmes, who had declared so eloquently in the first passages of *The Common Law* that the "life of the law has not been logic, it has been experience, the felt necessities of the time . . ." Furthermore, this had been transmuted into a general assumption which he was ready to apply everywhere. Still Sheehan insisted. "We, Catholics, believe that that revelation has been made to the Church. . . . You think that therefore the Church is bound to coerce and persecute. Certainly not . . . because to coerce conscience by punishment is totally opposed to the spirit of the Church . . . You will lift your eyebrows at this," Sheehan admitted, "and say: What about the 'Provincial Letters,' 'Jesuitism,' and all that? But, I am only stating the literal truth, no matter how Catholic doctrine has been twisted and abused by men." Finally he came to the assertion he was most eager to make to Holmes. "I am in thorough sympathy with you in your conviction of the sacredness of human liberty. It seems to me a kind of sacrilege to trespass on that Holy of Holies—the human conscience." A bold claim indeed, but one which Sheehan proceeded to qualify by adding: "whilst I would resent any attempt [by the state] to interfere with my principles or convictions in political or social matters, . . . whenever the Eternal speaks . . . either through divine inspiration or through the Vicariate He has established on this little planet of ours, I am a little child . . ."[43] Ultimately, Sheehan stood in awe of something outside himself, something which, in his contingent state, he had to accept and in his Faith he gladly embraced. At this precise point the elements of faith and doubt intersect to locate the prime meridian in the great circle of the Holmes-Sheehan intellectual affinity.

In contrast to Sheehan's almost bristling statement Holmes had to express his own distinctive faith more simply and more tentatively. Nor did his conviction hinge on any conception of truth. "As I must have said before," he commented to Sheehan, "all I mean by *true* is what I can't help thinking, and I define truth as the system of my limitations."[44] When it comes to truth, "I think science has changed our point of view, and for the better. But there I touch controversy," as Holmes put it another time.[45] On occasion, he could not do otherwise than equate himself with animal, "maggots preparing the way for a destiny they [do] not understand. If the maggots, why not man?"[46] Holmes's final vision was of man standing hopelessly before the Cosmos, yet strangely unique in that hopelessness. "The frame of mind that I am afraid I often am in and express is little better than one you would deem sinful," he confided. "I look at a man as a cosmic [speck], having neither merit or demerit except from a human and social point of view, working to some unknown end or no end, outside himself and having sufficient reasons, easily stated, for doing his best."[47]

Holmes and Sheehan each saw man, as an individual or as a race, reduced to a "cosmic speck." Sheehan was reassured by his beliefs. Holmes also was reassured, less simplistically, by his science. "I take comfort," he once wrote his friend, "in thinking of Fabre's grubs that prepare a dwelling for the beetles that they are to become and never see. I say to myself man also may have cosmic destinies beyond his ken."[48] Holmes was so thoroughly scientific, however, that he was "content to believe that probably I do not see the ultimate significance of things (to speak in human terms) . . . without inquiring too curiously what if any that ultimate significance may be."[49] Such concessions as he was willing to make in his scientific postulates do not destroy the image of the "bettabilitarian" so much as they soften the sharpness of the impression. These concessions, at the same time, speak Holmes's sensitivity to the spirit of Sheehan and to the values of the Western tradition which the Canon exemplified.

In any assessment of the relationship of Holmes and Sheehan the character of their personal attraction needs to be isolated and defined. Since Holmes was much the more important of the two figures, it is easy to appreciate Sheehan's admiration of him. Holmes was a famous man, and a kindly one, and his wide range of friends is testament to his magnetism. Sheehan could count himself fortunate, perhaps flattered, that Holmes esteemed him as he did. But what is the explanation of Holmes's fondness for Canon Sheehan. In a word it was his wisdom. Holmes loved him for what he wrote and for what he was, because of what Sheehan perceived in the human drama and what he had to say about it.[50] Passages from Sheehan's work brought Holmes face to face with history, with power and its temptations, and with the clear duty to wield power responsibly. Always something of a Reform Darwinist and frequently a champion of the underdog, Holmes could nonetheless proclaim his belief in force as the ultimate ratio. It was this *sturm und drang* element in Holmes's make-up to which Sheehan addressed himself quite artlessly, and to which Holmes listened attentively. Writing in *Under the Cedars and the Stars* he posed the complex question.

> Can the really humble rule? And must there not be the pride of strength in those who are called to govern? The question concerns individuals, limited communities, whole nations. Is humility, self-effacement, a qualification for the father of a family, the superior of a religious house, the captain of a great army, the premier of a world-ruling parliament? If it is, there seems to be no power of ruling, which means the enforcement of one's own will on the will of others. A family, a community, a commonwealth, without a strong, self-reliant hand to guide it, lapses into anarchy. On the other hand, how can humility consist with the absolute exercise of unlimited power? The problem may be put in other terms. We have seen

how the world, and our lower nature, worship
strength, even brute strength. . . . Say what we
like, the vast majority of mankind worship brute
force. . . .

On the other hand, gentle, refined natures love
simple and lowly lives, and humble and pleading
actions . . . If we were simple, and lowly, and
gentle, we would love them . . . But if we were
base and ignoble, if we worshiped strength and
distinction, we would despise them heartily as
beneath us. Why? Because, in the solitude of our
rooms we have no eye of public opinion upon us
to rebuke us for our weakness in loving the weak.
But, with the Argus eyes of society upon us, it
would be a grave test of our integrity to walk a
crowded street with the ragged companion of our
school-days; or to stand up in a heated ball–room
with the homely rustic, and face a hundred eyes of
criticism and contempt.51

For Holmes there was in such passages that prick of conscience,
often more salutary when delivered from without: the wisdom to realize
the frailty of human nature in worshiping strength, the potent obstacles
in maintaining the humility appropriate to that same frailty.

It is not too much to claim that *Under the Cedars and the Stars* cast a
spell upon Oliver Wendell Holmes. In successive letters from December
1903 through February 1904, he wrote Sheehan repeated words of
praise: ". . . greatly and unaffectedly charmed and moved by it . . .
the beauty and loftiness of your thought and of the song of the words in
which it is clothed."[52] He granted that he was "as far as possible from
being on your side" but the book moved him "more intimately by old
world feeling than anything that I have read for a great while."[53] A few
weeks later, he uttered fresh praise. "And now I must tell you once more
of the love and exaltation which your words have the skill to command,
as few words that I have read anywhere can." "It is true," he added, "that

I don't believe your philosophy—or shall I say, the religion you so beautifully exalt."[54] Had not Sheehan rendered distinctions in philosophy and denominations in religion incidental? He was speaking to Holmes in the fullness of the jurist's years, as Emerson had done in his youth, of the "infinite worthiness" of every individual. Holmes once related to Sheehan how, when he was still young, he saw Emerson from across the street, and ran over and said to him: "'If I ever do anything, I shall owe a great deal of it to you,' which was true. He was one of those who set one on fire—to impart a [thought] was the gift of genius."[55] Sheehan, like Emerson, was a moralist whose role it was to make others perceive truth and to realize how truth and good and beauty are one. Holmes believed in ideals, as Sheehan had detected from the first. In an early letter he wrote: "But I love an idealist—even while I doubt the cosmic significance of our judgments."[56] At another time Holmes was prompted to confess: "Oh, I am a regular Danton-Herod on paper and in theory. I am not very hard hearted in practice."[57] In an important way Holmes is better understood because of his affection for Canon Sheehan and, no less telling, because of Canon Sheehan's admiration for him.[58] In Holmes's own words: "an admirer is the vehicle of truth, it matters not that he is humble."[59] And so it was with the friendship of Oliver Wendell Holmes, Jr., and Patrick Augustine Sheehan.

NOTES

1. Herman J. Heuser, Canon Sheehan of Doneraile (New York, 1917), p. 133 Heuser's work comes close to a standard biography. It has some of the characteristics of an "authorized life" as well, though it is not completely uncritical. He and Sheehan were close personal friends from 1897 when they first corresponded down to Sheehan's death in 1913. Francis Boyle, Canon Sheehan (New York, 1927) is a slight piece of work.

2. The reality of Sheehan's popularity in the United States is illustrated by the story told him by Holmes. ". . . I stopped at a hotel in Boston and was talking with a waiter I knew and telling him I had been in Ireland, County Cork. He asked me if I had been in the neighborhood of Doneraile. I said yes. Whereupon he asked if I had seen Canon Sheehan. It seems that he was a reader and admirer of your works." Holmes to Sheehan, November 7, 1907, Heuser Letters, St. Charles Seminary, Overbrook, Pa. See also Holmes to Sheehan, February 5, 1913, ibid. Sheehan's letters to Holmes are in the Library

of the Harvard Law School, where copies of Holmes's letters to Sheehan are also deposited.

Shortly after this article went to press, the correspondence (both the letters from Sheehan to Holmes, which are cited here as printed in Heuser's Canon Sheehan of Doneraile, and those of Holmes to Sheehan, which are cited here as Heuser Letters) was published: Holmes-Sheehan Correspondence: The Letters of Justice Oliver Wendell Holmes and Canon Patrick Augustine Sheehan, Edited by David H. Burton (Port Washington, N.Y./London: National University Publications, Kennikat Press, 1976).

3. Holmes was asked by Heuser to read portions of his biography of Sheehan dealing with Holmes. Despite the press of his duties he agreed to do so. Holmes to Heuser, March 11, 1917, Heuser Letters. Once Holmes read Heuser's book, he wrote: "The life of Canon Sheehan has come and surpasses even my expectations . . . a beautiful memorial." Holmes to Heuser, November 17, 1917, ibid.

4. Catherine Drinker Bowen, Yankee from Olympus (Boston, 1944) is the only full-length study of Holmes. It is both intimate and scholarly. A definitive life of Holmes was begun by Mark DeWolfe Howe; only two volumes appeared before his death. These are: Mr. Justice Holmes, The Shaping Years 1841–1870 (Cambridge, Mass., 1957) and Mr. Justice Holmes, The Proving Years 1870–1882 (Cambridge, Mass., 1963). Critical for understanding Holmes are two major collections of his letters. These are: Holmes-Pollock Letters, Mark DeWolfe Howe, Editor, 2 vols. (Cambridge, Mass., 1941); hereafter cited Holmes-Pollock Letters, and Holmes-Laski Letters, 1916–1935, Mark DeWolfe Howe, Editor, 2 vols. (Cambridge, Mass., 1953); hereafter cited Holmes-Laski Letters.

5. Holmes to Pollock, August 21, 1919, Holmes-Pollock Letters, II, 22.

6. Heuser, op. cit., p. 389.

7. Sheehan to Holmes, August 26, 1910, ibid., p. 217.

8. Sheehan to Heuser, December 12, 1903, ibid., p. 185.

9. Sheehan to Holmes, August 26, 1910, ibid., p. 214.

10. Ibid., p. 186.

11. Ibid.

12. Ibid., p. 172.

13. Patrick A. Sheehan, Under the Cedars and the Stars (New York, 1903), p. 143.

14. Holmes to Sheehan, February ?, 1904, Heuser Letters.

15. Holmes to Laski, October 26, 1919, Holmes-Laski Letters, I, 217.

16. Holmes to Laski, May 8, 1918, ibid., I, 154.

17. Holmes to Sheehan, July 5, 1912, Heuser Letters.

18. Holmes to Sheehan, March 7, 1913, ibid.

19. Heuser, op. cit., p. 32, p. 177, p. 387.

20. Sheehan to Holmes, March 25, 1911, Heuser, op. cit., p. 237. Holmes wrote to disagree. "I love your [words . . . Dante gains] a new value from them." Holmes to Sheehan, April 1, 1911, Heuser Letters.

21. Holmes to Sheehan, August 14, 1910, ibid.

22. Holmes to Sheehan, April 1, 1911, ibid.

23. Antony Coleman, "Priest as Artist: The Dilemma of Canon Sheehan," Studies, LVII: 2 (Spring 1969), 30–40. The following passage from Heuser's biography is revealing: ". . . a few days before his death, the Canon called his brother and asked him to go over with him his letters and other papers. These he had already carefully arranged and tied together with notes indicating their dates and contents, evidently with a view to their final disposition. Placing his hand on the Memoirs of his own life, he said to his brother: 'These might do harm to others; let us destroy them.' And then and there the volumes of manuscript were thrown into the open grate . . ." Heuser, op. cit., pp. 250–251.
24. Holmes to Sheehan, August 14, 1910, Heuser Letters.
25. Heuser, op. cit., p. 387.
26. Holmes to Pollock, August 13, 1913, Holmes-Pollock Letters, I, 207–208.
27. Holmes to Pollock, ibid.; Holmes to Laski, September 15, 1929, Holmes-Laski Letters, II, 1183.
28. Holmes to Sheehan, July 17, 1909, Heuser Letters.
29. Holmes to Sheehan, September 17, 1907, ibid.
30. Holmes to Sheehan, July 5, 1912, ibid.
31. Sheehan to Holmes, October 6, 1912, Heuser, op. cit., p. 380; Holmes to Sheehan, October 18, 1912, Heuser Letters.
32. Sheehan to Holmes, August 26, 1910, Heuser, op. cit., p. 214.
33. Holmes to Sheehan, August 14, 1910, Heuser Letters.
34. Sheehan to Holmes, August 31, 1909, Heuser, op. cit., p. 254. Holmes to Sheehan, July 17, 1909, Heuser Letters.
35. Holmes to Sheehan, October 16, 1904, ibid.
36. Holmes to Sheehan, September 6, 1904, ibid.
37. Holmes to Sheehan, September 21, 1908, ibid.
38. Holmes to Sheehan, August 14, 1911, ibid.
39. Sheehan to Holmes, August 31, 1909, Heuser, op. cit., p. 254.
40. Sheehan to Holmes, December 2, 1912, ibid., p. 384.
41. Sheehan to Holmes, March 25, 1911, ibid., p. 237.
42. Sheehan to Holmes, August 31, 1909, ibid., p. 254; to Holmes, March 25, 1911, ibid., p. 236; to Holmes, October 16, 1912, ibid., p. 381.
43. Sheehan to Holmes, August 26, 1910, Heuser, op. cit., pp. 214–217, passim.
44. Holmes to Sheehan, August 14, 1911, Heuser Letters.
45. Holmes to Sheehan, March 1, 1911, ibid.
46. Holmes to Sheehan, October 18, 1912, ibid.
47. Holmes to Sheehan, April 1, 1911, ibid. Holmes had put the paradox neatly in an earlier letter. "My most constant associate among our judges is White, a Catholic, and the other day when I was speaking of the logic of persecution he agreed but said we, none of us live logically—you (Holmes) professing skepticism act on dogma; and those who profess dogma do not and could not carry it out dogmatically—the spirit of the times is too strong for us." Holmes to Sheehan, February ?, 1904, ibid.
48. Holmes to Sheehan, January 31, 1913, ibid. "You doubt if mysticism is in my line—and you are right if mysticism means belief in an ineffable direct intercourse with the higher powers. Yet I used to say, and still might, that every wise

man is a mystic at bottom. That is, he recognizes the probability that his ultimates are not cosmic ultimates." Holmes to Sheehan, October 27, 1912, ibid.

49. Holmes to Sheehan, October 18, 1912, ibid.

50. Holmes to Sheehan, November 23, 1912, a letter which ends: "I am thinking of and with you and . . . sending you my love." Ibid. Similarly: "Well, this comes pretty close to a letter of pure gossip doesn't it? but it takes you my love." Holmes to Sheehan, March 9, 1913, ibid. A like comment from a much earlier letter follows: "I remember hearing Emerson say once in a lecture, 'The lover writes "Meet me at half past seven precisely without fail. I have nothing particular to say. Thank God."' I have nothing particular to say and so I will give you a short account of my life since I last wrote." Holmes to Sheehan, September 6, 1904, ibid.

51. Sheehan, Under the Cedars and the Stars, pp. 181–183. Holmes shared his thoughts on such matters at various times. "If I put all my powers into deciding the case and writing my decision, I neither feel responsibility nor egotism, nor yet altruism—I am just all in the problem and doing my best." Holmes to Sheehan, March 21, 1908, Heuser Letters. ". . . When one fleetingly feels as if one has done one's work nobly and adequately, death doesn't seem so hard. But whenever for a minute and a half I feel cocky and as if I had done the trick, I at once begin to anticipate the revenge of fate and expect to get jolly well taken down within twenty-four hours." Holmes to Sheehan, November 23, 1912, ibid.

52. Holmes to Sheehan, December 27, 1903, ibid.

53. Holmes to Sheehan, January 2, 1904, ibid.

54. Holmes to Sheehan, February ?, 1904, ibid.

55. Holmes to Sheehan, October 27, 1912, ibid.

56. Holmes to Sheehan, February ?, 1904, ibid.

57. Holmes to Sheehan, November 7, 1907, ibid.

58. "Again you make me love and admire your tender poetic idealizing spirit . . . It is strange how little the difference in our point of view prevents my sympathizing with what seem to me your dominant feelings and attitude." Holmes to Sheehan, March 21, 1908, ibid.

59. Holmes to Sheehan, November 7, 1907, ibid. The depth of the friendship is well attested to by Holmes's words to Fr. Heuser. "I am disturbed to learn of the existence of my letters to him [Sheehan]. I sometimes wrote confidentially and always with the freedom one practices to an intimate, expecting no other eyes to see them." Holmes to Heuser, November 15, 1916, ibid.

HISTORIC FRIENDSHIPS
HOLMES, POLLOCK, AND LASKI

The friendships of Oliver Wendell Holmes, Jr., with a number of distinguished contemporaries formed an important part of his life of the mind. William James was among them, as well as Louis Brandeis, John Gray of the Harvard Law Faculty, and Felix Frankfurter. Each of these men, and others besides, gained much from their associations with Holmes. But not surprisingly, the friends the great jurist chose to make gave him special delight and in turn influenced him directly or otherwise. Such mutually nurturing experiences were especially evident in the friendships Holmes maintained with two leading British intellectuals, Frederick E. Pollock and Harold J. Laski. Though born fifty years apart and speaking with different intellectual accents, Pollock and Laski each had in Holmes (and Holmes in each of them) a friend to share fully in intellectual adventure. The letters which passed between Pollock and Holmes and Holmes and Laski, as these have been gathered together in printed editions, are ample evidence of this. In essence, Pollock and Holmes were companion legal scholars, fascinated by the history and the practice of Anglo-American legal processes, though by no means indifferent to the total human experience. Holmes and Laski, in turn, were fellow free-swinging intellectuals concerned ultimately with man himself. From the former, Holmes drew encouragement as well as knowledge at a time when he was making his mark in the world of legal learning. Laski, over the last twenty years of his life, gave him intellectual stimulation and solace from which in old age only such a mind as Holmes possessed could profit.

In 1889, one hundred years after the adoption of the Constitution of the United States, the supreme statement of American law, Frederick

William Maitland, the greatest historian of English law, was moved to write of a legal treatise but recently published in America: "for a long time to come it will leave its mark wide and deep on all the best thoughts of Americans and of Englishmen about the history of their common law." The book was *The Common Law,* the author, Oliver Wendell Holmes, Jr. Suitably enough, Frederick Pollock, Maitland's collaborator on their magisterial study, *History of English Law Before the Time of Edward I,* was already well known to Holmes, and out of their love of legal thought grew an abiding friendship. Centered as it was in the law, what Pollock spoke of as "Our Lady of the Common Law," the Pollock-Holmes relationship enjoyed a solid footing. But as both men maintained a wide range of interests, their exchange of ideas and opinions over the course of half a century presents a pattern of response suggestive of a common civilization towards the betterment of which Pollock and Holmes were to contribute. Conscious pride in that civilization combined with tempered assessments of the worth of their own efforts in its enrichment to reveal a singular set of Anglo-Americans.[1]

Frederick Pollock was born in London in the year 1845. By any measurement he seemed destined for the law. His grandfather, the first baronet, was Lord Chief Baron of the Court of the Exchequer; his father, Sir William Pollock, was Queen's Remembrancer and Senior Master of the Supreme Court of Judicature. Pollock himself was educated at Eton where he was a king's scholar, and at Trinity College, Cambridge. While at Cambridge he greatly prized his membership in the Conversazione Society, "The Apostles" as it was commonly called, a group distinguished by the intellectual reputation of its company. Pollock realized that he owed much to the Society—his friendship with Sir Henry Maine, for example—and "an earlier discovery of Maitland than I should have made otherwise."[2] Years later, in 1928, he told Holmes of presiding over the Society's annual dinner, where he talked "patriarchally about the past."[3] Pollock was chosen a Fellow of Trinity in 1868 and immediately began preparation for the legal profession. He was called to the bar by Lincoln's Inn in 1871. But his was to be a career as legal author, professor, and editor rather than barrister. Having come under the influence of both

Lord Lindley and Sir James Shaw Willes in his study of law, Pollock wanted to learn, in his own words, "the root of the matter which too many things in common legal practice inspired to obscure" since "the law is neither a trade nor a solemn jugglery but a science."[4] His legal scholarship first expressed itself in *Principles of Contract at Law and in Equity*, notable for a fresh awareness and renewed stress on basic principles, and *The Law of Torts*, in which he displayed a concern for the philosophy and the practice of law. Both books were published in the 1870s. Beyond a zeal for the law, Sir Frederick (he succeeded to the baronetcy in 1888) was a mountain climber of reputation, a fencer of real skill, and a poet, though he himself might have disclaimed the full implications of the latter. Like Holmes, he was drawn strongly in the direction of philosophy, publishing in 1880 a life of Spinoza which received wide critical acclaim in its own day and for years to come.[5] And like his American friend, Pollock was vouchsafed a long life, dying in his ninety-second year in 1937. Indeed, he lived long enough, this "Nestor of English lawyers," to offer some of the most decisive advice the government was to receive in the matter of the abdication of King Edward VIII.

Four years senior to Pollock, Oliver Wendell Holmes, Jr. was the only son of Dr. Oliver Wendell Holmes. Born in Boston, his name and background were distinguished. Among his forebears was Thomas Holmes, a lawyer of Gray's Inn in the sixteenth century. But all his grandparents traced descent from earlier colonial settlers, among them, Anne Bradstreet, "the tenth muse." Holmes's maternal grandfather, Charles Jackson, had been a justice of the Supreme Court of Massachusetts, while his father, physician, poet, and essayist, was widely and well known on the Continent and in England, where he had traveled extensively. Holmes was educated primarily at E.S. Dixwell's Private Latin School in preparation for college, entering Harvard with the class of 1861. When President Lincoln sent forth his appeal for volunteers after the attack on Fort Sumter in April, 1861, Holmes enlisted in the Union army. He was able to remain in Boston long enough to receive his bachelor's degree, then served as an officer in the Twentieth Massachusetts Volunteer Infantry, rising from the rank of lieutenant to colonel. Holmes saw hard fighting at Ball's Bluff, Antietam, and Fredericksburg and was thrice wounded before being mustered out of service in July, 1864. Two years later he was awarded a degree in law from Harvard and admitted to the Boston bar. Unlike Pollock, he engaged in the active practice of law for over a decade. In these years of apprenticeship he drew his lasting insights into the history and nature of the judicial process which were to sustain him as a legal theorist and as a judge. At the same time, along with William James, Charles Peirce, and Chauncey Wright, he was a member of the "Metaphysical Club." British empiricism, sharpened by skepticism and augmented by new directions in the sciences, helped these young thinkers formulate the first laws of that singularly American philosophy, pragmatism. Holmes's fondness for the utility principle of pragmatism was as characteristic of him and his work as that touch of mysticism which was evident in Pollock's intellectual make-up. Each friend thus found in the other's philosophy a corrective for his own thought.

Meanwhile Holmes had come to England in 1866 on the first of numerous visits. He met some of the memorable figures of the day: Sir Henry Maine, Benjamin Jowett, James Bryce, and A.V. Dicey among them. Fashionable London welcomed him not alone because his father had smoothed the way. He was, after all, a handsome, gallant, articulate and truly charming American cousin. English people, like his own countrymen, seemed to rejoice in his presence. Tel père, tel fils.[6]

The Pollock-Holmes friendship began when the American, visiting in London again in 1874, was introduced to Pollock by Leslie Stephen. Stephen had become acquainted with Holmes while in the United States some ten years before, meeting him as a young Union officer then in Boston recovering from his third wound. Stephen and Pollock were already friends and were to remain so for a life time. Fond of mountaineering, history, and philosophy, together they had founded the famous walking club, "The Sunday Tramps." What would be more natural than for Stephen to bring his mutual friends together. It is also probable that the elder Holmes knew Pollock's father and mother, Sir William and Lady (Juliet) Pollock who were acquainted with most of the leading literary figures of the day, and also Pollock's uncle, Walter Herries Pollock, the jurist. One thing is sure; Dr. Holmes, "the autocrat of the breakfast table," was a man greatly respected for his writings by the Pollock family. The verse which Frederick Pollock wrote when in America in 1884, and after meeting the elder Holmes for the first time, is tribute enough.

Paulo Post
To O.W. Holmes

On halting feet, all out of time
    It creeps, a month and more belated;
    Yet this one plea may save my rhyme—

For living sight and speech it waited,
    Sight long desired, at length attained,
    Speech heard in dreams when those bright pages
    Were music to the mind o'erstrained

By converse with less gentle sages.
    At Cambridge, mother of the fair
    And valiant daughter here before me,
    When picking bones of learning bare

At sundry times did somewhat bore me,
    As oft in weary mood I sat
    And wished the sum of books were lesser,
    My monarch was the Autocrat,

My chosen tutor the Professor.
    Subject and learner, now and then
    As then I felt it, now I knew it:
    My pen—a little Professor's pen—

Hails Autocrat, Professor, Poet:
    Take, wise and genial friend of man,
    Your reader's homage—ask not whether
    Of British or American,

But English one and all together.

F. Pollock
Cambridge, Mass., September 30, 1884[7]

Undoubtedly Pollock's admiration for Doctor Holmes prepared and advanced his friendship for the son.

Of that first meeting in 1874 with Holmes, Jr., Pollock has put his feelings well: "There was no stage of acquaintance ripening into friendship; we understood one another and were friends without more ado."[8] Leslie Stephen may have been the human link at first because what he valued was shared by his two friends; but, in fact, Holmes and Pollock had much of the incidental and the substantial in common. Both had recently married, Holmes in 1872 and Pollock in 1873. Both looked forward to the years of legal study ahead with an eagerness belying their sophistication. And with the passing of time, both men attained the rank and the honors which their work merited.

Success was one of the energizers of their long friendship. In 1883 Pollock became Corpus Professor of Jurisprudence at Oxford, a post he retained for twenty years. During this period he wrote numerous books on law, lectured widely (from India to North America!) and all the while retained his editorship of the *Law Quarterly Review* from 1885 to 1919. Furthermore he was, from 1895 to 1935, editor-in-chief of the *Law Reports*. This latter service, standing alone, would have earned him the gratitude of two generations of barristers. In these various activities the kinship with Holmes is striking. Holmes too served for a time as an editor—of the *American Law Review*—in the 1870s, held the Weld Professorship of Law at Harvard, and about the time Pollock's *Principles of Contract* appeared, brought out a carefully edited and fully annotated version of Kent's *Commentaries*. Yet there was more here than a fortuitous parallel. While in the late seventies Holmes undertook to do a series of articles for the *American Law Review* dealing with possession, trespass and negligence, and the like, he dispatched each piece, as soon as it came out, to Pollock in England. He wanted a critical reaction to his scholarship and trusted Pollock to provide the informed scrutiny. Pollock viewed Holmes's investigation into the common law with quiet enthusiasm. The articles were, in his judgment, important because they displayed a scientific understanding of the law.[9] At the end of the decade Holmes drew these articles and several lectures besides into a unified whole, *The*

Common Law. What Holmes had done in this his major work was to continue a series of scientific observations which initially had been brought forward by Sir Henry Maine and subsequently applied definitely to the common law by Pollock in his book, *Principles of Contract.* Holmes complemented the scholarship of his English friends and extended the whole of the investigation at the same time, gaining what was important recognition for him from leading English authorities.[10] Subsequent to his law professorship at Harvard, Holmes became a justice of the high court of Massachusetts and in 1902 was named an associate justice of the Supreme Court of the United States by President Theodore Roosevelt. He served as an associate justice until 1932. By reason of the opinions he wrote in a multitude of critical cases, many of which pointed the way to new constructions of the Constitution, Holmes became a veritable "Blackstone of American law."

Over the years from 1874 the two friends met frequently both in America and in England. The regard each held for the other's homeland was based more on what they perceived as respect for intellectual concerns in the two countries and less because of the superficialities of either American or English life. Holmes was always appreciative of the warm reception his early work received in England, especially as his countrymen were slower to recognize the worth of his researches into the origins of the common law; while Pollock said he detected a respect for learning in America equaling that of his homeland. Yet the real measure of this friendship is in the letters exchanged over the course of half a century. When Holmes quoted approvingly to Pollock in 1929 the old saying: "no gentleman can be a philosopher and no philosopher a gentleman: to the philosopher everything is fluid, even himself, while the gentleman is a little God over against the Cosmos"—a proposition Pollock flatly denied —he was evincing the critical property which consistently featured the Pollock-Holmes correspondence.[11] Pollock's observations could be equally tart. "On the vanity and mischief of dogmatizing, we don't differ at all," he once wrote Holmes, adding "as Flaubert said: *'la bêtise consiste à vouloir conclure.'"*[12] In their letters each man spoke his mind freely, confident that disagreements on specific points which often did arise were likely to enhance their understanding of the broader aspects of life and the law. Intensely preoccupied in the early years with analytical comparisons of legal thought and practice in England and America, the correspondence, as did the personal relationship, grew to encompass all there was to think and say.

Discussion of the place of Roman law as a starting point in the development of Anglo-American law is an interesting illustration of the interplay of their ideas. Holmes took a position that "our *corpus juris* and procedures are Frankish (with a varnish of Roman) and the most profitable sources before the Conquest are on the continent."[13] Pollock agreed, but with a typical, erudite caution. "As to early Roman law," he wrote in reply to Holmes, "its analogies are risky, but the Roman is in many ways less archaic than our medieval law," citing as an example "the Roman lawyer who could not have thought the fraudulent purchaser of goods as stealing the price, and therefore as the Scots say: 'theftuous.'"[14] The Pollock-Holmes approach to the law was hardly antiquarian, however, as the exchange regarding the proper extent of the due process clause of the Fourteenth Amendment of the American Constitution shows. In the case *Baldwin* vs. *Missouri*, Holmes had dissented, arguing that the state of Missouri had a right to place an inheritance tax on bank deposits transferred by a will. When Pollock received copies of the briefs and opinions of the case from the Clerk of the Supreme Court—a courtesy Holmes had arranged all the while he served on the Court—he sided with Holmes's judgment. Pollock held that both law and common sense combined to support his friend's position in the case.[15] Or again, when Holmes wrote one of his memorable dissents in *Abrams* vs. *United States*, he insisted that actions, to be treasonous under the law, had to hold a "clear and present danger" to the security of the nation and not merely a potential threat to the community. Pollock tended to disagree at first. But once full information became available he acknowledged the correctness of Holmes's opinion, observing simply, "there was nothing (in the counts) that could properly go to the jury."[16] In matters of justice the instincts of the two men were much alike.

If Pollock and Holmes tended to be realists according to the prescriptions of their age, when they took a hard look at life their particular views nonetheless differed enough to account for particular preference in philosophy, religion and morality. Pollock once wrote Holmes, "as Berkeley said long ago, it is idle to censure the creator as wasteful if you believe in a creator who has unlimited stuff to play with. . . . Any how there will be new ideas in the future that can't come into our knowledge in this world. . . ."[17] In contrast, Holmes's outlook was hardly mystic and definitely matter-of-fact. "On the whole I am on the side of the unregenerate who affirm the worth of life as an end in itself as against the saints who deny it."[18] Such a divergency in focusing on the ultimate of life produced no alienation. For example, Holmes and Pollock tended to approach Jesus, his trial and crucifixion as historians rather than believers, while dissociating themselves from the common strain of skepticism so frequently encountered in their contemporaries. As Pollock observed to Holmes, denying the historical Jesus was like denying that such a man as Charles the Great ever existed because there were incredible legends about him.[19] Both men retained a respect for Christian ethics, though they were sure of nothing about the cosmic importance of the human breed. Still Pollock was reluctant to accept a utilitarian definition of good,[20] while Holmes was typically ambiguous on the subject in writing to his friend. "As to Ethics I have called them a body of imperfect social generalizations expressed in terms of emotions. Of course I agree," he went on, "that there is such a body on which to a certain extent civilized men would agree—but how much less than would have been taken for granted fifty years ago."[21] In light of all this it is worth noting that Pollock and Holmes were to congratulate one another on their rediscovery of Boethius's *De Consolatione Philosophiae* in their later years.[22]

One of the striking features of the Pollock-Holmes letters is the relatively slight attention each man paid to the everyday events outside the ken of the law, even though some of these, such as the Boer War, must have appeared dominant issues. Occasional references to world politics or Anglo-American concerns surfaced, with asides on such matters as the Hay-Pauncefote Treaty or the state of affairs in England or America at a given moment. Inevitably after 1914 many allusions to the Great War cropped up, including comments on the League of Nations, Wilson, and Lloyd George. But by and large the letters disregard the contemporary and convey the impression of two friends who either assumed the compatibility of their respective countries because of their compatibility as individuals derived from and part of a common culture, or inclined to look upon such considerations as irrelevant. Logic supports the former contention, literary evidence the latter, adding a subtlety and a shading to the correspondence, as to the friendship, easier to sense than it is to specify.[23]

Harold Laski's birth and background form a natural contrast to Holmes and Pollock. Laski was born in 1893, though the obvious age disparity with Holmes was perhaps the least significant of their differences. Laski's heritage was Jewish, and he grew up in the Cheetham Hill section of Manchester which had strong overtones of a middle-class ghetto. Rebellious by nature, he repudiated his Jewish religion and married at an early age a woman unacceptable to his parents. All of this marked him off from the American and the British aristocrat. Indeed, despite Laski's brilliance which drew him to Holmes, the friendship remains a curious one unless a constant stress is placed on their common intellectual outlook.

Nathan Laski, Harold's father, was a successful cotton shipper, well known for his philanthropies within the Jewish community in Manchester and his liberalism in politics. The Laski household was a model of bourgeois comfort, displaying at the same time a concern for humanity and many of its "large causes." Though young Laski's early education included the usual emphasis on the Jewish sacred books and ritual, he benefited from a solid university preparation at the Manchester Grammar School. In 1910 he won a history exhibition at New College, Oxford. But before going up to Oxford, Laski had fallen in love.

Laski and Frida Kerry met in December, 1909. He was sixteen and she was twenty-four, a trained physiotherapist who had studied eugenics in Sweden, taught in Belgium, and was employed in Glasgow when the two were introduced. A long correspondence followed, mostly on the subject of eugenics. Laski in fact studied eugenics for six months at the University of London before entering Oxford in 1911. By then he and Frida were in love and, acknowledging parental opposition from both families, they decided to marry first and announce the event afterwards. Total catastrophe in the Laski household was barely averted, so overwhelming was Nathan Laski's grief at the action taken by his son. A compromise finally was arranged: Harold was to go to Oxford and live apart from his wife most of the year, the marriage being kept secret from all but a few. Such an arrangement was abnormal in the extreme but the young people were determined to make the best of it. Turning from eugenics after a year of reading science at Oxford, Laski plunged into a study of history. He was a pupil both of H.A.L. Fisher and Ernest Barker, explored the medieval epoch with Vinogradoff, and became the total disciple of Maitland. In June of 1914 he took a First Class degree and the Beit Essay Prize as well.

Graduation from Oxford, among other things, meant that Laski was on his own. The £200 per annum allowance his father had provided during his stay at Oxford was not to be continued. During the summer months of 1914 he wrote leading articles for the *Daily Herald*. More importantly, he and Frida were able to live together. Their idyll ended, as it seemed to do for all of England, when the war came in August. Laski's attempts to join the forces were to no avail; he was rejected for medical reasons. A second search for work was then launched. At the bidding of the warden of New College he accepted a lectureship at McGill University in Montreal.

McGill was very little to the liking of either Laski or his wife. Lonely, deprived of the stimulating intellectual companionship they had come to depend on, continually pressed for funds, Laski was not likely to remain long at McGill. In the spring of 1915 he had occasion to meet Norman Hapgood, editor of *Harper's Weekly*. Hapgood was a close friend of Felix Frankfurter, then a leading member of the Harvard law faculty. He told Frankfurter of his chance encounter with the precocious Laski. Some months later, when Frankfurter and Laski were introduced, the former was so impressed he went straight to Dean Haskins of the Harvard Graduate School. He argued forcefully in favor of a position for the young Englishman with the result that Laski was appointed instructor and tutor in the department of government in January, 1916. He was to stay at Harvard just over four years, becoming notorious in the university as a radical and at times a source of acute distress to President Lowell.[24]

Harold Laski first met Oliver Wendell Holmes on a July day in 1916 at the justice's summer home, Beverly Farms, situated some thirty miles north of Boston. Just as Felix Frankfurter had made it possible for Laski to join the Harvard faculty, so he introduced him to Holmes.[25] To have been a passionate student of Maitland at Oxford was more than enough to recommend him to Holmes. He now became a passionate intellectual friend of the distinguished American jurist. As Frankfurter described the relationship, "they found themselves drawn to one another at first sight by the magnetic attraction of two deep-ploughing minds full of disinterested zest for the adventure of ideas."[26] In important ways the Holmes-Laski friendship ran a different course from that of Holmes and Pollock. They had less in common by way of social position and corresponding experiences, a condition aggravated to some extent at least by the fifty years separating them in age. Not that Harold Laski was ever a vague academic figure in relation to the leading public people of his time; he met with many of the political greats and leading personalities from the world of arts and letters and enjoyed such contacts immensely. About this time, by way of contrast, Holmes had begun a slow retreat from intercourse with all but a few of his closest friends. After 1916 Laski became a secure and trusted member of that inner circle. As Holmes wrote in one of his very last letters, "I feel very remote from the business of judges," as from the larger business of life.[27] Without the stimulation of Laski's ever resourceful and wide-ranging intellect, and, be it remarked, his utter willingness to write numerous exhaustive, erudite, and delightful letters with no thought that his aging correspondent ought or would answer them, one must conclude that the last twenty years of Holmes's life would have meant much less to him.

Few matters were of more earnest common concern than the scope of law as it affected the rights of man. Evidence of this was discernible from the very earliest exchange of letters. Holmes could not divest his thinking of the concept of the sweeping sovereignty of the state. "It asserts itself as omnipotent in the sense that it asserts that what it sees fit to order, it will make you obey. You may very well argue that it ought not to order certain things and I agree," Holmes continued. "But if the government does see fit to order them, I conceive that order is as much law as any other . . . and it seems to me idle to say that it is not law because by a theory that you and I happen to hold (though I think it very disputable) it ought not to be."[28] Holmes was, in such a passage, reflecting the influence of Herbert Spencer, which was bound to be more emphatic for him than for Laski who looked at *Social Statics* many years after its appearance. While not quarreling with the main thesis Holmes advanced, Laski entered some reservations regarding Holmes's attitude. "Of course sovereignty usually does make you obey," he replied. "The trouble is that when it does it is hopelessly wrong. My problem is to take away from the state the superior morality with which we have involved its activities and give them back to the individual conscience." Laski, to be sure, was surveying the results of increased government action in the hands of the capitalist establishment which he thought unworthy of such responsibilities; or as he said, "a tendency to push things on to the government as an ultimate reservoir which excuses individual thinking."[29] Holmes stated his position on the matter of rights directly, a few years later, writing: "I take no stock in abstract rights."[30] Not that such a resounding statement meant the end of further discussion; Holmes had been saying as much for decades and the controversy remained ever vibrant. Laski continued to hammer away on his own views under the influence, as he noted, of John Stuart Mill. "There are all kinds of theories, e.g., Christian Science, which seem to me to be stupid and wrongheaded," he told Holmes, "but looking at the natural history of such theories I don't think either stupidity or wrongheadedness has a sufficient chance of survival to penalize the ideals themselves."[31]

With the onset of World War I, the subject of rights brought a fresh timeliness to the issue of such freedoms as those of speech and the press. Holmes is well known for his "clear and present danger" principle which he first enunciated in *Schenk* vs. *United States*. In a companion case, *Debs* vs. *United States*, he held to the principle, yet felt compelled to explain his position to Laski carefully because he greatly regretted that the government pressed action against Debs.[32] Holmes chose to judge Debs entirely with respect to the law, the Espionage Act, not on the morality of Debs's protests against the war. In other words, he explained, it was not the possible danger implicit in Debs's exercise of the freedom to protest the war, but the law as it was on the statute books which counted. Such a law was an expression of the will of the sovereign state, sufficient warrant for Holmes in this instance at least. Years later, in an article, "What is Sedition?" which appeared in the Manchester *Guardian* (December 12, 1925), Laski incorporated the "clear and present danger" criterion in urging the passage of an act to make seditious utterances punishable only if immediate harm impended. Like Holmes, he was fearful of the tyranny of the sovereign state.[33] Holmes spoke his feelings directly enough in 1919. "Little as I believe in freedom of speech as a theory I hope I would die for it and go as far as anyone whom I regard as competent to form an opinion in favor of it."[34] Laski's position was much less intellectually ambiguous, probably, as he remarked to Holmes, because twentieth-century history had produced a change of perspective alien to the century before.[35] The age gap between the two friends could count for something after all. To Laski, as to a whole generation in the 1930s and the 1940s, dying for a theory became a commonplace because belief in freedom went so deep and the challenge to it was so direct.

The views of Holmes and Laski concerning natural rights are further illuminated if considered in conjunction with their dialogue on the related aspects of science and religion. Laski took the lead in these matters in a letter of March, 1918. Holmes had been reading, at his friend's suggestion, John Theodore Merz, *A History of European Thought in the Nineteenth Century*. Some parts of this book were under question, largely on the ground that Holmes and Laski were considerably more skeptical about the potential of the human intellect than was Merz. Merz also had written *Religion and Science,* an optimistic version of man in the universe and had exhibited therein the kind of facile faith Laski rejected out of hand. To him the easy optimism of Merz was "the tap-root of most indifference to reality." Laski judged God not to be in his heaven and all not right with the world, and so he could not "obey him and be quiet."[36] While denying the teachings of religion he was prepared to admit its influence, which he ascribed to human sentimentality.[37] The conventional religious persuasion, were it to continue to affect the Anglo-Saxon mind, would make the outlook a very dismal one.[38] Laski's intellectual honesty on the matter of God is worth underscoring. Holding to the proposition that the beauty of religion was the only quality enabling it to lay claim to sanctions—"the inherent appeal of that beauty"[39]—he opposed any one who favored a particular religious profession under law. He also disagreed with those advocates who, arguing from a largely scientific, secular frame of reference, insisted on finding harmony between science and religion. Reacting to the efforts of Alfred North Whitehead in *Science and the Modern World,* wherein he attempted to square the theological-philosophical circle, Laski pointed out that Whitehead "doesn't mean by God anything that any theologian has ever meant, with the result that he quite unjustifiably leaves an impression of harmony between science and religion which is only reached by making words, *à la* Humpty-Dumpty, mean whatever he wants them to mean."[40] The scientist-philosopher who indulged in such exercises was naïve, the victim of sentimentality or cultural lag.[41] To Laski, as to Holmes, the "only adequate test for good we had was social utility and this meant response to demand of persons."[42] If there was a God it was an everyday God, discoverable in everyday good.[43]

Holmes, suspicious about anything supernatural, had no difficulty in equating utility and good. On one occasion, writing about the progress of mankind, he observed to Laski that, if it be true that Asia produced every religion which had ever commanded the reverence of man, while Europe gave us only the steam engine, he "would bet on the steam engine for it meant science and science is the root from which comes the flower of our thought."[44] He was convinced of "faith in the prevalence of reason in the long run. . . . But I am well aware how long reason may be kept under by what man wants to believe." And just as Laski was prepared to dispute Whitehead, Holmes was prepared to name his own *bête noire* when it came to belief: "I do despise *The Will To Believe*," he added emphatically.[45] Holmes was fond of saying, with Madame de Staël, that he did not believe in hell but he was afraid of it nonetheless. This is a deft expression of what he found to be the irrationality of supernatural religion. Faith was childish, it was devoid alike of historical and rational foundations. Therefore, he could not believe, but only admit to a semi-shudder when he thought of millions of intelligent men who would hold him debarred from the face of God unless he confessed a faith of some kind.[46] What is most striking in all this perhaps is that, despite the different eras in which these two friends had been born, Holmes's attitude toward the possibility of a God was much the same as Laski's. Or, it might be argued, despite the passage of time since the nineteenth-century scientific arguments against religion were first heard by Holmes, Laski continued to cling to aspects of the ancient superstition. He once mentioned that he thought religion ought to "build on small daily incidents—the joy of finding a rare book, the unexpected visit of a dear friend, the contemplation of a picture."[47] In neither mind is there discoverable any tension between faith and science which characterized the outlook of certain of their contemporaries. Yet the traces of a religious sense, the residual evidence of supernaturalism, should not be ignored.

Talk of natural rights, of faith, and of science suggests the need to represent the fundamental philosophical postures of Holmes and Laski. Their respective positions were made clear one to the other early in their correspondence. And it was a posture, rather than any pattern of ideas constituting a "philosophy," which the early letters revealed. As Holmes phrased it:

> Of course I know that ideas are merely
> shorthand for the collections of the facts I don't

care for. It is the eternal seesaw of the universe. A fact taken in its isolation (to quote myself) is gossip. Philosophy is an end of life yet philosophy is only cataloging the universe and the universe is simply an arbitrary fact so that as gossip should lead to philosophy, philosophy ends in gossip.[48]

Laski agreed, calling himself a not inept disciple of Holmes in the bargain.[49] In his very next letter Holmes elaborated this theme.

Well—the universe may be contemplated in two ways—one our usual one, at the point of contact where it is finite, measurable, predictable— the other as a whole, as an inexplicable mystery which one can help oneself to realize by thinking that a roomful of men would take us back to the unknown. If one dwells on that and becomes emotionally possessed by it one very well might accept any cult that he found at hand, never troubling about its finite fallacies, but taking it as a momentary expression of the eternal wonder.

You know my expression for it—as a betta-bilitarian. A spontaneity taking an irrational pleasure in a moment of rational sequence.[50]

As though to seal the ripening friendship Laski wrote: "So long as we have a veneration for reason and a skepticism in common there can be little ground for serious disagreement between us."[51]

The Holmes-Laski skepticism should be understood as a serious one, whether considering the content of philosophy or its history. For example, Laski took exception to the philosopher L.T. Hobhouse when he insisted that Plato and Aristotle were the indispensable foundation for contemplating the edifice of western thought. He took it to be more important to know Berkeley and Hume; as he argued to Holmes, "it

seems to me that today the grasp of metaphysics involves an understanding of certain scientific ideas unknown until our own day."[52] And
he went on. "I saw that, e.g., infanticide was only bad when it was
considered bad in intent and results; there was no unchanging goodness
in the act, true for the Greeks and ourselves."[53] To all of which Holmes
answered:

> I am entirely with you against the man who said
> begin with Plato and Aristotle. I did with Plato, with
> no modern advantages to be sure, but it was Plato. I
> always say whether it be philosophy or law or what
> you like, begin with the latest. The modern books
> start from your milieu, emotional and intellectual,
> and of course, whatever they say, has enormous
> advantages also from the advance of science. . . .
> As I said of Montesquieu, to read the great books of
> the past with intelligence and appreciation is one of
> the last achievements of a studious life.

"Oh, I am fierce on that theme," he continued.

> Ideas rarely are difficult to grasp. The difficulties
> come from the language and emphasis. Of course I
> agree with you as to morality and have uttered my
> barbaric yawp on that subject from time to time. It
> is amusing to see in the law how in a century what
> was thought natural and wholesome may become
> anathema—like rum and the lottery—but they
> generally are argued about as if the present view
> was an eternal truth.54

Pollock had taken much the same position regarding the learning of
law. "I have never understood," he recalled in his autobiographical
memoir, "why beginners in the law should be plunged, without the least
instruction in the general elements, into the most technical and
perplexed branch of a science wholly new to them."[55] Yet their philosophical skepticism led them in somewhat different directions. Laski

breathed a certain scientific optimism, whereas for Holmes man possessed no cosmic importance. Man was just another species, having "for his main business to live and propagate, and for his main interest food and sex. A few get a little further along and get pleasure in it, but are fools if they are proud."[56]

Granting the downbeat of this last observation by Holmes, it nonetheless provides a clue to a unifying characteristic for the thought of Pollock, Laski, and Holmes together. At bottom, all three men were individualists by birth and background, by temper, by training, in values and in vision. Their respective brands of individualism did not spell themselves out in the same form, of course. Laski, for example, was a Marxist, but a very special sort of Marxist. His response to a heckler points this up. "Yes, there are variations on Marx," he once told a man who interrupted him at a meeting. "You have yours and I have Marx's." The diverse intellectual journeys pursued by Pollock, Laski, and Holmes account for the differences in their individualism. It may be more useful, however, to stress the unifying principle of individualism ascertainable in their thought if their impact on history, as well as the influences they had on one another, is to become clear. For Pollock and Holmes the individual before the law was perennially fascinating. Even when, in Holmes's judgment, the sovereignty of the state ought to prevail, the fate of a man like Debs was of genuine concern to him. The individualism of Holmes, when contrasted with that of Laski, comes through as a subtle yet sturdy kind. Facing what each accepted as extinction at death, Holmes and Laski made their commitment to search for knowledge and wisdom a total effort—*contra mundum*. If they whispered despair in beholding the fate of mankind, they also raised strong voices in support of individual effort and success in life, a struggle carried forward as part of the force of destiny.

Furthermore, such commitments were congenial to Americans and Britons alike. The absence of nationalistic barriers across the terrain of intellectual friendships may be taken for granted without ever accounting for the natural blending of common premises leading to kindred conclusions. Pollock, Laski, and Holmes had many of the same heroes and suspected not a few of the same villains in the history they read and the theories they elaborated, long before they had come to know one another personally. They were all cast in a liberal mold. Were they liberal according to the dictum of Bertrand Russell, who insisted that the essence of liberalism lay not in what opinions were held, but in how they were held, i.e., tentatively and with a consciousness that new evidence might at any time require their abandonment? Perhaps never fully so, yet they all had a healthy respect for this kind of liberal prejudice, nurtured as it had been by individualism and providing the dimension of freedom exhibited in their thought.

NOTES

1. Mark DeW. Howe, editor, *Holmes-Pollock Letters* (2 v., Cambridge, Mass., 1941). These letters are basic for an appreciation of the friendship of Holmes and Pollock. The first volume includes an admirable introduction to the friendship by John Gorham Palfrey A later edition, published in 1961, has a fine biographical sketch of Pollock by his son, Sir John Pollock, Bart. The 1941 collection is used throughout except when noted and is hereafter cited *Pollock Letters*.
2. *Ibid.* 2: p. 174
3. *Ibid.* 2: p. 221.
4. Frederick E. Pollock, *For My Grandson* (London, 1933), p. 163.
5. Laski, writing to Holmes as late as 1927, described himself as going back to "F. Pollock's book with a satisfied sense that it is quite easily and pre-eminently the best account of Spinoza there is." Mark DeW. Howe, editor, *Holmes-Laski Letters*, 1916–1935 (2 v., Cambridge, Mass., 1953) 2: p. 919. This collection is hereafter cited *Laski Letters*.
6. Mark DeW. Howe, Mr. Justice Holmes, The Proving Years (Cambridge, Mass., 1963) fully discusses the intellectual growth of Holmes across the decade of the 1870s. Catherine Drinker Bowen, Yankee From Olympus (Boston, 1944) is useful as an informed, intimate portrait.
7. *Pollock Letters* (1961 edition), p. xxvi.
8. *Pollock Letters* 1: p. xv.
9. Bowen, *op. cit.*, p. 273.
10. Mark DeW. Howe, "Introduction," The Common Law (Boston, 1963), p. xx.
11. Pollock Letters 2: p. 239.
12. *Ibid.* 2: p. 255.
13. *Ibid.* 1: p. 34.
14. *Ibid.* 1: p. 79. For a treatment of some points of difference between Holmes and Pollock see Howe, *op. cit.*, p. 227ff.
15. *Pollock Letters* 2: pp. 267, 271.
16. *Ibid.* 2: pp. 31, 45.

17. *Ibid.* 2: p. 24.
18. *Ibid.* 1: p. 101.
19. *Ibid.* 2: p. 211.
20. *Ibid.* 1: p. 117.
21. *Ibid.* 2: p. 3.
22. *Ibid.* 2: pp. 6–7.
23. In the course of their friendship those institutions most dear to each saw fit to honor the other. In 1895 Harvard University awarded Pollock the LL.D. degree *honoris causa.* Even greater honors awaited Holmes. In 1931 he was made an Honorary Bencher of Lincoln's Inn.
24. Kingsley Martin, *Harold Laski (1893–1950) A Biographical Memoir* (New York, 1953) is the best approach to Laski, apart from his own writings. I have based my account of Laski's personal life largely on Martin's book.
25. *Pollock Letters* 1: p. 238.
26. Mark DeW. Howe, "Foreward," *Laski Letters* 1: p. xiv.
27. *Ibid.* 2: pp. 1415–1416.
28. *Ibid.* 1: p. 21.
29. *Ibid.* 1: pp. 22–23.
30. *Ibid.* 1: p. 769.
31. *Ibid.* 1: p. 160.
32. *Ibid.* 1: p. 190.
33. *Ibid.* 1: p. 807.
34. *Ibid.* 1: p. 217.
35. *Ibid.* 1: p. 160.
36. *Ibid.* 1: p. 141.
37. *Ibid.* 2: p. 1140.
38. *Ibid.* 1: p. 771.
39. *Ibid.* 2: p. 871.
40. *Ibid.* 2: p. 1205.
41. *Ibid.* 2: p. 898.
42. *Ibid.* 1: p. 697.
43. *Ibid.* 2: p. 909.
44. *Ibid.* 1: p. 210.
45. *Ibid.* 2: p. 1134.
46. *Ibid.* 1: p. 154.
47. *Ibid.* 2: p. 909.
48. *Ibid.* 1: p. 129.
49. *Ibid.* 1: p. 130.
50. *Ibid.* 1: p. 131.
51. *Ibid.*
52. *Ibid.* 1: p. 696.
53. *Ibid.* 1: p. 697.
54. *Ibid.* 1: p. 704.
55. *Pollock, op. cit.,* p. 161.
56. *Laski Letters* 2: p. 1125.

THE ANGLO-AMERICAN
RAPPROCHEMENT

The term "special relationship" has been used since the early days of World War II to identify the friendship of Great Britain and the United States, not alone in war and diplomacy but in the larger cultural sense as well. This has come about for a variety of reasons, undergirded by a common language and literature and shared ideas in law and society. But from the beginning of the century, and critical to this phenomenon, were personal friendships of a large number of individuals. These men championed the relationship of the two nations, articulating the reasons why the relationship should be sustained and, in fact, added to, as ease of communication developed during the twentieth century. H.C. Allen has written in his history of Anglo-American relations that "the cultural tie has probably been the most important of all the ties binding Great Britain to the United States." Yet when all is said and done it has been individuals who believed in and worked to promote this historic friendship. Premonitions of this can be found in the correspondence of Carlyle and Emerson in the nineteenth century which would come to fruition decades later. But it was meaningful personal friendships which had lighted and then carried the torch for others to admire and wonder at. Such was the amity between Theodore Roosevelt and high ranking Britons, Cecil Spring Rice, Arthur Hamilton Lee, St. Loe Strachey, James Bryce and G.O. Trevelyan among them, that the foundation of this entente was put down on solid ground.

THEODORE ROOSEVELT
AND HIS ENGLISH CORRESPONDENTS

In an era when public men continued to look upon letter-writing as a means of setting forth ideas, developing thought, and justifying actions, Theodore Roosevelt earned a wide reputation as one of the great correspondents of the day. His letters ran to many thousands and though frequently he wrote with a consciousness of history, his correspondence betrayed the candor and the assertiveness, the honesty and the self-right-eousness that characterized him as a public man. Among his most active correspondents were several well-known Englishmen, Cecil Spring Rice Arthur Hamilton Lee, James Bryce, St. Loe Strachey and George Otto Trevelyan. More as a result of letters than from the immediacy of their company Roosevelt came to know and to esteem these men as friends Their exchange of thoughts through letters in each instance extended over a period of years and ranged over a wide list of topics of common concern. On the whole the letters reveal agreement and conflict, deep friendship and occasional distemper, with family notes interspersed among the larger issues in which all the correspondents were vitally involved. To read these letters is to share in an intimate fashion the growth of lifelong friendships and to witness from a privileged vantage point the rise of the Anglo-American rapprochement. From the early personal letters between Spring Rice and Roosevelt to the long, serious policy discussions of the 1914–1918 period the correspondence inter-twines individual lives with great events, demonstrating the influence of men on the world in which they live. The letters tell persuasively how the Anglo-American entente came about and why it endured to become a "special relationship."

Historians have given the Anglo-American rapprochement appropriate attention. The present study is an effort to enlarge understanding of the great event by viewing it as the result, in part at least, of certain intellectual convictions shared by public men in England and the United States. The letters of Roosevelt and his English friends speak the character of the Anglo-American mind in a singular way. In these letters the intellectual roots of the alliance are evident, and though the focus is individualized, it is nonetheless suggestive of the large attitudes entertained by leaders in each country whose policies encouraged and then fructified the rapprochement. The alliance arose out of mutual advantage for England and America and their deliberate if piecemeal reaction to fast-changing conditions. Lacking certain common principles, well appreciated and sincerely believed in by both Roosevelt and his several correspondents—men who were in their own ways barometers of official and public opinion in the United States and Great Britain—it seems doubtful that the alliance would have blossomed as handsomely as it did. Nor is it likely that the friendship would have endured the strain fresh events exerted on it, save for those same underlying commitments.

Theodore Roosevelt corresponded with a great many English people, from King Edward VII to Parliamentary back benchers. He wrote and received letters from Cromer and Kipling and Edward Grey. But with five individuals in particular he corresponded consistently and at times intensively so that their letters over a period of years acquired a coherent pattern of thought. Of the five whose letters constitute the basis of this inquiry, not all were Roosevelt's friends in the conventional sense. St. Loe Strachey has pointed out in his autobiography that TR and he were in such accord and their ideas so confidentially shared he was amazed to realize what a comparatively few number of days, even hours, they had passed in each other's company. This was also the case with Trevelyan and Roosevelt. Bryce's dealings with TR while much more consistent were oftentimes official. Arthur Lee saw Roosevelt regularly only in 1898 and 1899, before his return to England to pursue his own career. Thereafter Lee made several trips to the United States while TR was in the White House; after that they were together briefly in 1910 and again in

1914. Spring Rice and Roosevelt were friends in a more usual fashion and saw much of each other in the late 1880s and early 1890s. Because of the exigencies of World War I they enjoyed little of each other's company while Spring Rice was British ambassador in Washington. Largely these men had a special kind of friendship, a friendship of letters. George O. Trevelyan chose to put it this way: "My vocation was only to return the balls struck over the net by the hand of the master." To a degree this judgment might be made regarding all the correspondents, though clearly it attributes too much to Roosevelt and far too little to the capacities of his friends. In the phrase of Dr. Johnson, each man "fairly put his mind" to the other. As TR remarked to Spring Rice in 1897: "You happen to have a mind which is interested in precisely the same things which interest me, and which I believe are of more vital consequences than any other to the future of the race and of the world; so naturally I am delighted to hear from you and I always want to answer your letters at length." For St. Loe Strachey it was a matter of minds "jumping together" like horses taking obstacles with the same stride.

Any number of hurdles along the course of Anglo-American relations had to be taken before the *de facto* entente of the two English-speaking nations assumed a clear and definite outline. The Spanish-American War saw England desert the continental Powers to sympathize with the United States and its war aims. Controversy over the fortification of an American-built canal at Panama and dissension growing out of the Alaska boundary feud were both serious obstacles to Anglo-American friendship, overcome only by British acquiescence to United States insistence on settlements favorable to America. In contrast the Boer War, like the Russo-Japanese War, involving vital British interests demanded and received circumspect United States consideration of British sensitivity and advantage. The total effect of Anglo-American diplomatic give-and-take encouraged leaders in America and England to look forward to the time when they could agree that all future differences between them were to be settled by arbitration. That the proposal for arbitration contained in the 1911 Arbitration Treaty died aborning reminded one and all that national interest and national sovereignty were not things lightly cast aside. The lesson of World War I for Anglo-American friendship was much the same. Genuine sympathy and mutual regard between the two countries did not lessen the height of the hurdles emplaced by the war in 1914, but gave to the riders the requisite seat and hands and nerve to clear these fresh barriers to understanding. America's entry into the war in 1917 worked to confirm the governing principle of an entente that got its first statement in 1898. This principle can be simply rendered: a clash of two national interests can always be resolved so long as there is the will and willingness to seek it.

Theodore Roosevelt was not a universally popular figure in England during the years 1898–1919. It could hardly have been otherwise because of the hard line he took with the London government on certain critical issues. Some of his actions were readily interpretable as anti-British. His strictures regarding certain English newspapermen, like Maurice Low, were pungent evidence of this; he once exclaimed that Low was a "circumcised skunk." More importantly, British officialdom, from the prime minister down, entertained a mixture of distrust and distemper toward the strongly nationalistic policies of the United States during Roosevelt's presidency when they were carried out at the expense of the British Empire. Even after the London government had acquiesced to American world pretension and accordingly had reformulated its policies, and Anglo-American accord was on the lips of many, among Foreign Office professionals America's friendship appeared little more than a tiresome necessity. Roosevelt overcame both public doubts and official reservations in part because his diplomacy, largely viewed, was consonant with Britain's advantage and in part because a host of friends in England made the man in the street there aware of this.

Of all Theodore Roosevelt's English friends none was more dear to him than Cecil Spring Rice. The two met in 1886 on a trans-Atlantic crossing to England, at a time when their careers, which were to be surprisingly important parts of the larger friendship of their two countries, promised much. They were diverse characters: Roosevelt, the man of action, Spring Rice of a poetic, reflective disposition. Born a year apart, scarcely twelve months separated them in death. The introspective strain in TR's makeup was resilient enough to provide a viable response to his friend's poetic instinct. Spring Rice's own career that included tenure at diplomatic stations halfway round the world only whetted Roosevelt's curiosity about Berlin or Constantinople, Persia or Russia, for he wrote numerous letters rich in description of the things he witnessed, the people he met, and the historical forces that appeared to be at work, shaping, and at times threatening, the future of their peoples. In composing these dispatches Spring Rice showed how well he knew his American friend. From Berlin in July of 1896 he offered his impressions of the German military.

> As a matter of fact soldiers one sees (and regiments go by every day) look splendidly—marching well, and looking proud and pleased. It must in the long run be good for a nation to take all the young men of a certain age for two years—clean them, feed them, drill them, teach them obedience and patri- otism, and train their bodies. The officers are rather different to ours. A prince (and there are numbers of them) has to do exactly as the others do—that is, get up at five and work his men and his own training till four in the afternoon.[1]

Here was the diplomat on station, in his own way a man of action, supplying Roosevelt with a vicarious sense of soldiering. Only partly did Spring Rice recount such an impression because of TR's martial enthu- siasms. Equally important, and equally valuable for seeing through to the essence of their friendship, was the possible implication for the Anglo-American peoples of the rise of the new Germany. In this same letter Spring Rice introduced another note that underscored his profound uneasiness about the future: the specter of Russia. "I think the Russians have got the Chinese now whenever they like," he told Roosevelt; "when they command and drill the Northern Chinese they will be a pretty big power—such a power as the world has never seen."[2] Often in years to come Roosevelt and Spring Rice pondered together the ambitions of Germany, the destiny of Russia, and the uncertainties in the Orient, and in what best ways Great Britain and the United States, or the two nations working as one, must act to protect themselves. For both of them it amounted to a combination of thought and action and though the mixture differed for each man, they enjoyed a common ground.

Roosevelt's reply to this early letter of Spring Rice disclosed further dimensions of their mutual fondness. He told how he and his wife had eagerly read and reread his letter and had repeated parts of it for their children. "As you know," Roosevelt wrote, "we are not fond of many people, and we are very fond of you, and if you don't come back to America for ten years, yet whenever you do, you will find us just as anxious to see you as we always were in the old days in Washington."[3] Spring Rice was witty, urbane, keen on the children, and in what were still bachelor days for him, the Roosevelt home-life was surely attractive. During these years he came to value the friendship of Edith Carow Roosevelt. "Mrs. Roosevelt always refers to your last visit as one during which she got really to be more and more glad that you were in the house, so that she felt as if one of the family had gone when you left," TR confided to Spring Rice on one occasion.[4] Few of the people Roosevelt enjoyed earned the affection of his wife so that Spring Rice was all the more welcomed in the household. As the years went by he wrote Edith Carow on frequent occasions, especially when Roosevelt was president. He had her confidence and felt that, at times, it was more discreet to express himself fully on some delicate pending issue to her, assured that the president would receive his message. Writing to Mrs. Roosevelt from St. Petersburg in December, 1903, he asked coyly: "Would you like a disquisition on politics here?" Whereupon several paragraphs concerned with taxation, the weaknesses of the Russian government, conformity in Russian society followed. Then he added: "All this is rather dull for you, but it is amusing to me, however dull it is to hear about." The president, in turn, would know his thoughts.[5]

Spring Rice was not, however, merely exploiting his acceptance by Edith Carow Roosevelt. As often their letters dealt with family and the children, with tales of happy adventure or nostalgic comments on past pleasures, and because Spring Rice was a poet, an occasional romantic description of Santa Sophia or the Persian countryside.[6] Perhaps he found it easier to write his deeper feelings about TR to his friend's wife than directly to him. "The more I think of Theodore, and I think of him constantly—I believe every day of my life—I think I know him as a pure, high, noble and devoted character as it is possible to find in our present world."[7] These lines to Edith Roosevelt leave small doubt of his affection. Occasionally sentiment did break through as when he wrote at length to TR himself congratulating him on his election as New York governor. The letter concluded: "the great thing is to retain the power of being fond of people and that I have done, and most especially of you."[8] Mrs. Roosevelt's letters reciprocated Spring Rice's feelings. "I wish you knew how often we speak of you and how much we want to see you," she wrote him while he was in Persia.

> Do you remember that year that little Ted was so ill, and you used to ride up to the steps of the tiny Jefferson Place house with your pockets full of wild flowers for him? I can see him and Alice now making a baby garden by sticking the flowers in the seat of the cane chair. . . . Please come back before we are all too staid and middle aged.[9]

Though much in the official careers of Roosevelt and Spring Rice related to the large affairs of state, the two watched with satisfaction the personal successes visited upon the other. TR's was the more meteoric rise to power, Spring Rice's the more conformable to pattern: steady, patient, and at the last impressive in its achievement. It was also predictable. Born in London in 1859 the second son of the Hon. Charles Spring Rice, he was educated at Eton and Balliol. In 1882 he entered the Foreign Office where his father had once served. After gaining valuable experience as private secretary to Lord Granville and as a précis-writer for Lord Roseberry, he was posted to the British legation in Washington in 1886. Meeting Roosevelt quite accidentally on shipboard in November of that year they quickly became such good friends that Spring Rice stood as best man at the Roosevelt-Carow wedding which took place at St. George's, Hanover Square, in December. With his usual thoughtfulness he made the stay in London a pleasurable one for his new friends.

By the mid-1890s the careers of both men had taken steps forward and each was eager for the promotion of the other. With an eye to the outcome of the presidential election of 1896 Spring Rice wrote from Berlin at a time when TR was New York City police commissioner: "I hope . . . that you will get something extremely nice in Washington if you wish to go back, and if not, something that will give you a change in New York."[10] And there was both congratulation and admiration as Roosevelt wrote his friend when he was posted to Berlin.[11] Meanwhile Roosevelt's march on history took on a quickened cadence. "I am perfectly delighted that you are Governor," Spring Rice enthused in November, 1898. "I wish you were a Senator, but that is to come."[12] When TR was elected president in his own right—the summit of his political success—his English friend "chortled with delight" and wished he could be in Washington to see him. "This is the very best news I have had for ages. . . . It is simply grand," his letter read.[13]

This same personal quality motivated the president to prefer Spring Rice as British ambassador to the United States when the London government undertook to name a successor to Sir Julian Pauncefote in 1903. "Great Heavens, how I wish you were Ambassador here!" he wrote quite frankly to Spring Rice. "There are fifty matters that came up that I would like to discuss with you, notably about affairs in the Far East, and you could be of great service to your own country as well as this country."[14] Spring Rice in fact came to Washington in 1905 with the approval of Lord Lansdowne at a time when the president was attempting to make arrangements for peace talks between Russia and Japan. At that time the British government was unwilling to exert pressure on her Japanese ally so that it made little difference if the president and the special emissary were old friends. In fact, as the letters of Roosevelt and his English correspondents reflect relations between the United States and Great Britain, friendship of a personal sort generally did not shape policy but greatly facilitated the formulation and execution of policies which appeared to be mutually attractive. But where, in the judgment of either Roosevelt or his friends, the national interests of the two countries were opposed then at best the friendships provided the means for a renewed effort at a solution acceptable to each side.

Spring Rice became ambassador to the United States in 1913, having served in the British legations in Persia and Sweden in the intervening years. Considered too inexperienced for the Washington assignment in the early years of the century, he served in Washington down to 1918, the critical period for testing and proving the Anglo-American rapprochement. From Stockholm, Spring Rice expressed his inner satisfaction at the prospect of being once more in America, and especially of reviving his association with the Roosevelts. With mock-cynicism he promised to abuse TR "as much as you like in public if you stand in need of such assistance. The condition being that Mrs. Roosevelt is kind to my wife."[15] It was to be like the good old days and his feelings were fully shared. "Three cheers!" exclaimed Roosevelt to his friend on learning of the appointment. "But now I feel horribly at not being President."[16] At about the same time TR wrote to Arthur Lee: "I am immensely pleased that Spring Rice is coming here. I hope it will make him brace up and remove that 'distressing resemblance to a sad shrunken Bulgarian king' which you say his beard has given him."[17] The career of each man had reached fruition, though the arc of success did not intersect at apogee. The stress of the Great War, and the diversity of national interest between America and England brought on by the conflict, troubled relations between the two friends as between the two nations. Yet there was something deeper between them, the shared experience of happier times which not even the large concerns of state could efface. The old affection was poignantly evident as Spring Rice wrote Roosevelt in 1915 about the death of Henry Cabot Lodge's wife.

> Mrs. Lodge's death is the end of many things—more than I can say. It is a blow quite irreparable to my wife and me. . . . What times we had in

Washington and what things we can remember!
What immense changes, not only in the friends
who used to meet and walk together but in the
background. At any rate, we are the masters of our
own souls.[18]

The demands of the war and the passing of time had made the old
days irrecoverable, and the meaning of them more dear.

"You must always remember that the President is about six," Spring
Rice had occasion to write Valentine Chirol. The remark is often quoted
to expose the childishness of Roosevelt or the cynicism of its author. But
can it tell something of the Roosevelt-Spring Rice relationship? Spring
Rice made the comment to Chirol to whom he had given a warm letter
of introduction to the president. Theirs was a disappointing meeting,
despite the ardor of Spring Rice's favor, so that in writing Chirol as he did
he was attempting to soothe the latter's frustration at not winning
Roosevelt's acceptance. No doubt his wit exceeded his good judgment in
the matter. Spring Rice himself must have felt let down that his two
friends, Roosevelt and Chirol, could not have been friends also. A similar
feeling of disappointment on the part of Roosevelt and his English
friends became visible when some practical issue arose between their
two countries. American and Englishman alike preferred a settlement of
such disputes along lines of their own national interest. In like fashion
Spring Rice found in Roosevelt and Chirol people of whom he was
genuinely fond. But he could not allow his liking for one to blind him
to the other. This was the strength of the Anglo-American special
relationship as well: national advantage ought to be pursued, even at the
expense of the other partner. That diverse national interests did not
finally divide England and America but curiously added strength to their
entente was due to the common Anglo-American commitments, which
TR and his English correspondents typified. As for the two men, disagreements and quirks of character aside: Roosevelt's frenetic ways and Spring
Rice's relentless wit, they remained brothers to the last.

Of the tributes Theodore Roosevelt might have offered to Arthur

Hamilton Lee, the proudest was that he had been with TR in Cuba. A captain at the time, Lee had been seconded from the Royal Canadian Military College to serve as the British military attaché with the American army operating in the Caribbean in 1898. The common experience as a Rough Rider commended and cemented a friendship that was as firm in 1918 as it had been promising in '98. The friendship ripened quickly. "You can treat him [Lee] as you can trust me," Roosevelt confided to Elihu Root, "and in speaking to him you are not only speaking to an officer and gentleman representing the country to which we are most closely bound but also a thorough expert in his business and as staunch a friend as America has."[19] Less than a year before his death, TR wrote Lee: "My dear Arthur, I have literally never had a friend who combined as you do absolute loyalty with complete understanding and sympathy. And you combine a further and even rarer combination—insight and common sense with courage and humor."[20]

Their early correspondence was taken up with military matters. Roosevelt discussed with Lee some of the difficulties of the Cuban campaign, commenting unsparingly on the United States Army: "the utter lack of administrative skill shown before Santiago as well as the fact that there was literally no generalship whatsoever."[21] The shortcomings of the American army were pretty well known throughout European military circles, Lee told the ex-Colonel of Rough Riders, writing what he termed "delicious" anecdotes to underscore his point.[22] As the occasion and need of concern with military affairs passed the mutual interests of the two friends broadened to historical and political views and to personal matters. In 1899 Lee married an American heiress, Ruth Ellen Moore, as was the becoming style of many English gentlemen of the day.[23] In September of 1899 he told Roosevelt of his engagement: "the biggest thing that can come into any decent man's life has just come into mine, and I am engaged to be married to the sweetest and best girl in America."[24] The marriage heightened Lee's devotion to Anglo-American friendship. When he returned to England to enter politics he became passionately pro-American. "One of the chief planks in my platform was 'Friendly with America'," he informed Roosevelt, "and you will be glad to hear that it was perhaps the most popular of all my planks—a fact which was no doubt largely due to the striking object lesson I was able to show in my American wife."[25] The reply sounded much the same note, TR pointing out that in his collection of essays published in 1900 under the title *The Strenuous Life,* "you will see that there was no allusion to England that was not friendly."[26]

Having entered Parliament in 1900, Lee spoke candidly and intimately to Roosevelt of his reasons motivating the career he hoped to make for himself.[27] He represented a safe conservative district, Fareham, in Hampshire, and in 1903 joined the Balfour government as the cabinet office charged with the responsibility for naval preparedness; he remained in Parliament until World War I. Throughout these years Lee was on the friendliest terms with TR, and visited Washington several times while Roosevelt was president. He played host to Roosevelt during part of his 1910 stay in England and again in 1914. When war broke that year Lee once more entered military service. He was immediately seconded to France with the British Expeditionary Force where he was on the staff of General Sir John French. Twice mentioned in dispatches, Roosevelt's admiration for him "at the front" was supreme. He wrote Lee's wife to praise his soldierly qualities, recalling their days together in Cuba and lamenting that he had to be content to view the war from the sidelines.[28]

In the course of their relationship Lee displayed toward Roosevelt an unstinted admiration, combined with an instinctive feeling that his friend was destined for great things. Shortly after he received the vice-presidential nomination, Lee wrote with typical intent: "I hardly know what to say." Nature, he thought, had not intended TR to be a vice-president; he was "peculiarly unfitted to languish in the role of 'second-fiddle.'" "When the rivers are thrown violently out of their courses in this way, Providence must have a purpose in view that is not necessarily apparent on the surface."[29] McKinley's tragic death and Roosevelt's corresponding good fortune might be judged, therefore, as literally providential, even though Lee's comment may have been made in a less than totally serious vein. Certainly from that time on Lee was prepared to do the president's bidding. "I would come any place, any time, to talk with you," he insisted to Roosevelt, who saw in Lee a trusted and useful informant respecting the British political scene.[30]

Unlike the Spring Rice-Roosevelt friendship which was throughout its time one of equals, Arthur Lee, even with the passing of years, inclined to approach TR with a sense of awe. He could never quite bring himself to expect of his friend some favor or kindness without a special pleading though he was eager to be of the greatest service to Roosevelt. Arrangements for the ex-president's stay in England in 1910 particularly demonstrated this. Lee was fully determined that Roosevelt should be *his* guest while in London that year. England was the last leg of the famous Teddyssey which had begun on safari in British East Africa and included a number of European capitals before the grand finale of the grand tour in London. Lee's importunities of Roosevelt began before the latter had left the White House. He announced himself completely prepared to put himself at his friend's disposal.

> It will not in the least matter when you arrive as we
> shall be ready for you any time next year, and your
> suite of rooms will be waiting for you and your
> party from now on. . . . We will in fact be your
> private hotel from which you can make side trips in
> visits wherever you like. . . .[31]

At about this time the Lees had come into possession of Chequers, the magnificent estate in Buckinghamshire subsequently given by them to the British government. Lee was anxious that Roosevelt should enjoy his hospitality there as well as at his town address. He even went so far as to arrange a proper English valet for the ex-president.[32] Roosevelt was forced to decline the total of Lee's generosity. For official reasons he first went to the American Embassy and learned that as arrangements had been made by the staff there it would be a week at least before he would be able to come to the Lees, punctuating his explanation with the rather unRooseveltian admission: "I had no choice."[33] Lee managed, nonetheless, to host a number of activities for his friend during the

London sojourn, functioning as a kind of appointment secretary—"the rest of the programme I am keeping in as fluid a state as possible"—and in some measure influenced TR's itinerary. The English phase of Roosevelt's tour was a great success, in spite of the death at the time of King Edward VII, dramatizing the possibilities of Anglo-American accord. The presence of so distinguished an American in the funeral procession of the king for example, left the English people with an exceedingly favorable impression. The visit was also an important episode in the Roosevelt-Lee relationship. They were to see each other only once more when Roosevelt went back to England in 1914, in what Lee spoke of as "five days of delightful and stimulating memory."[1] By this time it was apparent that Roosevelt's health had been undermined by fever contracted in the Amazonian jungle. Lee warned the ex-president against a "swing-round the Middle West in August and 30 speeches a day from the tail of a Pullman car!" His ideal was that "you will find yourself dwelling in all the odor of sanctity in a 'Wren' house, looking on Westminster Abbey. . . ."[35] Not a likely prospect, Roosevelt wrote thanking his host: "as soon as I got back here I was plunged into politics."[36] Shortly thereafter hostilities commenced in Europe; the war would bring Roosevelt and Lee closer together.

Despite Arthur Lee's inclination to defer to TR, especially in personal affairs, the health of their friendship derived in no small measure from Lee's willingness to make a temperate but unambiguous statement of the British point of view in a given controversy between the two English-speaking nations. Replying to a letter of March 18, 1901, wherein the vice-president had written forcefully of the American desire to fortify an Isthmian canal under direct United States control and of the justice of the American demands in the Alaskan boundary matter, Lee began by saying: "It is very good of you to write your views so frankly, and yet it is only by a frank interchange of views that our Peoples can hope to understand each other as they should." The mood of candor thus established, he spoke out against the American determination to build an American, as opposed to a neutral, canal.

> Against this your people, may, of course, argue that their stand in this matter involved the national interest, to such an extent that they will sooner fight than give an inch. But is this always to be the answer of the U.S. when they can't get everything they want; and can you expect England always to give way simply because she regards the prospect of war with the U.S. as unthinkable?

Lee expressed similar views with similar emphasis respecting the Alaskan boundary dispute.

> And now—as you raised the question in your letter—I must say a few words about the Alaska Boundary question, from our point of view. . . . It is here necessary to remember that in 1895–96 there was a boundary dispute between England and Venezuela. England thought she was right, whilst Venezuela was equally confident of her position. Whereupon the U.S. intervenes (with some aggressiveness!) and insists that England shall submit the whole dispute to arbitration. England agrees and the consequent proceedings vindicate her claims. Now, another boundary dispute arises with the U.S. as one of the parties concerned. England, mindful of the precedent of 1895–96, suggests arbitration. But the U.S. refuses—and says in effect, "Oh—no—we won't arbitrate about the boundary because Canada 'hasn't a leg to stand on.'" But . . . if the American case is so overwhelmingly sound why not accept arbitration, and so demonstrate the soundness of your claim before the whole world?[37]

Roosevelt valued such candor. "I was glad to hear from you," he replied; "it is not worthwhile writing at all if one cannot write frankly."[38] Cool appraisal generally characterized the correspondence of Roosevelt and his friends, a recognition that differences of opinion which were inevitable because of differing national interests, had to be faced squarely. The compelling consideration was to speak out freely on the issues, to learn the attitude of the other and to treat his position with respect, for in that way some workable resolution of the disagreement could be achieved. "I shall always cling hopefully to the belief that 'the better we get to know each other, the better we shall like each other,' " Lee once observed to Roosevelt.[39] Such hopes did not depend simply on the good will of Anglo-American statesmen or the friendliness of their peoples. Good will was present because of the kinship of the two peoples, a condition prompting mutual respect and trust on one hand and facilitating agreeable accommodation on another. Lee thought the common bond made England "always willing to go further in the way of concession and friendly service to the United States than to all other nations of the earth combined." "But it cannot be all give and no take, and your people should remember that we are also very proud and very powerful."[40] Throughout their friendship this conviction of an ultimate basis for Anglo-American solidarity was an unwritten presupposition, to be acted upon positively by those individuals who accepted it as a working principle but who were at the same time aware of the limitations imposed by national interests.

Not all English leaders (nor American for that matter) recognized this working principle. Part of Arthur Lee's political purpose was to persuade those Englishmen of importance whom he met. He once told Roosevelt of giving Lord Lansdowne, Balfour, and other members of the government "some new lights on the American side of the case [of the canal]"; and of a "useful talk with Lord Lansdowne, . . . and was I think able to correct in his mind a certain number of curious misapprehensions about your personality and your policy."[41] An awareness of England's "melancholy isolation" cast in far larger terms than "useful talks" with Arthur Lee did more to convince the British government of the need for a friendly America; yet Lee's personal diplomacy was at least a small force in the swelling tide of reassessment.

The personal element, it appeared to Lee, was critical. He urged upon Lansdowne the extreme desirability of appointing "none but the best men to any position on the staff of our Embassy in Washington" and explained to him "how detrimental it was to the interests of the two countries to place inferior or unsympathetic men in the most delicate position."[42] Noteworthy of the confidentiality with which he discussed such matters with President Roosevelt, Lee wrote deploring the practice and the likelihood of some one from the Diplomatic Service being named to the American ambassadorial post at a time when the advancing years of Lord Paunceforte made an opening probable. He went so far as to state his opposition to Sir Michael Herbert, whose appointment he deemed would be "unfortunate."[43] Herbert in fact won the position and as it developed, the president liked him. It can only be guessed that Herbert failed to become a White House intimate in the style of von Sternburg or Jusserand because of Lee's appraisal.

Not surprisingly the time came when Roosevelt preferred Lee as ambassador to Washington. On the day of McKinley's funeral the new president suggested to Lee that he send him an occasional, confidential report on the state of affairs and opinion in London for his information and use.[44] In 1906 Lee came for a White House visit and while there discussed a variety of topics from Chinese customs to Newfoundland fisheries. In some way therefore Lee was an unofficial ambassador. To make it official seemed both logical and suitable to the president. His choice of Lee was dictated by a desire to have someone "whom I know well and in whose judgment no less than his discretion I had complete confidence." Much of what was typical of the Roosevelt-Lee friendship, itself suggestive of the larger outlines of the Anglo-American rapprochement, was contained in the remainder of Roosevelt's argument in favor of Lee as ambassador to the United States.

> You and I have campaigned together. You stand for your country's interest first, and I should not respect you if this were not the case. But so far as is compatible with first serving the interests of your country you have a genuine desire to do what is friendly to America. These are reasons why I asked

you to come to see me and have made you my channel of communication.[45]

In 1906 the ambassadorial post fell vacant when Sir Mortimer Durand who had succeeded Herbert upon the latter's death, proved incapable of striding with the president, a critical qualification in TR's judgment for any British ambassador to Washington. Roosevelt's letter to Lee, dated November 5, 1906, left little doubt of his preference and, equally significant, spoke that very friendly, highly patriotic, supremely practical quality that characterized the Anglo-American entente.

I earnestly hope that if a change is made we shall have some man as nearly your stamp as possible. You are not one of those maudlin sentimentalists who will sacrifice the good of their country to an admirable but weak desire to be good to another country. I wouldn't request you if you were such a type because a representative of Great Britain who would not be true to Great Britain's interests would speedily lose weight in Great Britain, and I want to deal with some one who can influence Great Britain. But you know America. You can get on well with our people. You can speak to them and appear to advantage before them. You were an honorary member of my regiment and I can trust not merely your purpose but your judgment and sagacity. If you were here you would visit Newfoundland and the Alaska seal fisheries yourself. If as in the Jamaica business it was possible for England to do a good turn to America without hurt to herself I could call the matter to your attention. If I had you or some one exactly like you here, you would have known the entire Algeciras business just as Jusserand knew it.

In China you would be kept in touch day by day
with all that was going on, so that our two
countries could act exactly on the same line. Surely
all this is worthwhile.[46]

Roosevelt's disappointment at Lee's failure to get the post—his
chances even with strong presidential support were remote—was
somewhat softened by the appointment of James Bryce, another long-
term correspondent and friend of the president.

Though Theodore Roosevelt welcomed the prospect of James Bryce
as British ambassador, Bryce was never his intimate after the fashion of
Spring Rice or Arthur Lee. There were good reasons for this. Bryce, twenty
years Roosevelt's senior when they first became acquainted in the 1880s,
had an already established reputation as a scholar, politician, and man
of affairs. The advantage of years and in some ways of mind and
experience which Bryce enjoyed showed itself even when TR was in his
last months in the White House and Bryce was ambassador. Lord
Curzon, chancellor of Oxford University, had invited the president to
deliver the Romanes Lecture for 1910. Roosevelt looked forward to the
occasion as a rare opportunity to discuss the method and meaning of
history as well as providing some direction for future generations.
"Biological Analogies in History," as the lecture was entitled, was TR's
most ambitious foray into the intellectual world. He could have no
better mentor than James Bryce, sometime Regius Professor of Law at
Oxford, a student of many different lands and cultures, and a man who
was by all accounts an intellectual of the first rank. Several times in the
latter weeks of 1908 Bryce was at the White House, as the president
himself put it, to "suffer the wholly unwarrantable torments which I
design to inflict upon you by going over my Romanes lecture with
you."[47] As a good mentor, Bryce looked at various drafts of the address,
advising on two or three points the president was unsure of, and in effect
giving it the imprimatur of a senior scholar.[48]

Despite the disparity of age Roosevelt and Bryce had much in
common, making their friendship if not intimate, genuine, and mutually

stimulating. In their distinct ways both men were social Darwinists who accepted the idea of struggle as necessary and proper to progress, optimistic that man would treat evils which were considered inevitable yesterday to be altogether intolerable today. In addition Bryce and Roosevelt were supremely conscious of the similarities of Anglo-American institutions, the American republic issuing from English antecedents. As men of action, however, they were eager to translate their ideas into political realities, to promote the common good of the two peoples by a friendly but patriotic quest of their own country's best interest.

Roosevelt first met Bryce while the English savant was touring the United States gathering materials for a commentary on American politics which he planned to write. He immediately recognized in young Roosevelt a source of observation and information on the American scene, the kind of first-hand, informed yet candid opinion, that would explain the operation as well as the structure of the American system of governments. Roosevelt supplied Bryce with a great deal of comment on women suffrage, ethnic assimilation, religious affiliation, and civil service reform.[49] He sent him schedules of congressional bills, hoping they "meet your requirements. If not, or if you want additional information of any kind or sort, pray, write me at once."[50] Besides official reports, and in response to Bryce's requests, he passed along anecdotes and offhand observations. "For instance," he told Bryce,

> I happen to know that the Ohio Republican Campaign Committee in its attempts to collect money for the prosecution of the campaign in Ohio this year from Government clerks in Washington received but a couple of thousand dollars. Under the old system they would probably have gotten ten thousand dollars by sheer blackmail.

And, he added, "you can use this information just as you wish."[51] TR read some of the galley proofs of the first edition of *The American*

Commonwealth, complete with his own marginal critique. And he made a prediction.

> I think your book will mark an epoch as distinctly as that of De Tocqueville. . . . I think everyone must be struck by the singular success with which you have combined a perfectly friendly spirit to America with an exact truthfulness both of statement and comment.[52]

The reception of *The American Commonwealth* and the reputation it won marked a fulfillment of Roosevelt's estimate.

In the 1890s the Bryce-Roosevelt friendship ripened. TR continued to advise Bryce about revisions in his book, but their exchange of ideas now included discussion of the westward movement of the Anglo-American peoples across the world, a major phase of which Roosevelt had described in his own *The Winning of the West.* When the first volume appeared he promptly dispatched a copy to Bryce.[53] The Venezuelan boundary dispute of 1895–1896, straining Anglo-American diplomatic relations, also provided a topic pressing for discussion between the two friends. Bryce preferred to becalm the troubled atmosphere. Writing to Roosevelt early in 1896 about the "war scare" he expressed astonishment at the "apparent existence of ill-will towards Britain in a large part of your population. What in the world is the reason? There is nothing but friendliness on this side." Whereupon he proceeded to explain the position of his country in the controversy, taking direct issue with the American stand. Yet the total effect of Bryce's letter was friendly disagreement, which ended slyly: "But you really must not go to war with us—for then how should we be able to come and go and have our talks?"[54] The storm clouds of 1896 passed and under favorable skies the friendly talks were soon renewed.

Bryce made his fifth trip to the United States in 1897; he planned to visit Theodore Roosevelt who had been named assistant navy secretary in the spring of that year. Bryce had in mind one of those talks that would encompass the full catalog "of your political phenomena" "furnishing some opportunities for a persistent optimist like myself to show that he is not lightly discouraged."[55] Whatever the source of Bryce's misgivings in 1897 his appreciation of the world situation and the state of Anglo-American affairs in the wake of the Spanish-American War seemed brighter by 1898, though he was concerned about the possible internal effects of the American experiment in colonialism. "Our hearty congratulations on your safe return and on the laurels you have won." "How stupendous a change in the world these six months have brought." "It is a happy result . . . that your people and ours seem nearer together in sympathy than ever before."[56] These were all sentiments agreeable to Roosevelt. By the time Bryce assumed his ambassadorial post in 1907 events had provided London and Washington with numerous occasions for friendly understanding and cooperation, though there had been uneasy moments as well. As between Roosevelt and his other correspondents, trust and confidence became the established order in dealings between Bryce and TR. Bryce's biographer, H A L Fisher, related how in 1901 the two men spent an evening together in the White House during which the president "opened his mind upon the subject of the Trusts." Bryce argued that trusts were but an offspring of the tariff and suggested that the evil be attacked at its root. The new president accepted the diagnosis but not the prescription, for as he pointed out to his guest he did not possess the political power to wage war on the trusts and the tariff simultaneously. This kind of frank and confidential discussion later typified their dealings when Bryce was ambassador.[57]

James Bryce served in Washington from February, 1907, to April, 1913. His aim as ambassador was threefold: to cultivate the good will of the American people at large; to settle whatever outstanding differences there were between Britain and the United States; and to leave behind a structural framework which would facilitate harmonious relations between the two countries in the future.[58] In all these objectives he received the official cooperation of Theodore Roosevelt as president and his moral support after he left office. Even before TR departed the White House, Bryce managed to resolve several lesser but troublesome issues: a final boundary line between Canada and the United States and the regulation of fisheries on their inland contiguous waters among them. More significant, the president and the ambassador saw eye to eye on the role of the Anglo-American nations relative to the world situation. "I am delighted to see what a splendid reception your navy has had in Australia," Bryce informed the president as "the great white fleet" plowed the Pacific. "It seems to me that one of the best results of this wonderful voyage has been the heartiness of the greetings exchanged between your sailors and our own people."[59] Via Bryce Roosevelt undertook to communicate certain private American reports on conditions in India and China to the London government, indicative of his interest in maintaining British power in those areas. Similarly the ambassador had nothing but praise for the president's speech, "The Expansion of the White Race," which paraded the good effects for civilization of British conquests in the East and voiced the hope that Britain would preserve a tradition of imperialism.[60] "Let me thank you again," Bryce wrote, "for that admirable speech you made last night to the Methodists. I have never seen the case for missionary effort as it stands today put either with more force or with more perfect truth and insight. What you said about Africa as well as about India is most sound and most helpful."[61] Bryce also conveyed the warm endorsement of Sir Edward Grey, adding that what had been said would be "most highly appreciated both in England and in India."[62] Replying to these compliments, the president wrote pointedly: "If I have been of the least use in the matter, I am more than pleased."[63]

During his Afro-European trip, 1909–1910, Roosevelt kept in touch with Bryce. From Naples he reported: "I have been in rather stormy petrel condition ever since I left Khartoum. I hardly need say how deeply appreciative I am of all the courtesy shown me by your officials. It was rather difficult to remember I was not at home."[64] At journey's end the ambassador sent a "welcome home" note, telling of his pleasure that TR's bird walk with Earl Grey in the New Forest "came off" and congratulating him on the Romanes Lecture which, he remarked, "seems to have been as warmly appreciated as I felt it would be."[65] In the same year, 1910, another edition of *The American Commonwealth* appeared, a copy of

which Bryce sent along to Roosevelt. Much of the intellectual broth-
erhood and common purpose these men shared was present in TR's
letter of thanks.

> The two volumes of your work—your great classic
> work—have come. How well I remember nearly
> thirty years ago, when as a very young man in the
> New York Legislature, I, at your request, went over
> some of the proof of the first edition. Well, I am
> glad you feel as you say in your preface that things
> have grown a little better, rather than a little worse,
> during these thirty years. There is much that is evil,
> much that is menacing for the future. That is the
> way I feel about it myself. And there are points in
> which we are worse off than we were thirty years
> ago; but, on the whole, I think we stand ahead and
> not behind where we then stood.[66]

The 1914 war soon cast serious doubts over the future, just as it
placed no little burden on the relations of Bryce and the former
president.

Once Theodore Roosevelt became convinced of the immorality of
German policies in bringing on the war and in executing a military
campaign to implement those policies, he was loudly insistent that the
United States join forces with England and France against a common foe.
From the Bryce Report detailing German excesses Roosevelt obtained
ample ammunition to keep up his attacks on the Germans as agents of
destruction and doom. The British government, and Bryce himself to
some extent, were much more concerned with cultivating the Wilson
administration, whose posture toward the war TR dismissed as craven
and hypocritical, than the support, moral or vocal, of an ex-president.[67]
Once the United States came into the war the Roosevelt-Bryce friendship
began to run a smooth course once more, on personal as well as policy
levels. In March, 1917, Bryce commented on the pending state of war
between the United States and Germany: "Needless to tell you this has
long seemed to be practically unavoidable and desirable in the interests

of mankind."[68] In October of that year he wrote to TR:

> We hear that your sons are going to the Front in France. If they pass through England, or come across on leave to England, I trust you will let us know, that we may come and see them again and put them in touch with some people in England they would like to know and who would like to know them.[69]

Both old friends looked forward to peace, anxious that it should be achieved with victory, but somewhat apprehensive about the portending postwar radicalism.[70]

St. Loe Strachey, editor of the *Spectator*, was another prominent Englishman, vigorous in his espousal of Anglo-Americanism, with whom Theodore Roosevelt developed a deep feeling of kinship and understanding. He and TR began corresponding in the later 1890s, and as Strachey and his wife planned to visit America in 1899 Roosevelt invited them to see him in Albany. The visit did not take place until 1902, but in the intervening years through their letters they got to know and like each other. Strachey himself was rampantly pro-American, a voice calling for cooperation between the two leading English-speaking peoples on all fronts, from the day he assumed editorship of the *Spectator* in 1898.

Any number of Strachey's ideas and proposals made him attractive to TR. By background he was in the imperialist tradition, his great grandfather having served as secretary to Clive in India, and through the pages of the *Spectator* he sought always to strengthen imperialist ties. He was also an energetic proponent of military preparedness on a voluntary basis with individual citizens willing to train in military fashion out of a sense of loyalty and duty to country. Strachey set up his own Volunteer Company in Surrey as early as 1906, a practice that was so widely imitated in the years down to the First World War that in 1914 the War Office had a list of 250,000 trained men, thanks largely to the idea original with Strachey. As he once wrote to the president: "the purpose of four months or so of training would be to make a 'full man.' No man is a 'full man' unless he knows how to defend his home and country."[71] Finally Strachey was strongly anti-socialist, thoughts on which he exchanged on numerous occasions with Roosevelt. The sympathies of the two men were really quite extensive. The individualistic strain in their thinking doubtlessly drew them together which, when combined with a genuine admiration each held for the other's homeland, brought along their friendship.

Strachey's editorship of the *Spectator* imparted curious aspects to his relationship with Roosevelt, especially while the latter was in high public office. Critics of Anglo-American accord, especially in the early years of the twentieth century, were vocal and powerful on both sides of the Atlantic. Strachey realized that he had carefully to weigh his words in print, lest sensibility and prejudice be offended. In September, 1901, for example, he wrote TR saying that he hoped what he had written in the *Spectator* on the death of McKinley would not be judged too cold and unsympathetic. "I felt more warmly than I wrote, but I was anxious not to slop over and so be misunderstood on your side. . . . Knowing what harm is done in your country by anything which seems to ticket a man as a friend of England, I was careful to give no occasion for such misunderstanding." In the same letter he adds he was "only speaking the honest truth" in agreement with most Englishmen, that the one real consolation was the belief that "the executive office would fall into worthy hands."[72] The new president's reply gave indication of the future direction of his dealings with Strachey. "Now, if I had time I would write you with entire freedom and at great length on many subjects, for, my dear sir, though I have never met you, you are one of the men to whom I am willing to write with the most absolute confidence. . . ."[73] The effusiveness of Roosevelt's words do not destroy their sincerity as his subsequent letters to Strachey attest.

The president invited the Stracheys to stay with him at the White House for part of their American tour which took place in the autumn of 1902. Their two-day stay with Roosevelt, occupying a room that had been used by John Hay during Lincoln's time—a fact that deeply stirred

Strachey—was the high point of their American visit. Upon being introduced to them, President Roosevelt said: "I am very, very glad to see
you," and a kinship that had its source in letters took on a more affecting
quality. During the reception that followed this introduction Roosevelt
and his guests were soon completely at ease and before long were
discussing with force and candor the pros and cons of the Alaska
boundary controversy. The next morning the president took Strachey
with him into the executive office and once more they fell into earnest
conversation. Before Strachey realized it the room had filled with cabinet
officers and a cabinet session had spontaneously commenced. With
some embarrassment Strachey turned to John Hay and excused himself.
That afternoon, as Strachey was an expert and indefatigable horseman,
he and the president made a hard ride to the suburbs and their saddle
talk did not end until dusk. Writing to thank his host a few days later St.
Loe Strachey called the White House sojourn "the greatest of honours,"
and unable to resist a political jibe, added, "an infinitely greater honour
than to stop at the Winter Palace or the Hofburg. *There is no
comparison.*"[74] Years later he was to call this meeting with Roosevelt "one
of the most delightful memories" of his life.[75] In 1910 the Stracheys were
able to repay the presidential hospitality while Roosevelt was in London.
They arranged an intimate dinner for him that included only Lord and
Lady Cromer, and Sir Cecil Spring Rice and his wife. The talk that night
moved from current politics to the principles of self-government within
the British empire. So much of what Strachey and Roosevelt had
discussed over the years in their letters came into focus; so much of what
they would write each other in the days ahead was better understood and
appreciated because of this brief, personal encounter.[76]

Before 1910 the Roosevelt-Strachey correspondence displayed several
recurring themes. Socialism was among the most prominent. Both men
agreed that one of the forces making for socialist appeal to the masses
was the irresponsibility of the capitalist class which for its own aggran-
dizement fostered trusts and tariffs. Roosevelt's opposition to the trusts,
carefully orchestrated as it was to the beat of politics, was nonetheless
authentic. In Strachey's judgment TR gave the "lead to all those here as

well as in America who are determined on the one hand to fight socialism, and on the other to hold the trusts and the combines in check. That the victory in the end will be yours and ours," he insisted to Roosevelt, "I do not doubt because right, common sense, and the conscience of mankind are with us."[77] He wrote at length to the president about a lecture he had given on "Society and the Family" to a University Extension gathering at Oxford. A good many of the audience, he related, were "genuine working men and others were school masters and school mistresses in elementary schools."

> I am sorry to say I found a great majority of my audience strong Socialists. They were however a very straightforward, good sort of people, and in the hours discussion which followed the lecture, I think I was able to make some impression upon them and to make them face the destruction of the family which must follow the adoption of such measures as (1) universal, unearned old age pensions; (2) the endowment of motherhood; (3) feeding of all school children by the State; (4) the endowment of unemployment. Only one or two wild socialists were willing to say that if the family and socialism were in conflict, so much the worse for the family.[78]

In reply Roosevelt agreed. "I was greatly interested in your article on socialism and I was even more pleased with your letter. It is curious how exactly you and I agree on most of the great questions which are fundamentally the same in both countries."[79] In 1907–1908 Strachey published in the *Spectator* a series of "Letters to a working Man," setting forth his views of "the perils and problems" of Socialism. He planned to bring the series together in booklet form and sought TR's permission to dedicate the collected essays to him, a request the president granted.[80] "I have a special reason for making the request," he wrote.

> I have of course been accused, because I wrote

> against Socialism, of being a hardhearted supporter
> of Capital and the rich. . . . If I dedicate this
> book to you I shall bring home to people in a
> striking way that the enemies of Socialism are also
> the enemies of unrestrained Capitalism. I regard
> you, the opponent of Trusts and evil finances and
> selfish exploitation of the masses, as the greatest
> supporter to their common problems.[81]

The common destiny of the Anglo-American peoples was bound up in Strachey's mind with common solution to their common problems.[82]

During these same years, 1902–1910, the Roosevelt-Strachey friendship also became more personal. A second American voyage set for the fall of 1907 during which the two men planned to visit was forestalled by the death of Strachey's first son who succumbed to pneumonia while a student at Balliol. His letter of March 25, 1907, telling the president the sad news betrayed the deep kinship that had grown up between them.[83] In the same spirit Strachey both telegraphed and wrote his sympathy to TR and the American people upon learning of the San Francisco earthquake.[84] At another level, Roosevelt and Strachey exchanged private views of William Randolph Hearst and the English journalist, Edward Dicey, each willing to abide in the adverse judgment by the other.[85]

World War I had a solidifying effect on the Roosevelt-Strachey friendship. As with Arthur Lee, no recriminations came about between TR and the editor of the *Spectator* over what America ought to do about the war. By March, 1915, Roosevelt was writing Strachey that it was "utterly futile to be favorable to the Allies and yet uphold the [Wilson] administration," an attitude his English friend was in the fullest agreement with.[86] Both men saw German victory as a threat to their common culture and their common advantage.[87]

George Otto Trevelyan and Theodore Roosevelt were attracted to each other by reason of temperament and taste. Their fondness for history alone might have accomplished the friendship. Each man made history, Roosevelt in a remarkable way; each wrote history, Trevelyan with distinction. Through history they became imbued with the meaning of Anglo-American unity. Trevelyan's *The American Revolution* was a fairer presentation of the war for independence than had been offered theretofore by an English scholar; TR's *The Winning of the West* glorified conquest by the Anglo-Americans and placed that movement within the larger parameters of "the world movement" by men speaking English in the eighteenth and nineteenth centuries.

Like Bryce, Trevelyan was twenty years Theodore Roosevelt's senior and by the time they had commenced their correspondence he had already retired from public life in order to pursue his literary and historical vocation. He served in Parliament for many years and was a member of Gladstone's first ministry as civil lord of the Admiralty. While in the Commons in the 1870s he was known as a strenuous advocate of the working class franchise and held various cabinet posts as well. In all of this he had come to know many of the leading figures in English politics and to be in close touch with men like Lord Roseberry, John Morley, James Bryce, and Edward Grey. His friendship with Roosevelt was built upon history in the making as well as the written record. In his writings to TR, Trevelyan relied upon experience as much as anything to promote a growing understanding with Roosevelt and the American people. In these letters he alluded to Gladstone or Morley just as though his friend in America knew and viewed these persons as he did, drawing out the subtleties of Anglo-American unity.

Whatever direction their correspondence took, by whatever thoughts their friendship was cemented, this unity was discernible. Their liking for John Morley depicted this. Of Morley, Trevelyan had spoken to Roosevelt:

> For ten years I sat next to Morley in the House of Commons and it was a great anti-dote to the dreariness and bad rhetoric which was the prevailing atmosphere of that, as I suppose of all national assemblies. I have never heard from him a sentence, or read from him a letter that was dull or common.[88]

And Roosevelt responded with much the same estimate.

> . . . Morley spent three or four days with us and I
> found him as delightful a companion as one could
> wish to have, and I quite understand the comfort
> he must have been to you when you sat beside him
> in the House of Commons. Incidentally it is rather
> a relief to have you speak as you do about the
> tedious and trivial quality of most of the eloquence
> in the House. I am glad to find that it is character-
> istic of all parliamentary bodies and not merely
> that of my own country.[89]

The effect of such a good humored exchange is to recognize that
Trevelyan and Roosevelt really did see themselves as kinsmen, a
condition re-enforced by mutual friends and common institutional
experiences.

In their correspondence Roosevelt and Trevelyan spoke of Thackeray
or Dickens, of Hawthorne or Poe, feeling they shared a common past; of
James II, of Philip of Spain or Jefferson Davis, confident they enjoyed a
common prejudice.[90] They mourned together the death of John Hay,
refought the battles of the American Revolution and the Spanish-
American War. And they compared political systems.[91] Roosevelt wrote
to Trevelyan, by way of commenting on the cabinet form of government:
"it is not possible for the politicians to throw over the real party leader
and put up as a dummy some grey tinted person . . . or at least though
perhaps it is possible, the opportunity and the temptation are much less
than in the American system.[92] Trevelyan made a useful distinction in
reply. "With regard to what you say of the differences between us and you
in the selection of the man who is to govern, I should express it by saying
that in America, the country elects the *ruler*, and in England, the country
elects the *party*."[93] These two friends were supremely aware of the importance of the character of the men who operated through party or ruled in
the nation. Their moral camaraderie was again evident. "It does not seem

to me that it is fair to say that passionate earnestness and self-devotion, delicateness of conscience and lofty aim are likely to prove a hindrance instead of a help to a statesman or a politician. "Of course," as Roosevelt continued to explain himself to his confidant, "if he has no balance of common sense, then the man will go to pieces; but it will be because he is a fool, not because he has some qualities of a moral hero."[94] Trevelyan's agreement utilized germane examples.

> Washington . . . prevented a terrible war with England in 1795 at the cost of a great part of his popularity and at a time in life when his enormous personal position and moral dignity by which he was so universally and for so long surrounded wherever his name was known, rendered the brutalities and vulgarities of political detraction as directed against him, humiliating and almost grotesque. Lincoln, again under immense temptation and difficulties, prevented another desolating war with us at the time of the Trent.[95]

To prevent wars between America and England was to balance morality with common sense in a way that Anglo-Americans of the twentieth century especially could appreciate.

The Roosevelt-Trevelyan friendship had a more personal side as well. When Trevelyan's eldest son, Charles, was in the United States in 1897, TR befriended him and through him sent an invitation for Sir George to visit the United States. "I am glad to thank you for your great kindness to my son," came the answer. "Your extraordinary attention to a young stranger when you were Secretary to the Admiralty greatly struck one who had been a Secretary to the Admiralty himself." But he declined Roosevelt's invitation, saying: "I am getting too old for going to America . . . but I am not too old to enjoy the feeling of sympathy with such a career as yours. I expect a great deal more of that pleasure before our common sojourn on this planet is over."[96] To speak his gratitude Trevelyan sent Roosevelt a copy of the first volume of *The American*

Revolution. Their personal values, their taste for literature and history, and their passion for politics had combined from the start to launch a friendship.[97]

In December, 1907, the president along with Henry Cabot Lodge and Elihu Root sent a silver loving cup to Trevelyan with the inscription: "To the Historian of the American Revolution from his friends— Theodore Roosevelt, Henry Cabot Lodge, and Elihu Root." In this way they sought to acknowledge in a personal way the volumes describing the war for American independence which had appeared down to 1907. Trevelyan's answer told of his "pleasure and pride" at receiving the gift. "The cup is a noble piece," he wrote, "and the simplicity and singular beauty of proportion struck us much and impressed us with the notion that there must be much artistic feeling among the silver workers in America."[98] During TR's 1910 visit to England he and Sir George spent a quiet afternoon together at "Welcombe," Stratford on Avon, where the Trevelyans regularly summered. Looking back to that afternoon from the vantage point of somber days in World War I, Trevelyan recalled that Roosevelt's visit to "Welcombe" "always will be to me the greatest memory connected with it."[99] After returning to the United States, Roosevelt in 1911 gave a full account of his Afro-European tour in a famous letter to Sir George.[100] In the next year, when news reached England of the attempt on the ex-president's life in the 1912 Bull Moose campaign, Trevelyan wrote at once: "I have been unable to forebear sending you a few lines; although perhaps I should have waited. This matter has given me the full measure of the personal affection which I bear towards you."[101] The 1914 war drew Roosevelt and Trevelyan even closer together They agreed completely on the moral issue of the conflict, and were committed to the battle in the persons of their sons.[102] When two of TR's boys were wounded Trevelyan wrote in concern and sympathy. Roosevelt acknowledged his appreciation in what was the most suitable way for him by praising the "high and gallant valor" of George Trevelyan *fils* who was himself on active service.[103] By then Roosevelt had become to the older Trevelyan "the best and closest friend I have made in the evening of my life, when a man is very seldom fortunate enough to make such a friend."[104] On such a note the friendship closed in 1919 with the death of Theodore Roosevelt. Of the five major English correspondents, only Cecil Spring Rice predeceased TR, but not before he and the others, Lee and Bryce, Strachey and Trevelyan, had lived to witness America committed to England and the Allies in a test and a proof of an alliance, to the building of which they, by their friendships, had contributed.

NOTES

1. Spring Rice to Roosevelt, July 18, 1896, Gwynn, 1929: 1: p. 208.
2. *Ibid.*
3. Roosevelt to Spring Rice, Aug. 5, 1896, *Roosevelt Letters* 1: p. 553.
4. *Ibid.*
5. Spring Rice to Edith Carow Roosevelt, Dec. 9, 1903, Gwynn, 1929: 1: pp. 372–374.
6. For example, Edith Carow Roosevelt to Spring Rice, Dec. 15, 1897, *ibid.* 1: p. 326; Spring Rice to Edith Carow Roosevelt, Dec. 22, 1898, *ibid.* 1: p. 271.
7. Spring Rice to Edith Carow Roosevelt, July, 1898, Spring Rice Papers.
8. Spring Rice to Roosevelt, Nov. 1898. *ibid.*
9. Edith Carow Roosevelt to Spring Rice, Dec. 15, 1899, Gwynn, 1929: 1: p. 326; see also, to Spring Rice, March 25, 1900, Spring Rice Papers.
10. Spring Rice to Roosevelt, July 18, 1896, *ibid.*
11. Roosevelt to Spring Rice, Aug. 5, 1896, *Roosevelt Letters* 1: p. 555.
12. Spring Rice to Roosevelt, Nov. 15, 1898, Gwynn, 1929: 1: p. 268.
13. Spring Rice to Roosevelt, Nov. 9, 1904, ibid., p. 435; to Roosevelt, Dec. 7, 1904, *ibid.*, p. 438.
14. Roosevelt to Spring Rice, Nov. 9, 1904, *ibid.*, p. 434.
15. Spring Rice to Roosevelt, Dec. 11, 1912, *Roosevelt Papers.*
16. Roosevelt to Spring Rice, Nov. 12, 1912, *Roosevelt Letters* 7: p. 638.
17. Roosevelt to Lee, Dec. 31, 1912, *ibid.* 7: p. 683.
18. Spring Rice to Roosevelt, Oct. 10, 1915, Gwynn, 1929: 1: p. 293; see also Roosevelt to Spring Rice, Feb. 18, 1916, *Roosevelt Letters* 8: p. 891; also to Spring Rice, July 6, 1913, *ibid.* 7: p. 737.
19. Roosevelt to Root, Sept. 2, 1899, *Roosevelt Papers.*
20. Roosevelt to Lee, April 12, 1918, *Lee Papers.*
21. Roosevelt to Lee, Sept. 2, 1899, *ibid.*
22. Lee to Roosevelt, March 14, 1899, *Roosevelt Papers.* For highlights and sidelights of Lee's experience as a British observer with American forces in the Spanish-American War see E. Ranson, "British Military and Naval Observers in the Spanish-American War," *Jour. Amer. Studies* 3 (1969): pp. 33–56.
23. Lee himself commented to this effect. "My wife is enjoying her new life immensely and is the greatest possible help to me in my work," he told TR.

"Indeed it is the first essential to success over here now to have an American wife, and the latest music-hall joke describes English society as being controlled by 'Duchesses and other American ladies.'" Lee to Roosevelt, Nov. 22, 1903, Roosevelt Papers.

24. Lee to Roosevelt, Sept. 24, 1899, *ibid.*
25. Lee to Roosevelt, Nov. 12, 1900, *Roosevelt Papers.*
26. Roosevelt to Lee, Nov. 23, 1900, *Roosevelt Letters* 2: p. 1440.
27. Lee to Roosevelt, July 19, 1900, *Roosevelt Papers.*
28. Roosevelt to Ruth Ellen Moore Lee, Nov. 30, 1914; to Ruth Ellen Moore Lee, June 16, 1915, *Lee Papers.*
29. Lee to Roosevelt, July 19, 1900, *Roosevelt Papers.*
30. Lee to Roosevelt, Aug. 21, 1902, *ibid.*
31. Lee to Roosevelt, March 1, 1909, *ibid.*
32. Lee to Mr. Harper, May 9, 1910, *ibid.*
33. Roosevelt to Lee, March 10, 1910, *Roosevelt Letters* 7: p. 54.
34. Lee to Roosevelt, July 21, 1914, *Roosevelt Papers.*
35. Ibid.
36. Roosevelt to Lee, June 19, 1914, *Roosevelt Letters* 7: p. 769.
37. Lee to Roosevelt, April 2, 1901, Roosevelt Papers. (Italics in original.)
38. Roosevelt to Lee, April 24, 1901, *Roosevelt Letters* 3: p. 64.
39. Lee to Roosevelt, April 2, 1901, *Roosevelt Papers.*
40. *Ibid.*
41. Lee to Roosevelt, Dec. 17, 1901, Roosevelt Papers.
42. *Ibid.*
43. *Ibid.*
44. *Ibid.*
45. Roosevelt to Lee, Oct. 16, 1906, Lee Papers.
46. Roosevelt to Lee, Nov. 5, 1906, *ibid.* Lee previously had written to Roosevelt of Durand. "I hope you will like Sir Mortimer Durand and that he will prove a success. Personally, I know nothing of him at all and my only fear is that he may have made diplomacy too much of a profession." Lee to Roosevelt, Nov. 22, 1903, Roosevelt Papers.
47. Roosevelt to Bryce, Nov. 27, 1908, Bryce Papers.
48. Roosevelt to Bryce, late, 1908, *ibid.*
49. Roosevelt to Bryce, Nov. 20, 1887, *ibid.* See also, Roosevelt, 1913: p. 89.
50. Roosevelt to Bryce, Dec. 26, 1891, Bryce Papers.
51. Roosevelt to Bryce, Dec. 26, 1891, Roosevelt Papers.
52. Roosevelt to Bryce, Oct. 5, 1887, *Roosevelt Letters* 1: p. 134. For examples of the considerable exchange of information related to Bryce's book see: Roosevelt to Bryce, Nov., 1896, to Bryce, Nov. 12, 1897, Bryce Papers; Bryce to Roosevelt, Feb. 28, 1891, to Roosevelt, Dec. 12, 1891, to Roosevelt, Feb. 25, 1895, Roosevelt Papers.
53. Roosevelt to Bryce, Nov. 13, 1891, Bryce Papers.
54. Bryce to Roosevelt, Jan. 1, 1896, *ibid.*
55. Bryce to Roosevelt, July 7, 1897, Roosevelt Papers.
56. Bryce to Roosevelt, Sept. 12, 1898, *ibid.*

57. Fischer, 1920: 1: pp. 6–7.
58. For a discerning account of James Bryce as British ambassador to the United States see, Peter Neary, 1965.
59. Bryce to Roosevelt, Aug. 27, 1908, Bryce Papers. Roosevelt wrote to George O. Trevelyan that he was "extremely pleased" by the voyage and by the reception accorded the American navy in Australia. Roosevelt to Trevelyan, Nov. 6, 1908, Roosevelt Letters 6: p. 1330.
60. Roosevelt, "The Expansion of the White Race," Works 18: pp. 341–354.
61. Bryce to Roosevelt, Jan. 20, 1909, Bryce Papers.
62. Bryce to Roosevelt, Jan. 20, 1909, ibid. (This was a second letter written the same day about the same speech.)
63. Roosevelt to Bryce, Jan. 21, 1909, Roosevelt Letters 6: p. 1478. Lee wrote of the speech. "I can't tell you what wholehearted pleasure your tribute to our work in India has given to everyone with whom I have come in contact since, and moreover you chose a moment to say what you did which made your testimony of quite peculiar value to us." Lee to Roosevelt, Jan. 29, 1909, Roosevelt Papers.
64. Roosevelt to Bryce, April 2, 1910, Bryce Papers.
65. Bryce to Roosevelt, June 19, 1910, ibid.
66. Roosevelt to Bryce, June 10, 1911, ibid.
67. Roosevelt to Bryce, May 29, 1915, ibid.
68. Bryce to Roosevelt, March 21, 1917, ibid.
69. Bryce to Roosevelt, Oct. 25, 1917, ibid.
70. For example, Roosevelt to Bryce, Nov. 26, 1917, to Bryce, Aug. 7, 1918; Bryce to Roosevelt, Oct. 30, 1918, Ibid.
71. Strachey to Roosevelt, March 10, 1906, Strachey Papers.
72. Strachey to Roosevelt, Sept. 23, 1901, ibid. Strachey had confided to Roosevelt that "the truth is I like to keep the American articles in the Spectator whenever possible in my own hands." Strachey to Roosevelt, Dec. 29, 1904, Roosevelt Papers.
73. Roosevelt to Strachey, Oct. 15, 1901, Strachey Papers.
74. Strachey to Roosevelt, Oct. 29, 1902, Roosevelt Papers. (Italics in original.)
75. Strachey to Roosevelt, Nov. 24, 1904, ibid.
76. For an interesting description of the Stracheys at the White House see Amy Strachey, 1930: pp. 135–137.
77. Strachey to Roosevelt, Aug. 26, 1906, Roosevelt Papers.
78. Ibid.
79. Roosevelt to Strachey, Sept. 8, 1907, Roosevelt Letters 5: p. 768.
80. Roosevelt to Strachey, March 14, 1908, ibid. 6: p. 971.
81. Strachey to Roosevelt, March 4, 1908, Roosevelt Papers.
82. See also, Roosevelt to Strachey, Feb. 22, 1907, Roosevelt Letters, 5: p. 596, to Strachey, Sept. 16, 1904, Strachey Papers; to Strachey, Dec. 4, 1904, ibid; to Strachey, Sept. 11, 1905, ibid; also Strachey to Roosevelt, April 3, 1906, ibid; to Roosevelt, Jan. 3, 1908, Roosevelt Papers.
83. Strachey to Roosevelt, March 25, 1907, Roosevelt Papers.
84. Strachey to Roosevelt, April 23, 1906, Roosevelt Papers.

85. Roosevelt to Strachey, Oct. 25, 1906, *Roosevelt Letters* 5: p. 468; Strachey to Roosevelt, June 22, 1908, Roosevelt Papers.

86. Roosevelt to Strachey, March 23, 1915, Strachey Papers.

87. Their views are fully developed in chapter 4.

88. Trevelyan to Roosevelt, Nov. 10, 1904, Roosevelt Papers.

89. Roosevelt to Trevelyan, Nov. 24, 1904, Bishop, 1920: 2: p. 144.

90. Roosevelt to Trevelyan, Nov. 24, 1904, *ibid*, p. 144; Trevelyan to Roosevelt, Dec. 8, 1904, Roosevelt Papers; Roosevelt to Trevelyan, Jan. 22, 1906, *ibid*; Trevelyan to Roosevelt, Jan. 8, 1906, *ibid*.

91. Trevelyan to Roosevelt, July 15, 1905, Bishop, 1920: 2: pp. 150–152; Roosevelt to Trevelyan, Sept 12, 1905, *Roosevelt Letters* 5: pp. 22–25; Trevelyan to Roosevelt, Nov. 27, 1907, Bishop, 1920: 2: pp. 165–166; Roosevelt to Trevelyan, Jan. 1, 1908, *Roosevelt Letters* 6: pp. 880–883; Trevelyan to Roosevelt, Jan. 18, 1908, Bishop, 1920; 2: pp. 171–172.

92. Roosevelt to Trevelyan, May 28, 1904, *Roosevelt Letters* 5: p. 806.

93. Trevelyan to Roosevelt, Nov. 10, 1904, Bishop, 1920: 2: p. 143. (Italics in original.)

94. Roosevelt to Trevelyan, Sept. 12, 1905, *Roosevelt Letters* 5: p. 24.

95. Trevelyan to Roosevelt, Sept. 25, 1905, Roosevelt Papers.

96. Trevelyan to Roosevelt, Jan. 27, 1899, *ibid.*

97. Upon receipt of TR's thank-you note, Trevelyan wrote at the bottom: "This is the hero! I suppose he will some day be President. I sent the book to him as he was so kind to Charles." See Bishop, 1920, 2: p. 139.

98vTrevelyan to Roosevelt, Jan. 8, 1908, Roosevelt Papers.

99. Trevelyan to Roosevelt, Jan. 8, 1915, *ibid.*

100. Roosevelt to Trevelyan, Oct. 1, 1911, Roosevelt Letters 5: pp. 348–415.

101. Trevelyan to Roosevelt, Oct. 18, 1912, Roosevelt Papers.

102. Trevelyan to Roosevelt, May 13, 1915, *ibid*; Roosevelt to Trevelyan, May 29, 1915, *ibid.*

103. Trevelyan to Roosevelt, March 31, 1918, *ibid*; Roosevelt to Trevelyan, April 9, 1918, Bishop, 1920: 2: p. 181.

104. Trevelyan to Roosevelt, May 14, 1912, Roosevelt Papers; see also Roosevelt to Trevelyan, Jan. 8, 1915, *ibid.*

Jesuit Presence, Time and Place

The Jesuits have played a distinctive and distinguished role in the affairs of the Roman Catholic Church and in the history of the United States. In the eighteenth century Jesuit priests were living and working in Philadelphia, establishing a mission church, Saint Joseph's, located not far from the State House. As in other colonies the position of Catholics was ambiguous, laws proscribing their religion less and less enforced. Late in the century as the colonies drifted ever more in the direction of independence the two Jesuit pastors at Saint Joseph's, Fathers Harding and Molyneux, faced the decision that every thinking colonist had to make, to support rebellion or oppose it. History shows they were to favor independence, making the case for the Jesuit as Patriot, a curious but vital phenomenon. That growth proved to be fully secured in religious matters and public affairs with the decades giving way to centuries. As a result there was nothing incongruous about Jesuit professors of law bringing heavy criticism to bear on the reputation of one of the legal icons of the day, Justice Oliver Wendell Holmes. Inasmuch as Father Francis Lucey and others divined conflicts and inconsistencies between certain of the Justice's legal principles and the Constitution of the United States they created a firestorm of controversy. Clearly the Jesuits had gained a rightful place in the life of the nation. as educators and scholars, authorities in their chosen fields. They were heirs, so to speak, of Fathers Harding and Molyneux, among the first Jesuit Patriots.

Fathers Harding and Molyneux

Ours is the age of the computer, the evidence of which is everywhere. History, as with other disciplines remote from the marketplace, has adopted many of its ways. The historian often makes excellent use of computer methodology to rediscover the past by uncovering for the first time facts about the historical experience which could be read only from a printout. In consequence, fresh and exciting interpretations become increasingly common. Yet this is an age in which there may still be a place—and a useful place at that—for historical inquiry which begins with fragments of letters, diaries, and other records but which, at the crucial phase in the investigation, is carried forward by no force other than informed speculation. History thus considered is not scientific; but it is intensely human. What it lacks in scientific verifiability it makes up for in human awareness. As long as history remains in some sense an art, the Muse is honored by the effort to explore corners of the past alien to computer science. Failure to acknowledge the uses of such history may be as unfortunate as claiming too much for it.

In taking up an account of the response of Robert Harding, S.J. (1701–1772) and Robert Molyneux, S.J. (1738–1808) to the movement for American independence thoughts about the speculative possibilities of history seem appropriate.[1] This is especially so since their response rests upon an hypothesis which, with investigation, may lead to a thesis about the "Jesuit as patriot." The hypothesis is simply this: a large proportion of eighteenth century Englishmen, at home and in the colonies, had a strong preference for the Whig philosophy of government. Even George III had a touch of the Whig about him; if his claim be taken seriously that prior to the American Revolution he was attempting to return English government to that state of balance between King and Parliament which had been prescribed by the Settlement of 1690. Irrespective of background, training, experience, of religion, education, or vocation, scratch an eighteenth century Englishman and like as not he would be a Whig. The attitudes of Harding and Molyneux toward American independence when taken in combination may be a case in point.

Fathers Harding and Molyneux were successive pastors of Saint Joseph's Church, Willing's Alley, Philadelphia, located but a short distance from the State House (Independence Hall). Altogether the church was in their charge from 1749 when Harding arrived, down to 1785, Molyneux having been pastor from 1772, the date of his confrere's death. They were witness to momentous events associated with the movement toward independence, residing as they did in the first city of British North America and enjoying the friendship of several of those who took prominent parts in revolutionary activity. At the core of their response to the cause of independence was their commitment to natural rights as these obtained under secular government and man-made law.

Because they were Catholic, Harding and Molyneux had a Catholic conception of the natural order. Their view was derived from the natural rights school associated with the medieval schoolmen in general and with thinkers like Thomas Aquinas[2] and Marsilius of Padua[3] in particular. These philosophers, admittedly dominated by the doctrines of the ancient Church, upheld individual rights based on the natural condition of man. Harding and Molyneux, furthermore, were eighteenth-century Jesuits, trained in the style of the universities of Europe and thoroughly knowledgeable in the teachings of such earlier Jesuits as Bellarmine[4] and Suárez.[5] Bellarmine wrote in justification of mixed governments as a check on tyranny. Suárez, whose treatises on law exhibited concessions to voluntarism unusual in contemporary Catholic literature, also championed popular sovereignty. Typical of the instruction received by Harding and Molyneux in their continental schools were the lectures of Thomas Ellenker at the Jesuit College in

Liege.[6] In his *Tractibus Theologica de Jure Et Justitia* Ellenker not only presented the views of Aquinas but those of the radical Jesuit thinker, Luis Molina,[7] who held that God's grace depended on man's free acceptance. Ellenker's purpose was not so much to refute as to acquaint his students with traditional and contemporary notions as to the nature of man. Such exposure was sure to have had a pronounced influence on Jesuits in the making.

Harding and Molyneux were, moreover, Englishmen born and bred. In a sense they were English before they were Catholic or Jesuit. They were in some measure nurtured on Locke; life, liberty, and property; and the whole Whig tradition. Bernard Basset in his study, *The English Jesuits From Campion to Martindale,* relates how the Jesuits resisted the authority of the Crown in the days of Elizabeth I: Campion's brag led on to Tyburn's tree.[8] In contrast, he makes no mention of any such subversive activity after 1721, the implication being that the English Province of the Society of Jesus acquiesced in the political order. The era of resistance had waned. The time of accommodation, despite the formality and in a way the actuality of penal laws against papists, had set in. Mere "acquiescence" and "accommodation" are not likely to transform hypothesis into thesis, however. It must be realized, instead, that the lessons of Bellarmine and Suárez nicely complemented constitutional monarchy and rule by law which increasingly made up the way of political life in Great Britain in the eighteenth century. It is likely that Harding and Molyneux as Englishmen were conditioned to accept constitutional government and as Jesuits they were persuaded of its values by mentors who held with Bellarmine and Suárez.

The New World environment intensified Whig convictions among people living in the colonies. The pluralism of American society was well advanced by the eighteenth century and that fitted in with constitutional rule. Men came to an awareness of natural rights, for example, in various ways: Judaeo-Christian beliefs, rationalistic propositions, lessons from history, frontier hardships. If Jefferson's appeal in the Declaration of Independence was a general one: "we hold these truths to be self-evident, that all men are created equal . . .," he cast so wide a net because there were various fish to catch. Irrespective of why men believed in equality, Jefferson appears to have wanted them all on his side. The philosopher and the propagandist were astutely blended in the patriot. Among the variety of Americans were some Catholics who craved religious freedom as much as any sect, and for whom religious freedom, once experienced, became the first of the several natural rights expressions they would take up and defend. This is another way of saying that in the "Maryland tradition"[9] the Church of Rome—certainly strongly disposed to be authoritarian in the Old World and holding stiffly to that same line in Spanish America—had softened its stand on the subject of tolerating other faiths in British America. There has been no end of telling how the Puritan Mind was eroded by a remorseless wearing away due to the pressure of New World realities. Much the same thing happened to an equally hard nut, the Catholic Mind, once it faced the day to day demands of the frontier. The common denominator of the American Puritan and the American Catholic Minds was that these diverse sectaries were British in origin. As James I is reputed to have observed, Jesuits are nothing but Puritan-papists. The British factor is central for appreciating the response of the two Jesuits, Harding and Molyneux, to the Revolution.

What, more exactly, was the "Maryland tradition," which worked such an influence on Catholics in colonial America? The Calverts who founded Maryland intended it to be a colony of religious toleration. Charles M. Andrews has pointed out that Cecil Calvert's instructions of 1633 "disclose better than any formal document of authority the deep-lying desire of the proprietor to erect a colony free from religious animosity and contention in which Protestants and Roman Catholics might live together in peace and harmony."[10] The first Jesuit priests arrived in the colony in 1634, lodged themselves permanently in Maryland, and became elemental to the "Maryland tradition." Almost from the start there occurred a practical application of the theory of toleration. Priests who were property owners, for example, might be excused from attendance in the Assembly according to law and not by the favor of some medieval clerical immunity.[11] One William Lewis, to cite a different kind of evidence, who was a lay overseer of Jesuit estates, was fined for proselytizing Protestant indentured servants. His employer, Father Thomas Copley, S.J., rebuked him for his "contumelious speeches and his ill-governed zeal."[12] Such testimony may serve to illustrate the principle that at first in Maryland only those who attempted to carry over into America the conflict practices of the Old World ran afoul of the law.

The early history of the colony further demonstrated that the "Maryland tradition" included a code of laws which emphasized natural rights and liberties guaranteed by Magna Carta as a means of protecting freedom of individual conscience. The church's place became that of an autonomous spiritual society. Thus when a dispute arose between the Proprietor and the Jesuits over the ownership of land, the argument was resolved by the General of the Jesuit Order. He took the side of the Proprietor, making the point that Maryland was not Europe. He further advised his men to claim no right they would not have claimed in England itself. "I should be very sorry indeed," wrote Father Vitelleschi, the Jesuit General, "to see the first fruits which are so beautifully developing in the Lord, nipped in their growth by the frost of cupidity."[13]

The situation in the Maryland province changed after mid-seventeenth century with an influx of Puritans, reducing the Catholic population to a minority. Catholics were severely put upon, at least down to the time of Queen Anne. In spite of vicissitudes, Maryland Catholics once again came to enjoy freedom to practice their faith in the eighteenth century, a development which traditionalized religious liberty as founded on natural rights. In summing up the "Maryland tradition" no single individual illustrated it more convincingly than Charles Carroll of Carrollton, one of the Signers of the Declaration of Independence. Educated abroad in the Jesuit colleges in Flanders and at the College Louis le Grand in Paris as well as studying law at Westminster and the Temple, he was a man of the Enlightenment. His Jesuit tutors had introduced him to Locke and Montesquieu. In 1763 he wrote his father with typical enthusiasm that he regarded Jesuits to be "men of Republican principles who will not fail to inspire the youths with a love of liberty."[15] As priests, Father Harding and Molyneux were not primarily concerned with public matters. But their subconscious political attitude, as with their basic education, tended to resemble very much that of Carroll, with whom they were one in mind and spirit and faith.

Robert Harding was born on 6 October, 1701, in Nottingham, England. He was educated at first privately. Entering the Society of Jesus young Harding was sent to the Jesuit college at Liege for formal training in literature as well as in philosophy and theology. As Liege was judged to be a more liberal institution than, for example, the Jesuit college at Bruges, he probably imbibed something of its freer spirit. Harding was chosen for the Maryland Mission after ordination as a priest and arrived in America in 1732.[16] It was not until 1749 that he was assigned to the Jesuit parish of Saint Joseph's in Philadelphia. Because of repercussions from the Jacobite uprising in 1745, Catholics became somewhat suspect in Philadelphia as elsewhere in the colonies. Their credibility as loyal British subjects was again challenged by the French and Indian War in the 1750s. During that war there was heard talk of a "Popish plot" in Pennsylvania and indeed some evidence exists that a certain individual or individuals, identities unknown, supplied false letters to the Duke of Devonshire and others which were intended to incriminate Catholics in treasonable actions.

Possibly such moves were undertaken to stir up agitation against Catholics, especially in Maryland where their strength lay, which might have led to a sequestration of their property.[17] Property rather than subsidy might have been the reward given the marplots. But these rumors of treason came to naught. Nonetheless pamphleteers were busy pointing out the danger of a Catholic community possibly in league with the French enemy. One such defamatory tract, by Rev. William Smith, and entitled *A Brief Statement of the Province of Pennsylvania*, argued that the French, by means of "their Jesuitical Emmissaries," were seeking to win the German population of Philadelphia away from the British "in multitudes." The colony might be in grave peril in consequence. When copies of Smith's fusillade were distributed in the city Harding was quick to protest and to set forth his own views respecting British authority. He paid a visit to Dr. Thomas Graeme and in the words of Graeme's letter to

the Proprietor, Thomas Penn, made a strong case for his loyalty. In part
the report read:

> Doctor, says he [Harding], I am an English Man
> and have an English heart. I don't know if I shall be
> believed when I tell you and assure you that I
> should be extremely concerned ever to see the
> French possessed of a foot of English America, that
> though I may like something about them, their
> Government I should never desire to live under.

In any event Harding's reputation for loyalty to the English system
of rule appears to have gained a firm foothold.[18] When some French
settlers in Illinois country asked General Gage for a priest to minister to
their needs Gage in turn requested Harding to recommend a candidate,
one "well attached to His Majesty's person and government.[19]

In much the same vein in 1768 Father Harding presented to John
Dickinson the thanks of the Roman Catholics of Philadelphia upon the
latter's authorship of *Letters From A Pennsylvania Farmer*. Dickinson had
been forthright in his disagreement with British policy especially because
that policy seemed to fly in the face of British liberty. In that light
Harding's endorsement of Dickinson's argument is understandable. In
the same year, 1768, he was also elected a member of the American
Philosophical Society, Franklin's organization for promoting useful
knowledge. It may be presumed that Harding was acceptable on learned
as well as other grounds and that his political convictions were not
inconsistent with that of the Society's membership generally. Harding
was indeed a pious as well as an erudite man. He was renowned as a
preacher. Ezra Stiles, the noted Congregation clergyman who was later
president of Yale College, attended his chapel to hear him speak. In 1771
Harding in the name of the Catholic community assured the new
colonial governor that "our acts and behavior shall be the best proof of
the sentiments we express on this occasion."[20] The year he died Harding
acted as one of the founders of the Society of the Sons of Saint George.
Jacob Duché's estimate of Father Harding stands as an apt summary of

his work and reputation. "A decent, well-bred gentleman," Duché had found him, "much esteemed by all Christians in this city, for his preaching, his moderation, his known attachment to British liberty, and his unaffected, pious labors among the people to whom he officiated."[21]

As Robert Harding died in 1772 the question can not be definitely answered whether or not he would have been a patriot once war came. It is well to keep in mind that much revolutionary fervor before 1776 was fanned by the constant refrain that the colonists were only demanding their rights as Englishmen. Harding's attachment to British liberty therefore becomes a persuasive factor in any speculation about his possible attitude in 1776. He was, furthermore, so close a friend of George Meade that the latter was a witness to Harding's last will and testament. Meade himself was a staunch Catholic and a convinced patriot. Given his sensitivity to the cause of British liberty, might Harding not have followed the lead of certain of his friends like Meade when it came to making a commitment regarding the cause of American liberty?

Robert Molyneux was also a north of England man. Born at Formby, Lancashire, 24 July 1738, he was the son of a distinguished North Briton cavalier family with close ties to the Catholic Church and the Jesuit Order. Over the years the Molyneux family had given numerous sons to the service of the Church. After private schooling at home Molyneux attended St. Omers and thereafter the Jesuit College at Bruges. Of St. Omers the American Tory, Daniel Dulaney, observed in exasperation that it was "the best seminary in the universe of the champions of civil and religious liberty."[22] The influence of St. Omers on Molyneux at so formative a stage in his development is hard to measure but difficult to ignore.

Father Molyneux arrived in America in 1771 and almost at once succeeded Harding as pastor in Philadelphia. He was both a bookish and a priestly man, habits which stood him in good stead in the war years ahead. During the Revolution Molyneux showed himself a moderate patriot. With the British in occupation of Philadelphia he resorted to his worthwhile collection of books—"a library well fitted up in the choir of the old chapel" at Saint Joseph's—and it was there he buried himself in order to avoid association with the occupation forces. Molyneux had taken the all important oath of allegiance to the State constitution, the crucial test for differentiating loyalists from supporters of independence. As the leading Catholic clergyman in the city he had, in a sense, identified his congregation with the patriot cause. During his pastorate at Saint Joseph's Church he welcomed members of the Continental Congress to requiems for foreign envoys and had occasion to instruct the Chevalier de la Luzerne in the English language. When Don Juan de Mirailles died in 1780 a funeral Mass was offered at the Jesuit church. Father Molyneux officiated at the requiem attended by de la Luzerne, members of the Continental Congress and army officers. Toward the close of the war Molyneux signed the petition praying for the return of Congress to Philadelphia and on March 1, 1781 a *Te Deum* was chanted at the church in Willing's Alley to celebrate the ratification of the adoption of Government Under The Articles of Confederation.[23] Though primarily a priest with only peripheral interest in politics Molyneux's various actions and attitudes justify characterization as a patriot. Steeped in the "Maryland tradition" he was worried that religious liberty might well be eclipsed if political freedoms were denied by the mother country. That same "Maryland tradition" helps to explain his sympathy for the Revolutionary cause.

Having considered the postures of Harding and Molyneux, attention must be given to a seemingly extraneous development which may serve to throw additional light on "the Jesuit as American patriot." In 1773 the Society of Jesus was suppressed by Papal bull. This event had been a long time in the making and had come about as the result of machinations in high political places. The governments of both France and Spain had worked to clip the wings of the Society and no Jesuit could remain unaware or indifferent to the evil effects of unrestrained political power. Suspicions of the excesses of governmental authority, crucial to American patriot feelings, were likely elements in Jesuit thinking, rendering them hostile to the idea of unchecked power wherever it might be identified.[24] Further, as English Jesuits, they had to live with the constant possibility of running afoul the English penal laws—another sign of dangerous government authority. It is true that as the eighteenth century progressed religious toleration for Catholics became more common. But it is well to remember that into the 1720s summaries such as *The Penal Laws Against Papists and Popish Recusants* were still published while the Gordon riots of 1780 demonstrated the continued anti-Catholic feelings among the English people.[25] Given the circumstances surrounding the suppression of the Society of Jesus and official British religious intolerance, men like Harding and Molyneux had special reason to support the patriot cause.

At least one important corollary follows from suppression of the Society of Jesus. Jesuit priests became free agents, so to speak. Very probably they felt less need for caution in what they might say or do because they would be acting only for themselves as individuals and would not be associating the Society with their views in any way. The Society was defunct, and could not come under attack for what its members, or more precisely, ex-members, might undertake. Molyneux, who appears to have been less confident of himself as a public man than was Harding, could well have responded positively to this sense of freedom.

By way of summary speculation the Harding-Molyneux response to American Independence was composed of abstract and practical ingredients. Harding, it can be argued, exemplified the English Catholic in America who believed profoundly in the concept of English liberty. Molyneux, for his part, stood forth as the Englishman who, disposed to liberty, was swept along by events and the circumstances in which he found himself. Both ingredients had a share in generally determining men's loyalties and ultimately the achievement of independence. For Catholic priests like Harding and Molyneux the teachings of Bellarmine, Suárez, and other Jesuit philosophers provided a unique additive. Moreover each man had lived long enough in the New World to be persuaded that the scope of liberty, including freedom of religious conscience, should be enlarged beyond the habits of Europe. It would be unwise to deny that in their respective outlooks there was something frontier-related, something American. It would be no less wrong-headed to overlook the English inheritance. The attitudes of Fathers Robert

Harding and Robert Molyneux in sum appear to illustrate the American and the English elements in the large movement toward independence. John Adams undoubtedly had some such judgment in mind when he mused that the Revolution was in the hearts and the minds of the people. Whether Adams,[26] as a contemporary, would have subscribed to the thesis of "the Jesuit as American patriot" is dubious, rendering the thesis itself more provocative but no less likely true.

NOTES

*This article was researched on a grant from the Penrose Fund of the American Philosophical Society, which support is gratefully acknowledged.

1. There are good accounts of both Harding and Molyneux in Dumas Malone, editor, *Dictionary of American Biography*, (New York, 1932), 8: 250–1; 13: 81–2.

2. Thomas Aquinas' (1225–1274) interests embraced the political order. See especially *De regimine principum*.

3. Marsilius of Padua (d. ca 1342) argued in *Defensor Pacis* that all political power came from the people and that the ruler therefore was merely a delegate of the people.

4. Robert Bellarmine (1542–1621), in *De Potestate summi ponticifis*, developed many ideas regarding temporal political prerogatives.

5. Francisco Suárez (1548–1617) taught in *De Defensione Fidei* that kingly power came from the body of men, and thus opposed divine right kingship.

6. Ellenker was an eighteenth century Jesuit teacher-philosopher. An unpublished manuscript of his lecture on law and justice is in Ms B,v, Stonyhurst College Archives.

7. Luis Molina (1535–1600) was a Spanish Jesuit theologian who tried to reconcile God's power and man's freedom. His *Concordia* was the strongest Catholic statement of his day supporting the individual in God's scheme. His *De Justitia et jure*, in which he was both moralist and economist, may have been Ellenker's model.

8. Bernard Basset, *The English Jesuits From Campion to Martindale*, (New York, 1968).

9. Interestingly enough Jesuit copyists in Maryland in the seventeenth century spent much time in making multiple copies of the Maryland charter, interpolating such comments as Maryland established "for the propagation of the Christian Faith and the enlargement of our Empire and Dominion by the transplantation of an ample colony of the English nation." Province Notes, Folder 4 W1, Georgetown University Archives. For a critical yet sympathetic statement of the "Maryland tradition" consult Thomas O'B. Hanley, *Their Rights and Liberties The Beginnings of Religious and Political Freedom In Maryland*, (Westminster, Md., 1959).

10. Charles M. Andrews, *The Colonial Period of American History, The Settlements*,

(New Haven, 1936), 2: 290.

11. Hanley, *op. cit.*, pp. 85–6.

12. *Ibid*, 83–5.

13. Thomas A. Hughes, S.J., *History of the Society of Jesus in North America*, 4 vols. (London, 1907–1917), Documents, I, I, 31.

14. Charles Carroll (1737–1832), American patriot. For a full length portrait see Thomas O'B. Hanley, *Charles Carroll of Carrollton; The Making of a Revolutionary Gentleman*, (Washington, 1970) based on the latest scholarship.

15. *Ibid*, p. 133.

16. Whether Harding volunteered for the mission or was chosen is unclear. In any case, Harding found America and Philadelphia congenial.

17. The so-called "Popish plot" is analyzed in some detail in Thomas Hughes, S.J., "An Alleged Popish Plot in Pennsylvania 1756–1757," *Records of the American Catholic Historical Society*, (New York, 1899).

18. The entire episode is recounted in Joseph L.J. Kirlin, *Catholicity in Philadelphia*, (Philadelphia, 1909), pp. 79–80.

19. Province Notes, Folder 4 W1, Georgetown University Archives.

20. Kirlin, *op. cit.*, p. 96.

21. Ibid, p. 95.

22. Hanley, Carroll of Carrollton, p. 254.

23. Martin I. J. Griffin, History of Old Saint Joseph's, (Philadelphia, 1882), p. 4.

24. John Carroll wrote to Fr. Ellenker from Rome, 23 January 1772: "our catastrophe is near at hand . . . the date of our destruction has been fixed . . . our friends hope in nothing but the interposition of providence." Maryland Volume, Archives of the English Province of the Society of Jesus.

25. In England Catholics made this distinction: religion is a matter of conscience, patriotism is a matter of loyalty. Ms. Anglia IV, 31, Stonyhurst College Archives.

26. John Adams was not unfamiliar with the Catholic Church in Philadelphia. In October 1774 Adams in the company of Washington attended a Vesper service at St. Mary's Church, the daughter parish church of Saint Joseph's located on South Fourth Street. Father Molyneux officiated in all probability. Reflecting on his experience Adams wrote both his wife and in his diary of his impressions, observing in his diary: "The scenery and music are so calculated to take in mankind that I wonder the Reformation ever succeeded." L.H. Butterfield, editor, *Diary and Autobiography of John Adams* (Cambridge, Mass., 1961), 2:150.

FATHERS LUCEY, FORD AND GREGG

The reputation of Justice Oliver Wendell Holmes, Jr., one of the chief architects of twentieth century American law, has gone through a number of phases, changing from being altogether praiseworthy in the last years of his life and the first years after his death in 1935 to that of more sober evaluations. Writing at mid-century Henry Steele Commager offered the judgment that Holmes had had about him "much of the Olympian [and] something of the Mephistophelean."[1] The most useful account of how the winds of change swept along Holmes's reputation is an article by G. Edward White, "The Rise and Fall of Justice Holmes," which appeared in the *University of Chicago Law Review* in 1971. White examined the myth of Justice Holmes as it obtained from 1932 to 1940 and then proceeded to describe the demythologizing of Holmes from 1941 through 1949. What followed 1949, according to White, was a "sense of alienation," "a widening gulf" between Holmes and his critics. Originally considered dateless, the Justice quickly became dated, occupying an important place—but only a place like others—in the ongoing build-up of American law. The hero of legal realism became something of an icon, receiving increasingly perfunctory reverence. As Holmes' opinions were less and less pertinent, he was less and less quoted in the law reports. In his treatment White touched on the basis of Jesuit opposition to Holmes.[2] The significance of that opposition is such that it may be highly useful to canvas the Jesuit position thoroughly. It may also be useful to see how the controversy became part of the scholarship surrounding Holmes and his historical reputation.[3]

The surprisingly sudden fall from Olympus—the demythologizing began within six years of his death—came about not simply because of changing modes of thought at home due to threatening totalitarianism abroad. These were relevant factors and must figure in the account. But the abruptness of his decline and the steep gradient along which it proceeded were due in particular to a series of attacks on Holmes and his juristic philosophy by three Jesuit legal commentators, Francis E. Lucey, John C. Ford, and Paul L. Gregg. Until 1941 when Lucey first lashed out at Holmes the Justice had been virtually untouchable. Yet less than five years later Ben W. Palmer made a sweeping denunciation of Holmes in a piece for the *American Bar Association Journal*, entitled "Hobbes, Holmes, and Hitler," proposing to consign Holmes to the charnel house of history.[4] Many rushed to the defense of Holmes' reputation, including Fred Rodell, Charles Wyzanski, Mark Howe, and Francis Biddle. Nevertheless Holmes' image would never again be the same. The change was so decided, in fact, that the arguments used by the Jesuits, when analyzed, may explain why.

Francis Lucey was the leading Jesuit critic of Justice Holmes. Trained in theology, philosophy, and law, he was the Regent of the Law School of Georgetown University. Lucey came to his rejection of Holmes by stages and, as he had indicated, only with some reluctance. Like most students of law he had been taught to admire Holmes and especially the effects of many of his leading decisions. By 1941, however, with the tragedy of war in Europe about to engulf the United States, Lucey was brought to look at the legal philosophy of Holmes in light of the philosophies of Nazism and Communism.

Totalitarianism was very much on Lucey's mind in his essay "Jurisprudence and the Future Social Order."[5] In particular he singled out the menace of Nazism, calling it a "false philosophy of life, law, and government" because it "divorced itself from the moral dignity of man."[6] What the Nazis taught was directly opposed to American traditions. "In drawing up our Constitution," Lucey pointed out, "our forefathers did not presume to establish a government which would give individual rights. . . . They merely delineated and prescribed protections for those rights which were God-given."[7] American legal values had

changed, however, and that due, in Lucey's judgment, to the influence of
Comte, Hegel, Austin, Neitzsche, Kant, and William James.[8] The result
had been the adoption of a pragmatic test of truth, the same code as the
Nazi stormtroopers.[9]

With these preliminaries out of the way Lucey leveled an accusing
finger at Justice Holmes, referring to him as "the so-called great
liberal."[10] He insisted that Holmes "had no patience with the jurisprudence of the founding fathers,"[11] "no belief in absolute values nor the
importance and dignity of the individual."[12] For the most part he built
his case by quoting from Holmes' essay, "Natural Law," which had been
published as long ago as 1918.[13] Holmes had hardly disguised his view
at that time, and looking back the wonder is that he was not taken to task
soon after its publication.[14] Lucey would argue that it needed the ugly
fact of Nazism to show conclusively where Holmes' philosophy of law
would lead men and nations, that, ironically, it was the test of workability which had shown Holmes' jurisprudence for what it was. As the
Nazis had relied on force as the ultimate justification for their actions so
the Jesuit was at great pains to identify the place of force in Holmes'
version of natural law.[15]

In "Jurisprudence and the Future Social Order" Lucey had given over
less than one third of his attention to a castigation of Holmes. A fair
appraisal of the essay is to characterize it as a study in contrasts between
despotism and democracy, and to insist that in fighting despotism,
democracy did not have to forego its protection of the inalienable rights
of individuals.[16] But Oliver Wendell Holmes, Jr. had been a central
consideration in Lucey's criticism and the seeds of "Hobbes, Holmes,
and Hitler" had been planted.

In the same year, 1941, Lucey continued his attack on Holmes in a
second article, "Natural Law and American Legal Realism: Their
Respective Contribution to a Theory of Law in a Democratic Society."[17]
His leading argument was that natural law principles used by the
founding fathers had been weakened in the course of the late nineteenth
and early twentieth centuries by the theories of legal realism which
stressed the changing nature of truth and goodness.[18] Lucey's main

concern was with what he deemed the bad effects of legal realism, in which the external results of human behavior determined the law and in which the law had become what the Courts said it was.[19] As Holmes had had a major part in promoting these and kindred ideas he was once again Lucey's prime target. Briefly sketching the background of legal realism by examining analytical and sociological jurisprudence, Lucey found in the former, "the authority of the government consists in the force exercised by the dominant group on the dominated group by issuing imperatives which from the subjective viewpoint of the dominant group seem useful to society."[20] This position he associated with Hobbes and Bentham; the names Holmes and Roscoe Pound, Lucey used to identify sociological jurisprudence. Calling Holmes "the father of realism," he saw him combining the principle of force with the principle of utility.[21] Furthermore he condemned Holmes for resorting to "tastes" as a determinant of what the law should be, as he had in "Natural Law." "One detests his theory," Lucey wrote in dismay.

Tracing the influence of Holmes on legal developments Lucey showed how the realists embraced the utility principle but at the same time chose to soften the rule of "might makes right." The dominant social institution was substituted for "might" which translated "authority makes right" and the "will of majority makes right."[22] In any event the scholastic natural rights theory, which Lucey endorsed, i.e., some rights are eternal and immutable and therefore not subject to either authority or majority, had been rejected by the school of legal realism. Not that Lucey failed to recognize what to him had been the positive and indeed admirable work which the realists had done. He noted that they had led the assault on *stare decisis* and had been instrumental in promoting valuable social legislation and the extension of the administrative process.[23] But, for him, realism had given law "a shot in the arm" while threatening it with a "broken neck." Realism, when put fully in practice, would destroy the basis of democracy by eroding the natural rights of man. Lucey compared what could happen in America with what already had happened in Germany, observing that the dominant group, whether called class, race, or party, had acquired something more powerful than divine right of kings; it had acquired divinity itself.[24] He then closed his discussion by insisting that scholastic natural law principles were those upon which American democracy had depended from the outset. As such, it was a theory in which some elements were inflexible, but others were flexible. In his own phrase, the "leaves hide the tree."[25] The vast majority of human actions demand and can receive a mutable system of regulation under natural law provided the few enduring principles remain intact. The "present crisis," as Lucey spoke of the world situation, was reducible to "Democracy v. Absolute State, Natural Law v. Realism."[26]

By 1942 the Jesuits appeared to be in full cry against Holmes. Six months after Lucey's second article John C. Ford wrote an openly hostile account of "The Fundamentals of Holmes' Juristic Philosophy"[27] and within the year Paul L. Gregg delivered another salvo, "The Pragmatism of Justice Holmes."[28] In both instances the candid opinion and commentary of Holmes made available by the publication of the Holmes-Pollock letters in 1941 supplied critics with additional evidence of the toughness of the jurist.[29] [Holmes, of course, had stated openly his juristic fundamentals in several essays, including "The Path of the Law" (1897),[30] "Law in Science and Science in Law" (1899),[31] in addition to "Natural Law" (1918), but publication of hitherto private letters had provoked renewed interest in his legal philosophy.]

John C. Ford was not himself a lawyer but a moral theologian. He described his article dealing with Holmes as an effort to understand the "hard" side of his subject, to unmask it, and to disagree with it. As such his writing was largely expository. Given the state of Holmes scholarship today there is little that is unexpected or noteworthy in Ford's essay. "The essence of law in physical force;"[32] "divorce between the legal order and the ethical and moral is complete;"[33] "there is no such thing as a traditional morality;"[34] "man is but a part of the cosmos. That is enough;"[35] these and similar glosses on the mind and faith of Justice Holmes cause no raised eyebrows now. But delivered in November, 1942, at a time when America had mobilized in defense of liberty and when intellectuals had closed ranks with other Americans in the name of the historic natural rights doctrine, the effects were otherwise. Holmes' denial of a personal God, for example, became almost unthinkable and Ford pounded away on this and like features of Holmes' juristic philosophy with considerable effect.[36] Holmes' reputation was made to take on a sinister quality.

Gregg's essay, "The Pragmatism of Mr. Justice Holmes," added weight to the criticism. Gregg was both a priest and a lawyer and what he wrote seemed to smack of a determination to go beyond Lucey and Ford in a repudiation of Holmes. Gregg began his essay by noting that as a judge Holmes had given effect to the natural law theory as part of his duty under the Constitution. "But as a philosopher, he did not give intellectual assent to the theory of natural rights."[37] He accused Holmes, in other words, of double dealing.

Dividing his indictment into four main parts: Man, Truth, Natural Law and Morality, and Pragmatism and Positive Law, Gregg used numerous and lengthy quotations from the Holmes-Pollock letters to excoriate Holmes. Man was the "cosmic ganglion;"[38] Truth was "what I can't help believe;"[39] Natural Law and Morality "a spontaneous taking of an irrational pleasure in a moment of rational sequence;"[40] Pragmatism and Positive Law, seen as "a mirror reflecting the passions and desires of men both good and bad and right and wrong."[41] In conclusion Gregg offered the following:

> Holmes's pragmatism springs from his skepticism. Objective reason is cast off as the norm of right and wrong, and subjective desires are put in its place. Inalienable human rights and absolute principles of law are denied. Man is the tool of dominant powers. All that he has, even his life, is the proper subject for even the wildest social experiments. God, of course, is ruled out of the juridical scheme of things. In His place, the ultimate authority is brute force. Truth, man, the common good, even God, are nothing, desire and power are everything.[42]

At this point the prosecution rested.

The Jesuits had been the first to challenge Holmes and his reputation head-on. Where one or two others had intimated lapses in Holmes' legal philosophy, they had identified massive faults. The fallout from their blasts was significant, eventually involving some of the most prominent legal scholars. Their criticisms had prompted the extreme allegations made by Ben W. Palmer in "Hobbes, Holmes, and Hitler," and warned others, Harold R. McKinnon, for example, of the dangers of extremism. McKinnon published "The Secret of Mr. Justice Holmes"[43] in 1950, a tempered but nonetheless hostile critique of Holmes' legal thinking which owed an indirect debt to the Jesuit school of thought. Palmer's attack, in contrast, appeared directly Jesuit inspired.

Palmer was a member of the Minnesota Bar and a Lecturer at the University of Minnesota Law School. In his article he underlined the materialist philosophy of Holmes which led him, as it had others, back to the place of force. "The fact that Holmes was a polished gentleman who did not go about like a storm-trooper knocking people down and proclaiming the supremacy of the blonde beast," wrote Palmer, "should not blind us to his legal philosophy that might makes right, that law is the command of the dominant social group."[44] Predictably, he denounced Holmes as a moral relativist, observing that in Holmes, "since both law and morals represent a will and that will may change, certainly no one can hope to find in morals any absolute standards."[45] As for rights Palmer discovered in Holmes' skepticism "the very denial of any doctrines of inalienable rights . . . this is Hobbes and his Leviathan come to life."[46] "Holmes was directly in the tradition of Hobbes. Spiritually they were brothers."[47] "True, Holmes would have tinctured or softened his absolutism . . . but the gentility of its exercise should not disguise the iron fist of absolute power. . . ."[48] Throughout the article Palmer pressed Holmes hard on these and other particulars. But he saved his severest condemnation for the summing-up.

> He loved his country dearly. He was champion of
> liberty of mind and speech and press. But his basic

> principles lead straight to the abasement of man
> before the absolutist state and the enthronement of
> a legal autocrat—whether individual, minority or
> majority—a legal autocrat who may perhaps be
> genial as Holmes, benevolently paternalistic,
> perhaps grim and brutal as any Nazi or Japanese
> totalitarians, but none the less an autocrat in lineal
> succession from Caesar Augustus and Nero
> through Hobbes and Austin and Mr. Justice
> Holmes.[49]

As "Hobbes, Holmes, and Hitler" appeared in the columns of the *Journal of the American Bar Association* the reputation of Holmes was now widely discussed.[50] As it clearly echoed the condemnations of the Jesuit critics of Holmes, the Jesuits themselves became part of the controversy. What had been another "monks' squabble" promised more.

Three differing responses developed from the demythologizing of Oliver Wendell Holmes. The first of these, which deserves only limited examination in this context but which was the most fruitful of the three, was a series of measured and in the end invaluable reassessments of Holmes. This response is best exemplified perhaps in Harold R. McKinnon's "The Secret of Mr. Justice Holmes," published in 1950 in the *American Bar Association Journal* where it served as a corrective to Palmer's denunciation of five years before. McKinnon's analysis was conciliatory. He was in fundamental disagreement with Holmes' philosophy, beginning his essay with the observation that Holmes "had a very bad philosophy."[51] In striving to understand the Justice's great reputation he noted that so many of his decisions were in keeping with what the public wanted.[52] Furthermore, as America and Americans were pragmatic, so Holmes was a great judge because of this same pragmatic strain.[53] Holmes' reputation was high because he was "congenial" to his time and place.[54] Never throughout his analysis did McKinnon mention the Jesuit background to the controversy over Holmes and only once did he allude to it. It somehow seems appropriate, however, in this instance to argue *post hoc, ergo propter hoc*. In any event McKinnon's essay may be allowed to represent a number of fresh and provocative essays on Holmes in history which began to appear in the early 1950s.[55]

A second and differing response, despite similarities, was to be found in a defense of Holmes by Mark Howe, the senior Holmes scholar of the time. In the February, 1951 issue of the *Harvard Law Review* Howe presented a brilliant essay, "The Positivism of Mr. Justice Holmes;"[56] this was followed in the May issue by Henry M. Hart's "Holmes' Positivism: An Addendum,"[57] to which Howe replied with "A Brief Rejoinder"[58] which appeared in the May issue as well.

Howe's clear purpose was to enter the fray to exculpate Holmes and his legal philosophy. He began by saying that he had become aware of certain charges against Holmes as anti-democratic and anti-American and credited Ford and Lucey as sources of these accusations. Passing reference was made to Palmer and also the newspaper columnist, Westbrook Pegler.[59] But it was the Jesuits who had first made the pot boil and it was to them that Howe felt compelled to address himself. His response must be quoted in full as no paraphrase could do it justice.

> The criticism of Fathers Ford and Lucey . . . is so firmly grounded in the Catholic philosophy of law that were I to attempt to meet it directly I should find myself quickly engaged in a theological controversy beyond my competence to discuss. All I need say of the essays of Father Ford and Father Lucey is that they take a position which it was almost inevitable that members of the Jesuit order would take: Holmes not only proclaimed himself a skeptic in matters of religion and denounced man's relentless effort to give human values a more than human significance, but he denied the existence of that law of nature upon which the Catholic philosophy of law is based. It would have required no special insight to predict, twenty years ago, that Jesuit teachers of law would find Holmes's skepticism philosophically unacceptable.[60]

Having thereby dismissed the Jesuits, by implication if not innuendo, as hopelessly unintellectual, out of date, perhaps even "medieval," Howe slanted off in a somewhat unexpected direction to argue against the criticisms of Holmes made by Lon Fuller (of the Harvard Law School) in his 1940 book, *The Law in Quest of Itself.*[61] Howe's essay was unquestionably a finely wrought filigree of legal argumentation; just as surely had he written off the monstrous regiment of Jesuits as unworthy adversaries. Howe and Professor Fuller could exchange ideas; they were from the same intellectual world and spoke a common intellectual tongue. But Howe and the Jesuits were from different worlds, between which communication was difficult. If someone were to challenge the Jesuits directly, it was not to be Mark Howe, who did not choose to do so.

The final of the three different responses to the Jesuits was confrontation. The best of these, offered by Francis B. Biddle in *Justice Holmes, the Natural Law and the Supreme Court* (1961),[62] merits careful consideration. But before Biddle became party to the controversy Lucey had written still another long, anti-Holmes article, "Holmes-Liberal-Humanitarian-Believer in Democracy?"[63] appearing in the *Georgetown Law Journal* shortly after Howe's analysis, "The Positivism of Mr. Justice Holmes," was published at Harvard. In fact, it was written specifically to refute Howe as well as to answer an article by Fred Rodell, "Holmes and his Hecklers," in *The Progressive*, April, 1951.[64] The most interesting were the introductory and concluding pages; in between Lucey had simply sandwiched an extended restatement of the errors, as he thought of them, in Holmes' philosophy. In so doing, he added no new evidence, though there was a marked increase in the harshness of his tone. By way of introduction Lucey claimed credit for first challenging Holmes in his 1941 article, "Jurisprudence and the Future Social Order." He assured his readers that he had not exaggerated his previous charges and sought to refute Howe point after point.[65] Furthermore, Lucey accused Howe of trying to supply Holmes' philosophy with some moral "oughts" where Holmes wanted none,[66] of quoting Holmes out of context on the subject of morality so that it would appear the Justice believed in a conventional version of right and wrong and not the preference of the dominant group,[67] and lastly, of approving Holmes' substitution of human desires for the moral law.[68] Lucey then turned briefly to Rodell, asserting that Holmes himself would have had the courage to say he believed in nothing and would be shocked by Rodell's efforts to grant him a conscience.[69] In summary Lucey observed that the chief objection of Howe, Rodell, and many others for that matter, was they believed moral theologians were "incompetent witnesses . . . . They live in a cloud of misty abstractions. . . . They have not reached the adult stage. . . . They are not realists."[70] As Lucey's article was a lengthy one which rehearsed familiar arguments, his purpose, one may conclude, was to throw down a gauntlet to the "Holmes idolaters," to have a full, forthright, and, as it turned out, final say on the subject of Holmes' reputation. It was the kind of statement which Holmes' supporters were not likely to allow to go unanswered.

Francis Biddle's *apologia* for Holmes and his legal philosophy took up all aspects of the controversy. He led off by noting that a renewal of interest in scholastic natural law theory had taken place in Catholic law schools, rendering their teachings "somewhat doctrinaire."[71] The Jesuit criticisms of Holmes he termed "onslaughts, sometimes highly personal and ungoverned," so that Biddle saw himself coming "to the defense of a great man whom little men were trying to pull down."[72]

Respecting the essence of law as physical force, Biddle denied that Holmes meant this simplistically, interpreting it rather as the power of government to enforce the law and observing that even in St. Thomas Aquinas force had its place in putting law into effect.[73] On the universality of the scholastic natural law, Biddle asked: "Does natural law exist in a civilization dominated by Communist dogma? If not, was it ended at a certain time and place, or does it still hover [to] descend to earth when the time is ripe; or is there a natural law of Communism which has its own set of dogmatic absolutes?"[74] Obviously Biddle was not above drawing a little blood himself. He spoke of Lucey as "rushing to the attack,"[75] while noting the "ineptness" of his language;[76] he described Ford "trembling a little as he tries to hold his spear in place."[77] And he could adopt a mocking tone, as when he argued that in Nazi Germany the Jews did not enjoy rights as Ford meant the word, but he supposed that the rights of Jews "existed undiminished in Father Ford's head (or heart), or in that distant Heaven where Jews take their place with Christians and Mohammedans, since natural law is universal."[78] On another occasion he suggested that as Holmes wrote a lean and compacted prose, perhaps his critics had some trouble in understanding him correctly.[79]

Biddle rightly pointed out that the underlying difference between the views of Holmes and the Jesuits "boils down to whether or not you believe in absolutes."[80] He appears to be on less certain ground when he went on to assert that in the matter of scholastic natural law the Jesuits were Platonists, a contention which weakens a valid and major premise.[81] Attempting to demonstrate the impartiality of Holmes, Biddle also noted that as Holmes distrusted the churches and their clerics so also he questioned "the postulate of science that everything can be explained."[82] All of which is a reminder of the difficulty of evaluating Holmes. Biddle said as much when he remarked that Holmes could "for the sake of a telling *bon mot* or neat aphorism let out the most absurd generalities, worded as if they were self-evident truths."[83] Olympian and Delphic elements mixed at times in Holmes' pronouncements.

One of the characteristics of Biddle's defense of Holmes is that he was torn between a desire to make certain explanations of how the Justice's writings should be taken for proper meaning and "getting back at" the Jesuits. The retorts he made are some measure of his exasperation over the attacks on a man he "loved and admired."[84] Biddle's sentiments become part of the controversy, as were the slights offered Holmes by the Jesuits. In both cases *argumentum ad hominem,* while something of a distraction from the substance of philosophical disagreement, was integral to the dispute itself.

There are various ways of evaluating the controversy surrounding Justice Holmes and the Jesuits. What occurred can be thought of as an unprovoked attack on a jurist of great stature and respect; or as a justifiable exposé of the pernicious influence of Holmes on American law.

Between such extremes lie any number of points in a line, to the left or right of center, where one might be intellectually comfortable. But there is another, unexpected perhaps but nevertheless valuable, aspect to be noted. By standing apart from the controversy itself there is to be found in this war of words and ideas the most important single energizer of continued scholarly interest in Holmes across two decades and more. The controversy was the main source of the ongoing debate about Holmes in history, generating articles, lecturers, segments of commentary in books, not proper to the dispute, but not likely to have been written except for it. Inasmuch as the parties to the controversy were never going to agree, the stimulus given to Holmes scholarship should be appreciated as its lasting benefit.

NOTES

1. Henry Steele Commager, *The American Mind*, (New Haven, 1950), p. 390.
2. G. Edward White, "The Rise and Fall of Justice Holmes," *The University of Chicago Law Review*, No. 1 (1971), pp. 55–71 *passim*.
3. Important critical assessments of Holmes can be found in the following books. Silas Bent, *Justice Oliver Wendell Holmes*, (New York, 1932), useful despite its early date; Francis Biddle, *Mr. Justice Holmes*, (New York, 1942), a fond memoir by an admirer; Catherine Drinker Bowen, *Yankee From Olympus*, (Boston, 1944), a popular but informed biography; David H. Burton, *Oliver Wendell Holmes, Jr.*, (Boston, 1980), the most recent biography; David H. Burton, Ed., *Oliver Wendell Holmes Jr., What Manner of Liberal?*, (Huntington, N.Y., 1979), investigates the nature of Holmes' judicial outlook; Felix Frankfurter, Ed., *Mr. Justice Holmes*, (New York, 1931), a collection of essays by several including John Dewey and Benjamin Cardozo; Felix Frankfurter, *Mr. Justice Holmes and the Supreme Court*, (Cambridge, 1961), evaluates Holmes in history; Ralph H. Gabriel, *The Course of American Democratic Thought*, (New York, 1956) is critical but fair; Grant Gilmore, *The Ages of American Law*, (New Haven, 1977) offers a nonsentimental assessment; Mark W. Howe, *Oliver Wendell Holmes The Shaping Years 1841–1870*, (Cambridge, 1957); *The Proving Years 1870–1888*, (Cambridge, 1963) are definitive on the early life of Holmes; James W. Hurst, *Justice Holmes and Legal History*, (New York, 1964) is consistently useful; Max Lerner, Ed. *The Mind and Faith of Justice Holmes*, (Boston, 1943) has an exceptionally perceptive Introduction; John T. Noonan, *Persons and Masks of the Law*, (New York, 1976) identifies Holmes with legal change; G. Edward White, *The American Judicial Tradition*, (New York, 1976) deftly places Holmes in history; Philip P. Wiener, *Evolution and the Founders of Pragmatism*, (Cambridge, 1949) sets Holmes in the large framework of the scientific revolution.

4. Ben W. Palmer, "Hobbes, Holmes, and Hitler," *American Bar Association Journal*, (Nov., 1945), pp. 569–573.
5. Francis E. Lucey, "Jurisprudence and the Future Social Order," 16 *Social Science* (July, 1941), pp. 211–217.
6. *Ibid.*, p. 211.
7. *Ibid.*, p. 212.
8. *Ibid.*, p. 213
9. *Ibid.*
10. *Ibid.*
11. Ibid., p. 214.
12. Ibid.
13. Of the eight citations, four were from Holmes' essay, "Natural Law," 32 *Harvard Law Review* (Nov. 1918), pp. 40–44.
14. White cites only one scholarly challenge to "Natural Law," by Boyd H. Bode. Bode's criticism however was the 180° opposite of what the Jesuits would later say. Bode's objection was not that Holmes' "position is too revolutionary, but that it is not revolutionary enough. What it offers is, in the last analysis, but a continuation of the old tradition that right conduct consists in conformity to a pre-existent standard. Standards are repudiated for no other purpose than to set up in their place certain arbitrary and accidental preferences to rule over us by divine right." In place of these preferences, Bode called "for the emancipation of the moral life and not a perpetuation of its servitude" by using intelligence. Bode, "Justice Holmes on Natural Law and the Moral Ideal," 29 *The International Journal of Ethics* (July, 1919), pp. 397–404; p. 403; 404.
15. Lucey, *loc. cit.*, p. 215–6.
16. *Ibid.*, p. 216–7.
17. Francis E. Lucey, "Natural Law and American Legal Realism: Their Respective Contribution to a Theory of Law in a Democratic Society," 30 *The Georgetown Law Journal* (April, 1942), pp. 493–523.
18. *Ibid.*, p. 494–5.
19. *Ibid.*, p. 505–6.
20. *Ibid.*, p. 497.
21. *Ibid.*, p. 496.
22. *Ibid.*, p. 512–3.
23. *Ibid.*, p. 521–2.
24. *Ibid.*
25. *Ibid.*, p. 526.
26. *Ibid.*, p. 533.
27. John C. Ford, "The Fundamentals of Holmes' Juristic Philosophy," 11 *Fordham Law Review* (Nov. 1942), pp. 255–278. Ford was Professor of Moral Theology at Weston College, Weston, Massachusetts; Weston College was a Jesuit conducted school for the training of Jesuit priests.
28. Paul L. Gregg, "The Pragmatism of Justice Holmes," 31 *The Georgetown Law Journal* (March, 1943), pp. 262–295. Gregg was Professor of Law, School of Law, Creighton University, Omaha, Neb.
29. Mark DeW. Howe, Ed., *Holmes-Pollock Letters*, 2 vols. (Cambridge, 1941).

30. Oliver Wendell Holmes, Jr., "The Path of the Law," *Collected Legal Papers*, (New York, 1920), pp. 167–202.

31. Oliver Wendell Holmes, Jr., "Law in Science and Science in Law," *Harvard Law Review* (Feb., 1899), pp. 443–463.

32. Ford, *loc. cit.*, p. 256.

33. *Ibid.*, p. 259.

34. *Ibid.*, p. 264.

35. *Ibid.*, p. 268.

36. *Ibid.*, pp. 261, 267, 268.

37. Gregg, *loc. cit.*, 262.

38. *Ibid.*, p. 268.

39. *Ibid.*, p. 265.

40. *Ibid.*, p. 268.

41. *Ibid.*, p. 286.

42. *Ibid.*, p. 294.

43. Harold R. McKinnon, "The Secret of Mr. Justice Holmes: An Analysis," 36 *American Bar Association Journal* (April, 1950), pp. 261–4; 342–6.

44. Palmer, *loc. cit.*, p. 571.

45. *Ibid.*, p. 571.

46. *Ibid.*, p. 572.

47. *Ibid.*

48. *Ibid.*

49. *Ibid.*, p. 573.

50. Palmer also wrote a second article in like vein, "Defense Against Leviathan," 32 *American Bar Association Journal* (May, 1946), pp. 328–332, 360.

51. McKinnon, *loc. cit.*, p. 261.

52. *Ibid.*, p. 344.

53. *Ibid.*, p. 264–342.

54. *Ibid.*, p. 345.

55. See especially Irving Bernstein, "The Conservative Justice Holmes," 23 *The New England Quarterly* (Dec. 1950), pp. 435–452; H.B. Davis, "The End of the Holmes Tradition," 19 *University of Kansas City Law Review* (1950–1951), pp. 53–65; Max H. Fisch, "Justice Holmes, The Predictive Theory of Law and Pragmatism," 39 *The Journal of Philosophy* (Feb. 21, 1962), pp. 85–97; Nathan Green, "Mr. Justice Holmes and the Age of Man," 6 *Wayne Law Review* (Summer, 1960), pp. 394–412; Wallace Mendelson, "Mr. Justice Holmes— humility, skepticism, and democracy," 36 *Minnesota Law Review* (March, 1952), pp. 343–363; Yosal Rogart, "The Judge as Spectator," 31 *The University of Chicago Law Review* (Winter, 1964), pp. 213–256; Charles E. Wyzanski, "The Democracy of Justice Holmes," 7 *Vanderbilt Law Review* (April, 1954), pp. 311–324.

56. Mark Howe, "The Positivism of Mr. Justice Holmes," 64 *Harvard Law Review* (Feb., 1951), pp. 529–546.

57. Henry M. Hart, "Holmes' Positivism: An Addendum," 64 *Harvard Law Review* (April, 1951), pp. 929–937.

58. Mark Howe, "A Brief Rejoinder," *ibid.*, pp. 937–9.

59. Howe, "The Positivism of Mr. Justice Holmes," *loc. cit.*, p. 530.

60. *Ibid.*, p. 530-1.

61. *Ibid.*, 531 ff. The flavor of the exchange may be gained from the following excerpts. Fuller took exception to Holmes' "bad man" theory of the law, suggesting that "this bad man of Holmes' is himself an abstraction, in two senses. In the first place, it will be noted it is a peculiar sort of bad man who is worried about judicial decrees and is indifferent to extra-legal penalties. . . . In the second place, Holmes assumes that his bad man has already reached a conclusion concerning the legal risks of a particular line of conduct, and he neglects to inquire into the process by which this man would actually arrive at such a conclusion." As Fuller observed: "In short, our bad man, if he is effectively to look after his own interests, will have to learn to look at the law through the eyes of a good man. To be a good positivist, he will have to become a natural-law lawyer." Fuller, *The Law in Quest of Itself*, (New York, 1940) pp. 93-5. Responding to this point Howe wrote: "What Holmes was seeking to do was to put the familiar and valid thesis of *The Common Law* in dramatic terms, to suggest to his audience that their understanding of the law would be more penetrating if they washed its precepts in cynical acid, and in doing so, discover that its language of subjective morality was deceptive. Perhaps his effort was an artistic failure, possibly the dramatic image of the bad man was bound to distract the attention both of the speaker and the audience from the philosophic point in issue. If Holmes' failure was merely artistic, however, criticism of his effort should be concerned with that failure and not with the thesis which he sought to establish. Howe, *loc. cit.*, p. 543.

62. Francis Biddle, "The Attack on Justice Holmes," in Mr. Justice Holmes, Natural Law and the Supreme Court, (New York, 1961), pp. 28-49. This was one of three lectures delivered at the University of Texas in Dec., 1960.

63. Francis E. Lucey, "Holmes-Liberal-Humanitarian-Believer in Democracy?" 39 *The Georgetown Law Journal* (May, 1951), pp. 523-562.

64. Fred Rodell, "Holmes and His Hecklers," 15 *The Progressive* (April, 1951), pp. 9-11.

65. Lucey, "Holmes-Liberal-Humanitarian-Believer in Democracy?" *loc. cit.*, p. 523-4.

66. *Ibid.*, p. 554.

67. *Ibid.*, p. 555.

68. *Ibid.*, p. 556.

69. *Ibid.*, p. 557.

70. *Ibid.*, p. 558.

71. Biddle, *op. cit.*, p. 30.

72. *Ibid.*, p. 31.

73. *Ibid.*, p. 34-5.

74. *Ibid.*, p. 32.

75. *Ibid.*, p. 33.

76. *Ibid.*, p. 44.

77. *Ibid.*, p. 36.

78. *Ibid.*, p. 36-7.

79. *Ibid.*, p. 37–8.
80. *Ibid.*, p. 41.
81. *Ibid.*
82. *Ibid.*, p. 42.
83. *Ibid.*, p. 45.
84. *Ibid.*, p. 30.

Biography/Autobiography

Biography can be written in various forms, from the complete life to the thematic rendering to specific time periods or accomplishments, depending on the author's purpose or preference. Much the same may be true of autobiography, again a matter of purpose or preference. Biography and autobiography both run the risk of excessive praise or blame, which is not to claim that they may not also be balanced, based on an honest reading of the times and customs, the context of such a life (or lives, for example, the Founding Fathers), as well as an unprejudiced approach to the subject. When the biographer of a person must face and make use of an autobiography, problems of interpretation and judgments are likely to occur. Ordinarily these would not be insurmountable, and indeed could prove helpful overall with only the occasional pitfall. Whatever the pros and cons of biography and autobiography, they continue to be well-traveled roads leading to a more complete and sympathetic understanding of human history. The accounts provided here are a hard look at William Howard Taft as chief justice, during the years of his greatest accomplishments as a public servant and an autobiographical account by an obscure but memory-laden soldier in what has been termed "America's last good war."

CHIEF JUSTICE TAFT

William Howard Taft was nominated as Chief Justice of the Supreme Court of the United States on June 30, 1921, and the Senate confirmed the President's choice the same day, with only four dissenting votes. After years of waiting, the frustrations he had lived with were suddenly dissolved. That place in public service was now his which he believed he should have, by right of legal philosophy and ambition. The fact is, in 1921 Taft almost insisted that any appointment to the bench be that of Chief Justice. Had he accepted either of Theodore Roosevelt's earlier offers to name him, he would have been content as an Associate Justice. But, after the Presidency, nothing less than to become the high priest of the "sacred shrine," as he once termed the Court, would suffice. Such an attitude was not, however, based on pride of place. Taft had long been a critical, if friendly, observer of the operation of the High Court and of the entire federal judiciary. He realized better than most that it was a system which badly needed reorganization and leadership, that it required the hand of an experienced executive. Without the application of drastic reform measures, he feared that the Court, by falling further and further behind in its work—it might take up to two years for a case to be heard once it was entered on the Supreme Court docket—could simply become irrelevant. A dangerous prospect at any time, but the more so when the onslaught of Progressive legislation required the scrutiny of nine wise jurists. Only as Chief Justice could Taft have the opportunity to revitalize the operations of the court.

There had been an element of long-range calculation in Taft's hope to be the architect of Court reorganization when in 1910, as President, he promoted Edward Douglass White to be Chief Justice. White was a sixty-five-year-old Democrat from Louisiana who had slight claim to the position. His age and his party were presumably against him, especially when compared with Associate Justice Charles Evans Hughes, a New York Republican who was only forty-eight. The latter's apparent virtues were the very reason why Taft decided not to nominate him. The President was grimly aware of the truth of the old saying that "Supreme Court justices never resign and rarely die." White was a good bet to predecease both Taft and Hughes, which meant that in making his appointment the President was gaming with the gods. It caused him some inner qualms to have the duty of naming another to the post of his own desiring, but the choice proved to be the correct one for serving his own best interest. Charles Evans Hughes lived down to 1948 (he was named Chief Justice upon the death of Taft and served in that capacity until 1941), surviving his predecessor by many years. Once again the element of good fortune is discernible in Taft's final success.

Good fortune is sometimes the unintended result of good tactics. Taft could not have suspected the crucial contribution Warren Harding was to make in Taft's quest for the Chief Justiceship, but the fact remains that he greatly favored Harding's effort to win the Ohio statehouse in 1910. He discerned in the future President a man "attractive in many ways," and contributed $5,000 to the Republican campaign in Ohio that year. Though Harding did not win the governorship, he was elected to the Senate in 1914. Meanwhile, Elihu Root had chosen Harding to place Taft's name in nomination at the 1912 Republican Convention, with Taft's hearty approval. He predicted that Harding had a "great future." In playing the political game, Taft was taking the position that had gained him party favor as a young man in the 1880s: close to the seats of the mighty to profit from their favor, but distant enough to remain uncorrupted by either Foraker or Harding. Taft actively supported Harding's candidacy in 1920, and as a Republican ex-President, he proclaimed himself ready to help the new President in meeting the demands of office.

In late December Taft made the prescribed trip to Marion, Ohio, to visit the President-elect. People who knew Harding well were not surprised at what took place, though Taft himself was temporarily thrown off stride. After a pleasant breakfast, the two men retired to the parlor to discuss political affairs. Without warning, Harding interjected: "By the way, I want to ask you, would you accept a position on the Supreme Bench because if you would, I'll put you on the court." According to his own account, Taft responded at some length, his most salient point being that he could accept no appointment save that of Chief Justice. Harding remained noncommittal and the talks ended. Eager to exploit the opening which had been provided him, the next day Taft wrote Harding to thank him, and in the letter he went on to say that Chief Justice White had often voiced his preference for Taft as a successor. He could not have made his position more plain.

White was in poor health, in truth, a dying man. The end came in May, but Harding failed to act promptly to fill the Chief Justiceship. He had also made certain promises to George Sutherland of Utah regarding a Court position, and as the Court was not sitting at the time there was no pressing need to act. Taft did not propose to stand still, however. He enlisted the support of such powerful Republicans as Senator Lodge, and administration officials, including Attorney General Harry Daugherty. As a spokesman for the administration, Daugherty had gone on record as favoring Court reform to relieve the logjam of cases, and he, in turn, urged the President to avoid any delay in naming Taft as Chief Justice. Harding relented, and the announcement came at the end of June. William Howard Taft's plate remained right side up. At age sixty-four, the most exciting and productive part of his career lay just ahead. The safest of harbors had been reached at last.

The Taft Court, 1921–1930, revealed the influence of the Chief Justice in a variety of ways. Under his direction was carried out the most thorough reform of the Court system since Oliver Ellsworth had drafted the Judiciary Act of 1789. In order to persuade the Congress to pass the Judges Act of 1922 and the Judges Act of 1925, the Chief Justice became an activist, lobbying on Capitol Hill and before such interested parties as the American Bar Association, all with good effect. As an ex-President and a Republican, he felt pretty much at ease in offering advice—

sometimes solicited, sometimes gratuitous—which was sometimes taken by Presidents Harding, Coolidge, and Hoover. Though he had been a poor politician in elective politics, he was quite successful in playing the game as a jurist. He took pains to control the choice of federal judges, from the district courts far and wide to the High Court in Washington. Operating on the premise that the office of Chief Justice might be as big and as active as the person who occupied it—a premise he had formed about the Presidency in 1906—Taft used his considerable charm, skill, and willingness to compromise in order to "mass the Court" when it came to deciding cases. He participated fully in the processes of adjudication and in the writing of opinions. From 1921 to 1930 Taft wrote 253 of the 1,596 opinions delivered. Looked at in another way, he averaged thirty opinions a term to his colleagues' twenty. He was not simply the high priest but the workhorse of his own court. Of the opinions he wrote, several were especially noteworthy, including his dissent in *Adkins v. Children's Hospital* (1923) and the majority opinion in *Myers v. United States* (1926).

Taft dominated the Court for a decade. Given the strong personalities of Justices Holmes and Brandeis and their legal philosophies, which were often at odds with Taft's, this is a remarkable assertion. It suggests that all along Taft had been correct in his self-assessment: the highest court in the land was his natural milieu. As for the Chief Justiceship, his effectiveness in that position was the result of wide experience as an administrator in Manila and Washington. This merely underscores one of the ironies of Taft's career. Without the administrative experience which came about because he had reluctantly walked a political path after 1900, his achievements as Chief Justice could have been considerably less impressive. It was the combination of legal knowledge, judicial temperament, and administrative know-how which gave the Taft Court a distinctive dimension. Nellie Taft, to compound the irony, had a vital, if unintentional, part in making William Howard Taft a successful Chief Justice. She had insisted that her husband forsake his first federal judgeship for such rewards and training as politics had to offer.

William Howard Taft's first purpose was to streamline the federal judiciary, from the district level to the Supreme Court. It was a system much in need of renovation. Congress had never used its power to construct a unified and well-coordinated system of courts. District courts had become virtually self-contained and were rule unto themselves with regard to the handling of cases. Certain districts were overloaded with work while others had relatively few cases to deal with. But there was no authority vested in the Chief Justice or any other officer to direct an equitable distribution of the case load to achieve a speedier disposition of cases and, not incidentally, a speedier dispensation of justice. The Chief Justice was at best a nominal head of the national courts system. The situation at the Supreme Court was complicated because the Court could exercise little discretion in the cases which came before it: a case of no great constitutional consequence vied with one of significance, and both cases had to be heard in turn. The delays involved were not only exasperating; they were negative in effect because they tended to reflect a poor image of justice.

Taft's concern for improving the operation of the whole judiciary went back to his circuit court days. As he also served as dean of the Cincinnati Law School at the time, his experience as a sitting judge and as a law school administrator/professor made the faults of the system particularly glaring to him. Despite a nonjudicial career after 1900, Taft continued to study the courts in operation. In June 1908 he wrote an article, "The Law of the Country," for the *North American Review*, which amounted to a point-after-point critique of the judicial system. He argued that "our failure to secure expedition and thoroughness in the enforcement of public and private rights in our Courts" was the case in which we had fallen farthest short of the ideal conditions in the whole of our Government." Taft accounted it worse than the "defects in our system of municipal government which are notorious." In particular he identified the number of allowable appeals, overelaborate codes of procedure, expense of litigation, and dilatory judges as among the chief evils calling for reform.

Taft pressed for action in these and other areas once he became President. In his annual messages to Congress he dwelt on the situation.

"In my judgment a change of judicial procedure, with a view to reducing its expense to private litigants in civil cases and facilitating the dispatch of business and final decisions in both civil and criminal cases, constitutes the greatest need in our American institutions," he announced in his first annual message. On another occasion he urged Congress to confine the jurisdiction of the Supreme Court "almost wholly to statutory and constitutional questions," and asked the legislature to appoint a committee to investigate the entire federal court system to determine what measures of reform should be pursued. While President, Taft also took care that only well-qualified men entered the federal judiciary. "The party leaders may name the political office holders, but as long as I am President, no man shall ascend [the federal bench] except for reason of qualification for that high and sacred office, regardless of politics."

By 1914 Taft had clarified his ideas for modernizing the courts. In "Attacks on the Courts and Legal Procedures" he proposed that power be conferred "upon the head of the Federal judicial system, either the Chief Justice or a council of judges appointed by him, or by the Supreme Court, to consider each year the pending judicial business of the country and to distribute the Federal judicial force of the country through the various district courts and intermediate appeals courts." Taft was to modify this proposal at a later time, but he would seek to have the basic idea of his 1914 statement enacted into law once he was Chief Justice.

The inherent deficiencies which Taft deplored were worsened by the great mass of litigation growing out of World War I and the passing of the Eighteenth Amendment. Both civil and criminal cases involving espionage, civil liberties, wartime business contracts, and like cases crowded court dockets, while the government's efforts to enforce national prohibition added to a growing backlog. Litigation arising from prohibition alone accounted for an 8 percent rise in the number of cases. Only Congress had the authority to revise court procedures, provide for more judges, and impart the badly needed flexibility to the system. Without leadership from the judiciary, however, to explain fully the growing desperation of the courts' situation, little was going to be done. Chief Justice White had no stomach for this line of action, which he thought might break down the separation of the political branches of government from the judiciary. Taft, in contrast, was eager to take up the fight. It was a formidable task, certain to invoke legislative suspicions and leading to opposition, but Taft embraced leadership as his primary responsibility upon becoming Chief Justice.

He had been in office only two months when he opened his campaign for reform. Addressing the American Bar Association in Cincinnati in August 1921, the Chief Justice complained of the congestion in the district courts. "Because of the general enlargement of the jurisdiction of the courts under the enactment by Congress of laws which are the exercise of its heretofore dormant powers something must be done to give to the federal courts a judicial force that can grapple these arrears and end them." Four months later, speaking before the ABA in Chicago, Taft proposed three major reforms: "first, an increase in the judicial force in the trial federal courts and an organization and effective distribution of the force by a council of judges; second, simplicity of procedure in the trial federal courts; and third, a reduction in the obligatory jurisdiction of the Supreme Court and an increase in the field of its discretionary jurisdiction by certiorari." The proposal that a council of judges would organize and administer the federal courts was immediately controversial.

Taft's particularization of the council-of-judges idea (that is, administrative power to be exercised by the Chief Justice and the nine senior circuit judges), upon conference with the Attorney General, was cast in statutory form by Attorney General Daugherty. Taft had a look at the draft and, after making one or two technical adjustments, approved the proposal. The bill was submitted to the Senate and referred to the Judiciary Committee. The Chief Justice testified before this Committee on two occasions, as he actively sought passage of the bill. He told the senators that "the principle of this bill is the executive principle of having some head to apply judicial force at the strategic points where the arrears have so increased that it needs a mass of judges to get rid of them." In following up this general comment Taft made any number of criticisms, which he addressed specifically before the Judiciary Committee: that there was much stuffing of dockets, so that many cases could be readily dismissed; that judges and their clerks could discern an important constitutional issue in a case; that district judges "not infrequently" grew indifferent to their responsibilities because they were answerable to no one. In essence, Taft was appealing for efficiency based on responsibility, very much in the Progressive mode and a useful reminder that instrumentalism in government may be appropriated by conservatives to help achieve their purposes.

The Chief Justice was both angered and scandalized by some of the senatorial objections to the judicial conference, since many of the criticisms seemed to trivialize the whole concept. Senator Shields of Tennessee described it "as a great social function of the Judiciary of the United States, presided over by the Chief Justice in Washington or some other nice place. All expenses are to be paid or at least $10 a day and travelling expenses are allowed. Let any Senator examine this provision, and if he can really find any merit except that of a social function, I shall be astonished." Senator Walsh of Montana dismissed the judicial conference in much the same fashion: "It means absolutely nothing on earth except a junket and a dinner."

But opposition to the bill was deadly serious as well. On the whole, Congress was dubious about the wisdom of authorizing the conference to assign judges. Shields argued that it was "not a judicial power and does not in the remotest manner concern the exercise of the jurisdiction of the Supreme Court. The judicial power is the power to try and determine controversies . . . the power to establish courts and provide them with judges is a legislative power. Congress alone has this power."

Because Taft had been so forthright and forceful in expressing his views to the Senate Judiciary Committee, he had put the passage of the bill at some risk. Senator Shields charged that the Anti-Saloon League (it was well-known that the Chief favored prohibition) was backing the bill because it would give the Chief Justice the power to assign more and more judges to try cases involving violations of the Volstead Act. Beyond that, any kind of special interest might seek to influence the selection of judges, with justice ill served as a result. Some senators questioned the propriety of the Chief Justice coming before the Judiciary Committee at all, on the grounds that such action violated the separation-of-powers principle and was therefore possibly unconstitutional. Others contended that the presence of the Attorney General at the judicial conference marked an explicit rejection of the separation-of-powers rule.

The considerable opposition which the bill faced required the submission of an alternate proposal in 1922. Soon Congressmen were coming to support the fundamental proposition that the courts as then organized were unequal to their constitutionally assigned tasks. Representative Joseph Walsh of Massachusetts agreed that a conference could accomplish a good deal more than "letters written from all over the country. . . . A Conference would result in uniformity and tend toward the dispatch of business." Senator Cummins of Iowa, a force to be reckoned with in the Senate, was more positive: "Instead of having disjointed and disconnected communications between the Chief Justice and the various circuit judges, we have provided for a meeting at which the requirements of all the districts can be considered and compared, and if it is necessary to designate judges for work outside their districts, it can be done with some comprehension of the real needs of the country, and it can be done in no other way." The Chief Justice could not have said it better.

The obvious need for judicial reform, Taft's persistence, and the support of the American Bar Association crystallized Congressional endorsement. The Judges Act passed the Senate by a vote of 36 to 16 and the House by 139 to 78. It was signed into law in September 1922. Admittedly, Taft did not get all he wanted in the legislation as it was finally written, but the power was now in the hands of the Chief Justice to relieve crowded dockets, while the judicial conference clothed him with an undeniable executive character. The national judiciary was now more self-directed.

In spite of the dire predictions of judicial usurpation, the conferences under Taft's direction were matter-of-fact affairs. The Chief presided; reports were submitted by the Attorney General with regard to the amount of business facing each court, along with an assessment of state dockets. The Attorney General also made known to the conference complaints against judges which his office had received and offered recommendations for improving court operations. The 1922 and 1923 conferences took up the matter of proposed legislation, which was enacted in 1925, respecting the reduction in the number of cases to come before the Supreme Court on writ of certiorari. The first conference also established committees to make recommendations regarding the transfer of judges, rules of procedure, dead litigation, and similar technical matters. On occasion, the Chief Justice made use of the conference in ways not specifically provided for in the statute. He was concerned, for example, with uniform sentences for prohibition violators, called for improved libraries for district judges, and sought to lay down guidelines to expedite the handling of cases. Taft became the first Chief Justice to lead the federal judiciary in a meaningful way. Not that the conferences amounted to a grab for power. As always, Taft was careful of the Constitution and continued to hold that the meetings of judges should be confined largely to "an examination of a judge's capacity to dispose of his caseload." Only when this new state of affairs is compared with the total lack of such authority on the part of his immediate predecessors, Chief Justices Fuller and White, does the power of Chief Justice Taft stand out. Passage of the Judges Act of 1922 amounted to a "great victory," with other challenges lying directly ahead.

The second objective in Taft's overall plans for judicial reform was the limitation of cases heard on appeal by the Supreme Court. He aimed to give the Court the authority to allow only cases of Constitutional importance to come before it by certifying them on writ. Even before the passage of the 1922 Act, Taft had begun to stress the burdens under which the High Court was laboring. "The situation is rendered critical," he told an ABA gathering in the summer of 1922, "by the accumulating mass of litigation growing out of the war, and especially claims against the government which, if allowed to come under the present law to the Supreme Court, will throw us hopelessly behind schedule." As his profile had been highly visible in the fight for the 1922 statute, Taft appointed a committee of Associate Justices to help in drafting this legislation, to be known as the Judges Act of 1925. He did so at the behest of Senator Cummins, Chairman of the Judiciary Committee. Despite this maneuver, the familiar opponents of reform had their say. Senator Walsh insisted that the bill was another power grab. It was a truism, he said, that "a good court always seeks to extend its jurisdiction," and that "the appetite for power grows as it is gratified." Even former Associate Justice Hughes was heard to express some reservations about the proposed changes. Such doubts combined with the need of Congress to attend to more pressing legislative matters to delay passage of the second Judges Act until February 1925. The significant Senate vote was seventy-six to one. It was a second major victory for reform, and as the Chief Justice had had a part in formulating the proposal for consideration by the Judiciary Committee—though his role was somewhat clandestine—he must share the credit.

For the remainder of his tenure, Taft looked to the enactment of additional measures to complete the modernizing process. Ideally this would have included a thorough revision of the Judicial Code, but for that there was little real prospect. His more modest suggestion of allowing the Supreme Court—in pursuance of specific legislative grants—to simplify rules of procedure for federal courts got insufficient support, for that matter. The limits of judicial reform had been reached. Taft's contribution to the administration of the law, both substantively and in terms of executive leadership, had been impressive notwithstanding, earning him an important place in the history of the federal judiciary.

Chief Justice Taft displayed an unusual flair in an office historically looked upon as a place remote from both politics and society. This came about because of his zest for judging, which was carried to ultimate heights as head of the Supreme Court. As he once remarked, the Chief Justiceship is "comfort, dignity, and power without worry." He was happy in his work because it suited him, and he was eager to share his enthusiasm with all around him. Down to 1927 at least, Taft was a singularly successful Chief. "Things go happily in the conference room with Taft," Justice Brandeis reported; "the Judges go home less tired emotionally and less weary physically than in White's day." Taft made it a point to encourage his colleagues, and especially the narrow-minded Justice McReynolds, to adopt a tolerant attitude toward Brandeis, the first Jewish member of the Supreme Court. The maladroit President had become the persuasive jurist. Only in his last year in office, which was the last year of his life, did Taft slacken his pace, though after 1926 the Court was sharply divided in its constitutional philosophy, and its decisions were based on divergent assessments of the law.

As the Chief Justice was not a man inclined to forego the pleasures of society—he was really an outgoing, genial, and winning person—he looked forward to a 1922 summer visit to England, where he had been invited to receive an honorary degree from Oxford University. He was equally prepared to enjoy the peculiar delights of aristocratic society. At the same time, Taft considered his visit an opportunity to view firsthand the working of the English court system, which he had admired in theory as a student of the common law. His verdict was stated simply to his son Robert: "the English administration of justice is the best in the world." No doubt he came to such a conclusion in part because of the presence and power of the Lord Chancellor, who supervised the judiciary as befit an executive with real authority, and in part because the freedom to litigate was more restricted than in the United States. Taft returned home in July more convinced than ever of the urgency of judicial reforms along the lines he had already announced.

While in England, the Chief Justice and his wife greatly enjoyed themselves. As guests of the American ambassador, George Harvey, they dined with royalty, gossiped with nobility, and were patronized by the Prince of Wales who, upon meeting Taft, said to him: "By the way . . . haven't you been made a secretary or put in the Cabinet or something?" The less frivolous among his English contacts quickly understood that he was a man of solid legal learning. Luncheon at No. 10 Downing Street gave the Chief Justice a chance to meet Lloyd George—"a fascinating man . . . anxious to be agreeable, but not unpleasantly so"—and to be treated to the Welsh wizard's stinging critique of Woodrow Wilson. For its part, England had had a glimpse of an American of aristocratic manner, but plain and unpretentious by Old World standards, who knew the meaning and value of service.

Taft's flair for action was registered also in his work as a lobbyist in the name of the federal judiciary. He cooperated directly with Senator Knute Nelson of the Senate Judiciary Committee and enlisted the aid of Arthur C. Denison, circuit court judge, to win Congressional approval for the creation of twenty-four new district judgeships. On occasion, the Chief made use of newspaper editorial opinion to win support for his ideas. To thwart the effort of Senator George Norris to have cases dealing with diversity of citizenship withdrawn from federal jurisdiction (Norris sought to protect farmers from suits in federal courts by out-of-state corporations) Taft got help from the *St. Louis Globe-Democrat* and the *Times* and *Tribune* of New York. One consistently effective way of exerting pressure was through Taft's willingness to use the American Bar Association as a forum for his views. He thought of his cooperation with the bar association as "one of the most important extracurricular things I have to do as Chief Justice."

Taft not only lobbied the Congress and the country but the Presidents as well. He was closest and most confident with Harding. Both Solicitor General James M. Beck and Attorney General Daugherty offered him assistance with the first Judges Act, while his influence extended to the State Department because of his friendship with the Secretary of State, Charles Evans Hughes. But when Coolidge came into office, Taft was suddenly less persuasive. Coolidge was as much an enigma to him as to the rest of the American people. Still, he applauded "Silent Cal's" veto of a series of appropriation bills, including a veteran's pension proposal, agreeing with the President that these were little else than raids on the treasury.

Taft fared poorly with Hoover, but again not for lack of trying. He resisted Hoover's efforts to encourage one or more members of the Supreme Court to resign in order to become members of a special Commission on Law Observance, an anticrime body and one of the President's pet projects. Taft had to remind him that the Court was a coordinate office with the Presidency and not subordinate to the executive. At first the Chief Justice admired Hoover as a strong and forceful leader, but as he got to know him better, Taft dismissed Hoover as "a good deal of a dreamer in respect to matters of which he knows nothing, like the judicial machinery of our government." On many counts Hoover was too Progressive, always a negative sign to the victim of the Bull Moose. In these dealings—with the Congress, the press, the ABA, the chief executives—the surprising thing is how aggressive and confident the Chief Justice was, hardly predictable in light of his Presidency and his professorship.

Taft's energetic style carried over into his direction of the business of the Court, and he was to work himself relentlessly during nearly ten years in office. This was an outward expression of his respect for, and devotion to, an institution which he revered beyond all others, in which he was reluctant to admit, or to abide, imperfection. The most glaring fault of the Court, in Taft's view, was the split decision, especially when rendered by a five to four vote. The disputability of such action reflected negatively on the wisdom of the judicial process where it was thought to be most refined. The great achievement, conversely, was the unanimous opinion, which Taft consciously strove to promote. Unanimity meant that the ruling was hardly contestable. It added strength to the Constitution and to government under law. When the Court spoke with one voice, its decision could not be lightly questioned. According to Taft, it was the duty of the Chief Justice to bring this about. He had to be "strong in his responsibility to the court, earnest in his desire to avoid divisions and highly skilled in reconciling differences in the midst of his brethren."

By no means indifferent or totally antagonistic to the changing place of government in the developing economic and social orders, Taft held tenaciously to the conviction that the law must change slowly if it were to change safely. A clear majority of the membership of the Taft Court was in accord with the legal philosophy of the Chief Justice, but two members, Associate Justices Oliver Wendell Holmes, Jr. and Louis D. Brandeis, were not. From the outset they were a source of distraction and worry to Taft, who proposed to disarm them by his geniality, edify them by his legal argumentation, and win them to join the majority of the

Court by his willingness to compromise on more or less abstruse legal points, to produce the solid front which he so ardently desired. In these endeavors he was not always successful.

Of the two Justices who tended to be court mavericks, Taft was more likely to respect the reasoning of Holmes than of Brandeis. By 1921 Holmes was already on the way to becoming a legend. In his eightieth year when Taft took charge of the court, Holmes had not so much altered his legal outlook as he had softened its expression, though still ready to deliver a sardonic thrust if the opportunity seemed appropriate. The Chief felt a certain kinship with Holmes because he was a New Englander, a feeling traceable perhaps to the Emersonian idealism which Holmes had imbibed in his youth, as had Taft's father, who passed it on to his son. Speaking of Holmes, the Chief Justice deemed it a "great comfort to have such a well of pure common law undefiled immediately next to one so that one can drink and be sure of getting the pure article." Though he often disagreed with the Chief's interpretation of the Constitution and the law, Holmes had the utmost respect for Taft. At first the venerable Justice found him a great tonic after the less-than-dynamic White. He liked Taft's friendly manner, his easy laughter, and his determination to "keep things moving pleasantly." As the years passed, while there was no falling out, a cooling was perceptible in their relationship. Taft complained of Holmes's dissents, to which the Justice responded that he had no choice but to dissent from bad legal opinions. Taft came to believe that Holmes's reading of the Constitution was flawed by a questionable ethical relativity and that he lacked experience in affairs of government, which would have kept him sound on the Constitution. Furthermore, was not Holmes getting too old, and if not that, was he not under the sway of Justice Brandeis to the degree that Brandeis usually had two votes in a case, his own and that of O.W. Holmes, Jr.? Despite such strains, Taft never lost his affection for his colleague. When Fanny Holmes, the Justice's wife of more than fifty years, died, it was the Chief Justice who stepped in to relieve his grieving partner of the cares of arranging for funeral and burial. Taft had a plot at Arlington set aside where Holmes himself would be laid to rest amidst his old comrades of the 20th Massachusetts Volunteers. As was the case in his relationship with Theodore Roosevelt, it was Taft who extended the hand of forgiveness or of help.

Justice Brandeis was a more formidable opponent of "massing the court." Whereas Holmes was neither liberal nor conservative—merely Holmesian and a coincidental Progressive besides—Brandeis was one of the principal liberals of the era. Because of his profession as a lawyer and advocate before the High Court, he had dramatized the difference between judicial conservatism and political liberalism on numerous occasions. Brandeis was a Democrat as well. Taft and he had first clashed when, as legal counsel to Louis Glavis at the time of the Ballinger-Pinchot controversy, Brandeis made public the President's falsification of a date on a certain document which helped to exonerate Ballinger. Taft's integrity had been more than slightly tarnished. When President Wilson nominated Brandeis to be an Associate Justice, Taft's reaction was hostile to the extreme. "It is one of the deepest wounds that I have suffered as an American and as a lover of the Constitution and a believer in progressive conservatism that such a man as Brandeis could be put on the court. . . . He is a muckraker, an emotionalist for his own purposes, a socialist . . . a man who has certain ideals . . . of great tenacity of purpose, and in my judgment of much power for evil." This was a fearful condemnation. Furthermore, Taft lent his voice to a general clamor of opposition by "people of quality." Along with five other past presidents of the American Bar Association, he put his signature to a declaration that "Mr. Louis D. Brandeis is not a fit person to be a member of the Supreme Court of the United States." Wilson's appointment, which Taft thought well calculated to win votes in an election year, 1916, was added reason to hate the President. In some part, Taft's animosity stemmed from his private hope, now doomed, that the Democratic chief executive would rise above party and name him to the court as Taft had promoted the Democrat, White.

William Howard Taft was not inclined to carry a grudge forever, or, for that matter, for very long. He had forgiven Roosevelt, he was to succor Holmes, and his treatment of Brandeis was usually, if not always, in the same vein. Let Brandeis tell the story of their initial reconciliation as he conveyed it to his wife. "Had an experience yesterday I did not expect to encounter in this life. As I was walking toward the Stoneleigh about 1 p.m. Taft and I met. There was a moment's hesitation and when he had almost passed, he stopped and said in a charming manner, 'Isn't this Justice Brandeis? I don't think we have ever met.' I answered, 'Yes, we met at Harvard after you returned from the Philippines.' He, at once, began to talk about my views on regularity of employment. After a moment I asked him to come in with me. He spent a half hour in 809, talking labor and War Labor Board experiences—was most confidential. I told him of the great service he had rendered the country by his action on the Labor Board and we parted with his saying in effect—he hoped we would meet often." Such an account perhaps says more about Taft than it does of Brandeis. The date of the encounter was December 4, 1918. Within three years the old adversaries would be colleagues on the bench.

A month after his appointment as Chief Justice, Brandeis wrote Taft a cordial note, congratulating him and stressing among other things the need to solve the problem of congestion in the district courts. In reply, Taft stated that he was looking forward "with pleasure to joint consideration and cooperation with you in this and all other matters of the Court." The ice had been broken altogether. In this exchange and in their years together as Justices, neither proposed to forego scruple or surrender principle. But each was prepared to compromise on *obiter dicta* while holding securely to his own interpretation of the points of law. As Brandeis once told Felix Frankfurter: "I can't always dissent . . . sometimes . . . I acquiesce." Taft had no difficulty appreciating Brandeis's virtues. He was a "very hard worker, who thinks much of the court and is anxious to have it consistent, and strong, and he pulls his weight in the boat." The Chief confided to his daughter: "I have come to like Brandeis very much indeed."

After 1926, however, Taft's estimate of Brandeis altered drastically. Reacting to the latter's dissent in an important case, he put Brandeis in that "class of people that have no loyalty to the Court and sacrifice almost everything to the gratification of their own publicity. . . . "

How to account for the Chief Justice's change of heart? As it was just that, a change of heart, his hostility sprung from the Associate Justice's accumulating dissenting opinions, particularly in those cases where he went against Taft's own preference in favor of private property. Apart from his altered attitude toward Brandeis (and Holmes), Taft was consistently conservative in his outlook after 1926, determined to build a wall of protection against the enemies of private property who might come on the bench after he was gone.

Except for Holmes and Brandeis, the personnel of the Taft Court was conservative to the point of favoring reaction. One Justice who might have tried Taft's patience by siding with the dissenters was John H. Clarke, who resigned his seat in 1922 to work for the principles of the League of Nations. He was replaced by George Sutherland, a trustworthy Republican conservative and a Justice the Chief came to lean on more and more. Only when Harlan Fiske Stone came to the Court in 1924 and soon thereafter joined the Holmes-Brandeis connection was there much meaningful deviation from Taft's strategy to mass the Court. The others could almost always be relied upon to constitute a conservative majority.

During his Chief Justiceship Taft wrote over 250 opinions (of which only 20 were in dissent), and by sheer weight of numbers his legal philosophy of constitutional conservatism was woven into the fabric of American law. Only occasionally did the Chief find himself sufficiently at odds with his brethren to offer a "ringing" dissent, based on a large principle. His determination to mass the Court and the conservative cast of Court membership made the Chief Justice the authentic voice of the Taft Court. The business coming before the Justices during the 1920s was significant and varied enough to draw from him opinions which, when taken together, trace a profile of a moderate conservative. This was especially true down to the year 1927, by which time Taft's energies began to decline along with his patience for those who disagreed with his rulings. In matters of female and child labor, Presidential executive authority, the right to strike, interstate commerce, and property rights, the Chief expressed strong views, and because of that his opinions were often controversial. Subsequent Court decisions have done much to alter or erase the imprint which the Taft Court left on constitutional law—not an uncommon fate for any judge—but certain of his constitutional positions have displayed a stubborn will to live on.

Taft's reputation as an antilabor judge, quick to issue injunctions in order to protect private property, was well established before he came to the Supreme Court. During the 1908 Presidential campaign, Democratic speakers constantly reminded audiences of his fondness for rule by injunction during his years as an Ohio judge. As serious disputes between capital and labor were rife in the 1920s, the Court heard any number of cases dealing with strikes, laws regulating hours and wages, and boycotts, and other aspects of industrial conflict. For the most part the Chief Justice's position favored property rights at the expense of organized labor.

The first Taft opinion involving the rights of workers grew out of the *American Steel Foundries v. Tri-City Central Trades Council* (1921). Workers on strike had resorted to aggressive picketing in response to wage cuts by the company. For Taft the issue boiled down to a difference between peaceful picketing, which he deemed a right guaranteed by the Constitution, and violent picketing, which could never be condoned. It was a fine line of distinction in most circumstances and one on which parties might honestly differ. Taft's rule of thumb was, when in doubt, prefer property rights over labor.

A more celebrated case of much the same character as the American Steel Foundries suit was *Truax v. Corrigan* (1922), one of the Chiefs most controversial opinions. Employees of a restaurant in Arizona had picketed the premises to protest wage reductions. A complicating circumstance was a state law which prohibited any judge from issuing an injunction in a labor dispute unless it was required to prevent irreparable property damage. Taft, speaking for the Court, asserted that "a law which operates to make lawful such a wrong as described . . . deprives the owner of the business and premises of its property without due process." The Arizona law "disregarded the fundamental right of liberty and of property." Taft was barely able to carry the Court with him, however, the vote coming to five to four. Brandeis, in dissent, was greatly disturbed by the willingness of the Court to go so far in interfering with the police power of a state.

In still another instance, the Chief Justice offended organized labor when in *United Mine Workers of America v. Coronado Coal Company* (1922) his majority opinion reaffirmed that unions were suable for damages arising from industrial actions. This was anything but an idle threat, because by the 1920s many unions had sizable strike funds which were definitely under the legal gun. Taft stopped short of accepting the coal company's claim that the disruption caused by the workers amounted to a violation of the Sherman Antitrust Act, a suggestion that there were limits to his pro-property stance.

Ever since the decision in *Hammer v. Dagenhart* (1917), which invalidated the Keating-Owens Child Labor Act, efforts had been afoot to promote new legislation to deal with what was admitted to be a profound social evil. In 1920 Congress passed a law laying a heavy excise tax on profits of companies which employed children under the age of sixteen in mines and under fourteen in factories and shops. Violators were to be punished by a levy of a 10 percent tax on net profits. The constitutional questions raised in the resulting case, *Bailey v. Drexel Furniture Company* (1922), involved two distinct Constitutional issues: the scope of the Tenth Amendment, which reserved certain powers to the states, and the purpose of the tax—was it a mere excise or was it designed to regulate working conditions, making the revenue raised incidental? If the law was found valid, the scope of the Tenth Amendment would be drastically reduced. Taft wrote: "To give such magic to the word 'Tax' would be to break down all constitutional limitations of the power of Congress and completely wipe out the sovereignty of the states." The power to tax was the power to destroy, in this case to destroy the delicate balance between the authority of states and that of the national government within the framework of the federal union. It is worth noting that both Holmes and Brandeis voted with the majority in striking down the law, Justice Clarke alone dissenting.

Taft's dissenting opinion in *Adkins v. Children's Hospital* (1923) softens the image of a highly conservative jurist. Congress, legislating for the District of Columbia, set minimum wages for women and children workers. A majority of the Court thought the law unconstitutional on the grounds that it was an unwarranted deprivation of private property. The Chief Justice wrote a vigorous dissent, while Holmes contributed a concurring dissenting opinion. (Brandeis did not participate in the ruling.) Taft deplored the evils of the sweat shop and insisted that neither women nor children were "on a full level of equality with their employers," that they were "prone to accept pretty much anything that is offered," becoming victims of "the harsh and greedy employer." In all likelihood Taft's experiences on the National War Labor Board, which had brought him face to face with the exploitation of workers, had considerable influence on his outlook. Contrary to the majority view, he considered that Congress was within its constitutional right to establish judicial restraint in the matter, especially as the District of Columbia could not call upon the reserve powers of a state, as contained in the Tenth Amendment. Was Taft's dissent in the Adkins case nothing more than an aberration, as has been suggested by some critics? Or did it reveal in the Chief a strain of residual Progressivism which broke through his conservatism when the circumstances of the case made the rights of property obnoxious? Whichever of these it was, Taft's action has been rightly termed "a fine dissent."

William Howard Taft was an unabashed admirer of John Marshall, whom he believed to be not only the greatest American jurist but very probably the greatest of all American public men. Marshall was, of course, a nationalist, who freely interpreted the Constitution to promote nationalistic objectives. The New Nationalism of Theodore Roosevelt, which Taft had deplored, exhibited much of the quality of Marshall, whom T.R. also esteemed. What the Chief Justice rejected as a political formula in 1912 he promoted when it came dressed in judicial clothes. Several of the Chief's opinions in cases dealing with the regulation of interstate commerce bear this out, though once again it must be stressed that he was not completely consistent. One such case was *Railroad Commission of Wisconsin v. Chicago, Burlington and Quincy Railroad Company* (1922). Congress had passed the Transportation Act of 1920, which allowed the Interstate Commerce Commission to set passenger rates on all interstate railroads, with a view to providing the roads with a fair rate of return on investment. In Wisconsin the rate set by the I.C.C. was lower than that allowed by the State Railroad Commission, thereby depriving the railroad of revenue. It was more than a question of differing rates, it was a matter of differing jurisdictions. Taft, speaking for the Court, wrote a Marshall-like view of the problem. As he argued, "under the constitution interstate and intrastate commerce are ordinarily subject to regulation by different sovereignties, yet when they are so mingled together that the supreme authority, the nation, can not exercise complete effective control over interstate commerce without incidental regulation of intrastate commerce, such regulation is not an invasion of state authority." "This," he added, "is because of the national power."

One specific provision of the 1920 Transportation Act was the limit of 6 percent which a railroad could earn, based on property evaluation. The Dayton-Goose Creek Railway Company refused to comply with the law, which required that earnings in excess of 6 percent be placed in reserve, and it brought suit against the United States to test the constitutionality of the limitation of earnings provision of the law. Taft went on the offensive in the name of federal regulation in *Dayton-Goose Creek Railway Company v. United States* (1922). Part of the purpose of the law, he noted, was to "build up a system of railroads prepared to handle promptly all the interstate traffic of the country." In sustaining the earnings limitation provision, Taft, in the name of the Court, urged that railroads were "dedicated to the public service," and were subject to a degree of regulation not appropriate to ordinary private business. Such a doctrine was not only reminiscent of John Marshall, it was also Progressive, the expression of a liberal attitude in an important area of government regulation.

Still another example of the Chief Justice's broad interpretation of the commerce clause occurred in *Stafford v. Wallace* (1922). Congress had acted to regulate trading in futures on the Chicago Board of Trade. Such an institution might be brought under Congressional scrutiny because it was "affected with a public interest." In short, the Chief Justice favored a loose construction of federal power under the commerce clause, the kind which Progressives thought essential to their reform purposes. In consequence, they greatly favored what they considered the statesmanlike position of the Court.

To imply that Taft was Progressive during his tenure on the Court is to confuse rather than to clarify the matter, however. Alongside the Dayton-Goose Creek case must be placed the Bailey decision. The Adkins ruling should be contrasted with *Wolff Packing Company v. Court of Industrial Relations* (1923) in which Taft, again speaking for the Court, rejected a Kansas law designed to require a settlement of wage disputes by compulsory arbitration. Such a law, it was held, ran afoul of liberty of contract. There is no doubt that Taft's rulings sometimes went in opposite directions. If Justice Holmes was neither liberal nor conservative but only Holmesian, Chief Justice Taft was both conservative and liberal. This is a less subtle distinction than that applied to Holmes, but it does undercut the contention that Taft was a single-minded conservative jurist.

Theodore Roosevelt, William Howard Taft, and Woodrow Wilson were the first of the modern Presidents, investing the office with power well beyond that enjoyed by any previous peacetime occupant of the White House. Taft contributed less to the early modern Presidency than did either Roosevelt or Wilson, but he made his mark, nonetheless. As the principal spokesman of the Taft Court, he put forth a singularly important recognition of the power of the executive in his majority opinion in *Myers v. United States* (1926). The case was pedestrian: removal by Presidential order of one Myers, a first class postmaster in Portland, Oregon. The implications of the Court's vote, in a six to three decision to uphold the executive removal, were far-reaching. The executive was greatly strengthened, the separation of legislative and executive prerogative more exactly defined, and Presidents in the future would be much more in control of the administrative machinery.

Taft worked long and hard on his opinion in the Myers case and was pleased with the results of his labors. "I never wrote an opinion," he said, "that I felt to be so important in its effects." It was based on two main supports, one historical and the other constitutional. The historical argument was built on what the Chief Justice called the "decision of 1789." This decision took the form of a vote or series of votes in the first Congress upon the establishment of a department of foreign affairs. It was originally voted in the House that the department be created under a secretary named by the President. After debate, this was augmented in two ways. First, a clause was inserted which clearly implied an unrestricted removal power in the President by alluding to vacancies created in that way. Second, the clause granting the power of removal to the President was deleted on the grounds that such a grant implied that without it the President would not have the power. The Senate agreed to these conditions. By this decision, declared the Chief Justice, Congress recognized and established the exclusive power of the President to command executive officers whom he had appointed. Taft appealed to a mass of historical documentation to show that this had been the accepted theory of removal power throughout American history, save for the post–Civil War era. Such an exception was judged to be outweighed by the force of almost continuous practice.

The constitutional argument advanced by the opinion was even more emphatic. It was clear, Taft commented, that power of removal was an implied power, which had its source in the general grant of executive authority in Article II of the Constitution, and from the injunction in that article that the President "shall take care that the laws be faithfully executed." By placing it on this broad ground, the Court avoided the difficulties which might result from implying removal power solely from the President's power of appointment. It is likely that this argument also derived from the conviction, based on Taft's Presidential experiences, that the President cannot effectively and responsibly administer his office unless he can control his subordinates through an unrestricted removal authority. This was a necessary and an inherent part of the broad executive power stated in the Constitution, so that any attempt by Congress to delimit or to interfere would be a violation of the doctrine of separation of powers.

Whether Taft's position in the Myers case softens or hardens the outlines of a constitutional conservative is itself open to interpretation. There is less question that it greatly added to the strength of future chief executives at a time in history when the exigencies of a domestic economic crisis and a world political crisis were to require greatly expanded powers on the part of American Presidents. In the hands of Franklin Roosevelt, the objectives of contemporary liberalism were especially well served, in part because of Taft's ruling.

The mixture of conservative and liberal strains identifiable in Taft's Supreme Court decisions is further illustrated in three cases dealing with the rights of individual citizens before the law. At first glance *Ex parte Grossman* (1925) is another example of the Chief's determination to uphold executive authority in the form of Presidential pardoning power. Grossman, an Illinois citizen, had been convicted of violating the Volstead Act, and an injunction subsequently issued had forbidden him to sell liquor. He was fined and imprisoned for contempt when he disregarded the court order. A Presidential pardon of the prison sentence was granted on condition that he pay the fine. The Chief Justice held that the pardoning power of the President was broad enough to encompass the contempt citation issued by the court. What is of special interest is that the ex-President argued that, there being no jury trial, sometimes "the desire of the judge allowed the personal element to enter into his verdict." In such circumstances, recourse had to be available to the citizen. Civil rights stood in need of guarantees against possible judicial tyranny. "May it fairly be said that in order to avoid possible mistakes, undue prejudice or needless severity, the chance of pardon should exist at least as much in favor of a person convicted by a judge without a jury as in favor of one convicted in a jury trial?" Such a statement by Taft is a rare admission indeed on his part of the frailty of men who sit as judges.

In contrast are two better known Taft opinions, in *United States v. Lanza* (1922) and *Olmstead v. United States* (1928), cases in which the Chief Justice appeared to come down hard on civil rights. Lanza had been convicted by a state court of Washington for violations of a state prohibition law and was sentenced to pay a fine. He was also indicted by the federal government for the manufacture and transportation of alcoholic beverages. Lanza claimed that the second prosecution was a violation of the Fifth Amendment because he had been placed in double jeopardy. The district court had rejected this contention and the High Court sustained its ruling. Taft, for the majority, wrote in part: "We have two sovereignties deriving power from different sources. . . . Each may enact laws to secure prohibition. . . . Each government, in determining what shall be an offense against its peace and dignity, is exercising its own sovereignty. . . . It follows that an act denounced as a crime by both . . . sovereignties . . . may be punished by each," due to the peculiarity of the federal system of government.

More intriguing are the facts of the Olmstead case. Olmstead was the ringleader of a gigantic rum-running and bootlegging business. The yearly income from these illegal activities was some $2 million. Federal officers had tapped the telephone wires of the building where Olmstead had his headquarters. For some five months a careful record was kept of the telephone conversations of the defendant and his employees, 770 pages in length. This evidence proved the guilt of the accused, but it was the sole evidence which the government submitted at the trial. Olmstead claimed that wiretapping was an unreasonable search and that the use of evidence thereby obtained constituted self-incrimination as proscribed by the Fifth Amendment. Taft, in handing down a six to three verdict, said: "There is no room in the present case for applying the Fifth Amendment unless the Fourth was first violated. There is no evidence of compulsion to induce the defendants to talk over their many telephones. They were continuously and voluntarily transacting business without knowledge of the interception. Our consideration must be confined to the Fourth Amendment." In considering the search and seizure protections of the amendment Taft protested: "The amendment does not forbid what was done here. There was no searching. There was no seizure. The evidence was secured by the use of hearing and that only. There was no entry of the house or offices of the defendant. . . . The language of the amendment can not be extended to include telephone wires reaching to the whole world from the defendant's home or office. . . ." Granting that Congress might legislate to protect the secrecy of telephone messages, "the courts may not adopt such a policy by attributing an enlarged and unusual meaning to the Fourth Amendment."

No doubt the controversy arising from this opinion was energized by the vigorous dissents of Holmes, Brandeis, and Pierce Butler. Holmes cast his doubts in the oft-quoted remark: ". . . for my part I think it a less evil that some criminal should escape than that the government should play an ignoble part." Brandeis upbraided the Chief Justice by lecturing him on the "progress of science" which would surely enlarge and multiply the number of ways the government might invade the privacy of the individual citizen. Butler likened telephone conversations to privileged communications between a physician and patient or between a lawyer and client.

In Taft's view—if not that of all the justices who concurred in his ruling—the criminal must pay for his crimes. "The common law rule is that the admissibility of evidence is not affected by the illegality of the means by which it was obtained. . . . The rule is supported by many English and American cases." This was a scholarly parting shot by a Chief Justice who was primarily concerned with putting law breakers in jail. Whether Taft was truly hostile to the exercise of civil rights in the Lanza and Olmstead cases needs to be placed in perspective. The rule in the second case was good law until the latter days of the Warren Court, being overturned only in 1967, while the Lanza decision has survived altogether.

Taft's constitutional philosophy was unquestionably conservative, as he had basically been so at each stage of his career. A knowing critic might argue that his conservatism was often enlightened, informed, and positive, that he was capable of a nonconservative (liberal?) response to issues raised in the Philippines, in the Presidency, or on the Supreme Court. He well understood the wisdom of occasionally acting without reference to theory. Some of Taft's conservative responses might be viewed as wholesome by his critics in much the same way that opponents of liberal jurisprudence discovered praiseworthy elements in the rulings of Brandeis. Taft could be doctrinaire without being doctrinal, i.e., wedded indissolubly to the conservative creed. He was known for his tolerance as well as for his conservatism. To make a comparison, Theodore Roosevelt was not as progressive or Taft as conservative as they appeared to be. Roosevelt simply took consistent advantage of the opportunity to tell the people that he was a Progressive, a proposition which became exaggerated in the telling. Taft, in general, and by not campaigning in the fall of 1912, in particular, threw away chance after chance to tell the people what he was. People who believe what they are told are not always fools, but neither are they oracles—as the state of Taft's reputation amply shows.

History has left us with two remarkable but unlike testaments to William Howard Taft as Chief Justice. One is of high visibility: the Supreme Court building, which sits like some "sacred shrine" across the plaza from the Capitol. The second is discoverable only through a search of the written record of the Court.

Taft had not been Chief Justice more than a few months before he began to think and talk seriously about a new building for the Justices. Traditionalist members preferred to remain in the old Senate chamber in the Capitol itself, but as the work of the Justices accelerated, the inadequacy of their facilities was increasingly felt. In 1925 a bill was introduced in the Senate to provide $50 million for public buildings. This gave the Chief Justice the opening he needed, and when the proposal was finally readied for approval by both houses, provision for a new Court building was included. In the process Taft had done some "gentle lobbying." Yet the Congressional mills grind exceedingly slow, and it was not until December 1929 that the President signed into law the appropriation of almost $10 million for the planned Court structure. Chief Justice Charles Evans Hughes laid the cornerstone in October 1932, praising Taft on this occasion for his "intelligent persistence" in bringing the enterprise to fruition. This new and separate structure was intended to symbolize the dignity of the Court and its complete independence under the Constitution—resting at the apex of the federal judiciary.

Meanwhile the Chief Justice's health had failed badly. By the opening of the 1929 fall term of the Court, he was barely able to continue doing what he had done for so long—writing judicial opinions. On the following February 3, fully cognizant that the work of the tribunal was too important to be impeded by the ill health of one member, he resigned his office.

It fell to Associate Justice Holmes to respond in the name of the Court. In a letter dated February 10 and signed by all the Justices, Holmes wrote:

We call you Chief Justice still—for we can not give up the title by which we have known you all these later years and which you have made dear to us. We can not let you leave us without trying to tell you how dear you have made it. You came to us from achievement in other fields and with the prestige of the illustrious place that you lately held and you showed us in new form your voluminous capacity for getting work done, your humor that smoothed the rough places, your golden heart that brought you love from every side and most of all from your brethren whose tasks you have made happy and light. We grieve at your illness, but your spirit has given life and impulse that will abide whether you are with us or away.

The venerable Holmes had offered a touching salute to a life well led and to service on the Court gladly given. William Howard Taft died on March 8, 1930. His two great monuments endure, one in marble and the other in lofty thought, demonstrating in singular ways his realism and his idealism.

UNIT

AT FIRST

"What's that, you say, the war has been over for more than half a century, and you are going to write about it? What kind of recall, a good bit less than total, do you think you have when it comes to all those names and faces and places and well, you know what I mean, all that death and suffering, and fear, all that loss of life and limb, and friends, don't forget the friends, yes, don't forget the friends, mostly the ones that went down, but others as well. Remember that First Cook, the one who refused to bring up hot chow for the guys because he heard there was heavy gun fire where you were dug in. What was his name?" "You know his name well enough. It was Reed, Herman Reed." Funny there were three Reeds in G Company, Cow-Hide/White. I guess Herman thought he was in "I'll Hide/White" (or was it to be "yellow" for him?) when he decided to duck out of front line duty, ignore the Captain's order, leaving the troops, as far as Reed was concerned, with K-rations on a very cold night in Belgium in December of '44. Three days later he was reduced from First Cook to rifleman as G Company was about to go on an attack. There he was kneeling in the snow begging the C.O. not to send him with the first platoon . . . the first platoon always seemed to lead off . . . babbling like a baby, tugging at the Captain's coat. Clearly he would have been useless and he was sent to the rear. Court-martialed? Who knew, who cared? The other two Reeds, L.J. and B.S. were to die good soldiers. About all there is to ask of a man, or a boy-man (19 or younger) in those days so many years ago.

"The fact is I remember plenty, let me tell you." "Sounds like you are going to, whether I like it or not." "I don't want you to like it. I don't care if you even listen. I just want to get it on paper, this story of being in G Company Cow-Hide/White. Believe me, there was nothing special about it or the battalion of just another infantry regiment in the ETO. If it was special in any way at all, it was because I was in it! And as with most 19-year-olds I did not expect to die but I knew I might, and I didn't, which, I suppose, gives me the right to tell the story as I still remember it. A 19-year-old has pretty much a blank slate for a memory. Not much there to begin with so that those wartime impressions stick. Don't ask me to remember names and faces from the 70s or 80s because they are indistinct, but I am good at recalling the 40s. Those memories last and last. I have been harboring my thoughts about the so-called good war (a saying, by the way, you would not have heard in the foxholes because war is lousy when you are in the thick of it, and where else are infantry companies but in the thick of it?). Americans had few self-doubts about the war and the fall back position, this is a good war, didn't figure."

"So what did matter?" "Hard to say in a few words and then I would be speaking only for myself, but this is what recall is all about. So let me have my say. Guys mattered. Not just buddies but anybody in the unit, from an old soldier like B.S. Reed to some kid just up from the repple-depple. The unit was the company, full stop. The company was what kept us together, thinking about each other but in an action it could narrow to a platoon or even a squad . . . ten guys more or less, not quite family and not all likable but squad members from sergeant to BAR man. But the riflemen were the guts of the squad. For one thing there were more of us. The real workhorses. U.S. small arms were o.k. but maybe could have been better. The M1 rifle was a good semi-automatic easy to re-load. But the BAR gave such a burst of fire from a 20-round-clip re-load was a problem. Why else was there an ammunition bearer, tagging along trying to keep ammo supplied. Besides, the bullets being spit out of the BAR tended to rise, wasting a lot of ammo. It would have been better to have an air-cooled 30 caliber machine gun integral to each squad, or at least, platoon. Nothing like level automatic fire to keep heads down. But then that is only a combat soldier's view. Ten years later I was working as a civilian research analyst for the Ordnance Corps in the Pentagon, but even then I did not have a chance to set things straight. Of course, I was never asked!"

The Outfit

The regiment, the 334th Infantry of the 84th Division, was lucky enough to have a historian in its ranks. His name was Perry S. Wolff, and he wrote immediately after the end of fighting in Germany, year zero. The tiny print on page four referring to its publication reads: "Mannheimer Grosdrückerei August, 1945." The book, *Fortune Favored the Brave*, is titled with no sense of irony, I am sure. But it will no doubt occur to some who were there, that it might have better been named "Fortune Favored The Fortunate." No disrespect intended to the officers and men who made up the regiment. These very same guys will have seen battle for what it was, if you zigged when you should have zagged, it could be all over, dog tags in the mouth and ready for the Graves Registration detail. But to get back to Perry Wolff who wrote at the close of his introductory reflections: "On the 7th we entrucked for a cold ride to Wittem, Holland, arriving in the morning hours of the 8th. As we stepped from the trucks, to east we could hear our artillery firing against The Siegfried Line. The preparation was over. We were ready for battle." Which was true, up to a point, but it is doubtful if we were ready in the literal sense. We were there, we would be in action, but it is only after the baptism of fire that men are likely to be ready for battle in the fuller sense. And even then, it may be only a temporary state of mind. After the first fire fight, or is it after the second one, men, aware of what is ahead, can steel themselves to, in the old army phrase, "move out."

Something else happens after the initial shock. The company, which had been a unit on paper, becomes the unit within which men will live and die. The table of organization, in the European Theater of Operations, for example, listed units from Army Group to Army to Corps to Division to Regiment to Battalion to Company. The most interpersonal, the most cohesive, the most tragic, the most self-conscious, the most penetrable was the company. It was at the company level we can get the closest to life and death, where numbers count for less and names count for more, where towns taken (or not taken) are not dots on a map but where buddies give their all, or gave their all. It is the company commander who knows his men, and they know him well enough to follow his orders. The battalion commander may be killed in battle, coming down on the line to assess the progress of an attack, but except for his uniform he is not one with the privates and the non-coms. If the individual soldier was aware that Colonel Williams was hunching next to him exposed to grazing fire, he would likely think: "What the hell is *he* doing here!" In other words, he doesn't belong. The Colonel's officers, or some of them at least, might admire "the old man" but they would also rue the day he was killed . . . for coming under grazing fire. As every infantryman knows grazing fire is lethal . . . there is no place to hide when the order is to move forward. Never mind, between a rock and a hard place. It becomes between a death trap and a hospital bed and the choice is not his. We're back to zig and zag.

This is a story of G Company but it has more to do with company than it has to do with "G." It could have been any letter from A to M as identification: it just happens to have been G . . . one of the basic units of the regiment. What was the origin of G Company? The division of which it was a basic component, the 84th, the "Railsplitters," (that was a nod in the direction of Abraham Lincoln, THE railsplitter) was just another division called into being as part of Army Ground Forces in October, 1942. Quartered at Camp Howze, Texas, its beginnings were not promising. Down to the spring of 1944 the 84th was rarely up to full strength. A lot of the draftees proved unfit for infantry and many others left the division as replacements, supplying manpower to cover the combat losses by divisions already in the fight. After much training, including "D" series in the Texas-Louisiana maneuver area the 84th was sent to Camp Claiborne, Louisiana, its future still uncertain.

In the spring of 1944 the Army High Command decided to kill ASTP, Army Specialized Training Program. Some thought it was an unwise use of manpower from the start. When men were inducted they took an Army General Classification Test. If you scored high enough the army was ready to send you to college to study to be an engineer. But with the D-day landings being readied for late spring and a heavy loss of infantry expected, the so-called "college boys" were pulled out of schools across the country, many finding themselves assigned to various infantry divisions still states-side. The 84th Division received upwards of a thousand high I.Q. "college boys," and among them was one Henry Kissinger.

Friction quickly developed between the newcomers and men long in the ranks. Not many men in pre-war America went to college making the ASTP-ers a bit cocky and the old timers more than a bit anxious when it came to competing for promotion as non-coms. The mix was pretty quickly homogenized when the men settled into the training routine and friendships soon developed. Not that some of the college-types did not think they had gotten a raw deal. But in the army it was easy to come to believe you had it bad and that ain't good. Most men learned to adjust. The fact is the 84th Division needed the ASTP-ers to bring it up to combat strength, which meant that overseas duty was less than a few months away.

Camp Claiborne was no garden spot, but then, what training camp is? It was hot, it was humid, it was dusty, and it was fullfield packs, 25-mile-hikes, 10-mile-forced-marches, obstacle course with live ammo, and no place to go on a weekend. Sure there was Alexandria, Louisiana, which was near to Camp Polk and Camp van Dorn, as well as Claiborne, not to mention Alexandria Army Air Field, so going to town (after waiting in line for hours to get on a bus) was a matter of competing with thousands of G.I.s for a beer, a movie, a whatever. Most guys were satisfied with the PX and a post movie and quite a few went to the post chapel on Sunday morning. Over the late spring and early summer of 1944, G Company began to take on the character of a unit. It was just a matter of time before it was fully firmed up, time, and a shooting war.

In June orders came down that every man must have a furlough during the six month period before going overseas. That was good news to the ASTP-ers and the others besides: but it was also a matter of fond, if not last, good-byes, for the thinking-man's soldier. The company even had its picture taken, everybody in dress khakis, some faces smiling, some sober, and some sullen. The officers sitting in the first row, the men standing behind them, many seemed to be wearing a grin. Little did they know. Oddly enough, not every soldier took advantage of the furlough offer. One man was heard to say, he couldn't go home because he was not a commissioned officer. His girlfriend wouldn't understand. Damn college boy. Many years after the war he became governor of his home state. Names come later.

By September, 1944, the Germans were falling back in both France and Italy and the prediction was sometimes voiced "the boys will be home by Christmas." Nonetheless fresh divisions were headed to the ETO because the generals were taking no chances. Given the role of the 84th Division in the crucial Battle of the Bulge (along with several other divisions freshly arrived) the generals got it right. More manpower meant insurance against the unforeseeable, such is the nature of warfare. Port of Embarkation was Camp Kilmer, N.J. POE as the last stop in the U.S. was supposed to be the point at which those unfit for combat were screened out. That was the theory, but it didn't work like that for G Company. If VD was not detected, you shipped out. As the first platoon made its way up the gang plank of the troop ship *Barry* a sergeant was seen to be carrying two duffel bags, one was his and the other belonged to a private who was unable to carry his own equipment. Seems he did not have VD when he had his physical and so off to war he went. Talk about a raw deal. The guy was 39 years old, he had a mild case of polio when he was 20 and never went out to the field to train at Claiborne. Instead, he was on permanent latrine duty, which needs no explanation. Oh yes, his wife was pregnant at the time. Once in a combat zone he finally got a "break." He was assigned to the Graves Registration detail of the division and thereafter saw mostly dead G.I.s. But he survived, his wife had the baby, and he made it back to Cicero, Illinois.

Life aboard the *Barry* was pleasant enough. The weather was warm and breezy, the waves were gentle, but the journey took ten days. German

U-boats were stalking enemy ships, the *Barry* among them. Not the sort of information that came across the p.a. system. Docking was in Southampton and after a short train ride to Winchester the regiment marched to the Barracks of the Royal Winchester Rifles, situated just above the cathedral. Light training in England followed the trans-Atlantic crossing, then the move across the Channel, and into France by truck combined to produce a tangible sense of the trials that lay ahead. Not even the glimpse of Paris by passing down the Champs Élysées or the bivouac at Le Bourget airport, where Lindbergh had landed in 1927, worked to lighten the mood of the men of G Company. Battle was ahead and battle was the pay-off.

Men: Leaders

A Captain, lieutenants, sergeants make up the leadership of an infantry company, and the two hundred or so of men under them are responsible to them. Much is expected of them and in the case of G Company, by and large they measured up, one or more exceeding a common standard of performance, and perhaps none proved to do less than what duty called for. This is a somewhat bland characterization of the leaders once in battle, but it certainly tends to be accurate looking at them in the training phase of the company's experience. Some would grow in stature, others would not. Only at the end of the day may true leadership be gauged. This is especially so in the person of the company commander, Captain Charles Hiatt. There was to be no more fearless officer. It was difficult to read Captain Hiatt in the States. To begin with he was not an imposing man at all. Of medium height, fair of complexion, almost boyish in appearance. And quite a contrast to his second in command, Lieutenant John Griffin. Griffin, tall and lean and mean, from the ranks it seemed he really ran the company. On a day to day basis at Claiborne, Griffin and the First Sergeant, Claude Hinsley, gave the daily orders to the four platoons assembled each morning on the company street. If Griffin was tough, Hinsley was tougher, behind his spectacles. His six stripes, three up and three down, carried more authority than Griffin's silver lieutenant's bar. And when the time came he proved it, a battlefield commission is no mean feat. Griffin was brave enough but he was wounded early on, and a definite loss to the company's leadership. Hinsley was a soldier's soldier to the end of his life.

In training camp Captain Hiatt was around, all right, but he never seemed to be visible to the naked eye of the private soldier. When it came to the 25-mile-marches he was with the column only part of the way. When it came to a field exercise, Lieutenant Griffin was always at his side, helping him, or so it appeared, to use his compass or to read a map. He simply failed to establish a connection with the guys who would be fighting under him. Perhaps the Captain was simply waiting for the real thing. He might get lost on a night exercise in Louisiana, but in the combat zone he was peerless. And fearless to boot, and fully in command of himself and the men. He became the battalion commander with the rank of major by the end of fighting in Germany. Yet he made little of his accomplishments as befit the hero he was. Why hero? Be patient, wait and see.

The other commissioned officers were the typical 90-day-wonders, officers and gentlemen by act of Congress. Which is not to say they did not lead well. Lieutenant Harris who commanded the first platoon tried hard to be "one of the boys," down to earth, but the line between enlisted men and an officer was so deeply ingrained as to make that attitude unworkable. Griffin never forgot he was an officer and never let you forget you were an enlisted man and he got the kind of respect Harris envied. That very attitude on Griffin's part almost cost him his life and did cost him a leg once the battle was joined. Then there was Baker; he came to the company just prior to shipping out and worse still, rumor had it in civilian life he had been a lingerie salesman in Detroit. He quickly got the nick-name, "Buddy Boy," and like most of us would have to prove himself. As the lieutenant in charge of the third rifle platoon he was a good combat officer, but at the same time he refused to be de-humanized by the demands of war. A curious thing to say but the evidence is there for later examination. Griffin was tough but not crude. He had been a practicing attorney before coming into the army and had a professional air about him people were reluctant to challenge. Indeed his fellow officers were intimidated, and not simply because he was a first lieutenant and they were second looys. Jack Schaper was both tough and crude and he did not care who knew it. That very combination made him popular with his men of the second platoon. He was there to fight and to kill. At Claiborne this looked like swagger; on the battlefield it became guts. He would as soon pop a Kraut as blow his nose. And he popped many a Kraut without himself going down. Dead, I mean. For him leading a patrol was daring fate. The C.O. called on him, confident that Schaper and his men would scout ahead and get a handle on the terrain and the enemy. Captain Hiatt could then better work out the tactics. But Schaper was not of a mind to waste his men so that volunteering for patrol duty under him became a pattern in company operations. If Jack said it was possible, not necessarily safe, but possible to move ahead, G Company moved ahead.

The non-commissioned officers were the sinew—that tough fibrous tissue uniting muscle to bone—of the company. It had been that way in training and remained so in battle action. The men in the ranks, the muscle of the organism, relied on the non-coms in a way that was a matter of equal station. Relations were relaxed, much more so than the interactions between lieutenants and private soldiers. And G Company was blessed with good platoon sergeants, you have to believe that. Ethridge, Hartline, Martin and Rabinowitz had it all together. Ethridge who headed up the first platoon was a model in camp and in battle. John Hartline was a big strapping guy, with a lot of lung power and a lot of courage; forceful when he had to be, he was basically decent and caring. He had a protégé, a young fellow-Oklahoman by the name of L.J. Reed: he was grooming Reed to take charge of the third platoon if it came to that. But it was Hartline who survived and L.J. who was killed. But more of that later on. Billy Martin was an ace who took charge of the second platoon shortly after the fighting started while Rube Rabinowitz, the sergeant of the weapons platoon, won a battle-field commission, one of the three such awards to G Company sergeants.

Each rifle squad had a buck sergeant and at that level the ASTP-ers came into their own. Angelo Genitti, "Gubby" to his squad, was a natural leader and somewhat like Marion Ethridge, a warm and friendly sort. Perhaps too much that way. Within the first two weeks of the fighting Genitti encountered a lone German soldier behind our lines. Unwisely he lowered his rifle, perhaps expecting the man facing him would know he was within enemy lines and would surrender. But instead, he opened fire wounding Genitti. The sergeant was found lying in his blood a couple of minutes later but prompt medical attention pulled him through. Arch Moore was another "college boy" who made buck sergeant and led a squad. It would be a safe bet that his girlfriend would have been proud of him for his duty done, even if he was "only" a sergeant. And if she had realized he would one day be governor of West Virginia, she would have understood it is not the rank that makes the man. Then there was Reed, B.S. He was an old army hand, having enlisted in 1937 in the hey day of American neutrality. There was not even a war on at the time. As with many guys of that vintage he considered himself "old army." He had been promoted and broken in rank, he said, more times than he remembered. But what a soldier! He not only died with his boots on, he died with his staff sergeant stripes showing. It took the god of war to break Reed, B.S., for the last time. But staff sergeants could have a short life expectancy. How short? How does twenty minutes sound? That was as long as Bill Hawk was a platoon sergeant. Details follow.

MEN: SOLDIERS

The men were the muscle of G Company whatever way you look at it. They did most of the fighting and the dying. As with the human anatomy, there must be the bone of the officers and the sinew of the non-coms, but lacking muscle there can be no action. And the stronger the muscle the more may be accomplished. And for a company made up of men who had trained together over a long period of time they formed the nucleus of the unit. Some of these "originals" would be killed, many more would be wounded, and replacements would come to fill in the squads. This new muscle was able to respond effectively to the weight on its shoulders in no small part because it was added to muscle already toned, already practiced, already able to carry the battle forward.

These citizen soldiers represented the mixture of strains in the general population. A study of the necrology of the company plainly bears this out. From Guillermo Gomez and Mariano Rodriguez to Severin Meldgaard, a naturalized citizen born in Norway, to Mike Adamczyk and Emil Schenkal to Christopher Schiraldi and Salvatore Connici to Elsworth Seel and Arnal Ryan the melting pot was well supplied. If there was one racial strain missing such were the times and the customs. The total KIA count was three officers (of whom two were battlefield commissions) seven non-coms, and thirty-seven soldiers of the line. For a guesstimate of the total wounded: upwards of sixty. The company was so depleted at one time late in the war that it was taken off the line and used to guard division headquarters. No one was about to complain.

Geographically the men were from many different parts of the country. Californians served along side New Yorkers, big city guys and farm boys were as one. But perhaps the states of Oklahoma, Texas, and Louisiana had the heaviest numbers. East met west with a reassuring ease, and while there could be a good bit of razzing about accents, the New York City accent was a ripe target, it was humor not rancor fostering it. Nothing like a card game to get people together back at Howze or Claiborne, the camaraderie born there paying off in Germany and Belgium when a different set of chips were down.

And sure there were class differences. Bill Deihm's father was an Episcopal bishop in contrast to Willy Baker, from a dirt poor family in Alabama. Deihm was smart and educated (an ASTP-er) and Willy was, to use the p.c. term, mentally challenged. Willy was a good soldier although on one occasion with a BAR on his hip he opened fire on a dozen or so Germans who had just surrendered: none killed but some wounded. Willy would have re-loaded only to be knocked down by one of his buddies after the first clip was emptied. *C'est la guerre.*

If G Company men-at-arms were leveled down so that the best and the worst (however those words may be defined) were indistinguishable they were at the same time raised up to a standard which many if not most of us could not have attained except as members of the unit. Tell an individual, selected at random, to cross a road and enter a house afire to rescue a child, chances are he would be unable to work up the courage to do so. But tell a squad of riflemen to cross a road in order to take out a machine gun and in all likelihood the sinew would activate the muscle. The risks are similar. In the non-military situation the individual's action would be exceptional and he would be hailed a hero if he entered the house. In the military context the individuals would rise to the level of heroism because acting as a unit they were able to measure up. Not that on occasion soldiers have been known to flinch, but battles are won and wars are won because on balance soldiers find the will to do what, in a home-town set of circumstances, they could not. Wars bring out the worst in human nature but paradoxically, they also bring out the best. This is what the citizen soldiers of G Company, 84th Division, were to learn and to learn quickly in the heat of battle. And any battle was more likely to convince leaders and soldiers alike that team work, coordination of movement, the unit cohesion, from company to squad were key to neutralizing the first enemy strong point in order to move ahead. The Siegfried Line was ready-made to teach that lesson, and to go a long way in defining the character of G Company.

THE SIEGFRIED LINE

Once the action begins, the so-called big picture loses its meaning—if it ever has a meaning to men in the foxholes—and threatened death is not long in coming. His name was Rudy Klemenic, a machinist by trade from Cleveland, the first guy I saw go down, his back sliced open like a giant knife had laid his innards bare. The only thing about him moving was the flow of blood as the wound widened. An aid man was quickly at his side, kneeling over him trying to stanch the bleeding. I thought sure Rudy was a goner but somehow he made it—not one of the forty GIs of G Company who did not come back. Nothing can make a war seem real more certainly than the fallen comrade. When it comes to the real thing Hollywood should butt out. All that simulation, but those are not casualties you see on the wide screen, only a lucrative piece of make-believe. You want to see the real thing, find yourself a war, any war will do, as long as the bullets are real. Better still, stay home, go to the war movies, they are the next worst thing to being there. And speaking of being there just after Klemenic was hit, out of the corner of my eye, I saw one of the lieutenants, couldn't tell which one, peel off his officer's pink trench coat—maybe thought he was in the movies, dunno,—judging I suppose, it made him an obvious target. But those mortar rounds which were dropping did not differentiate between the well-dressed officer and the ordinary dogface.

It could not have been more than a week later that KIA took on a personal meaning. Mike Adamczyk and I occupied the same hut at Claiborne from the start. He was in his mid-thirties, and I was nineteen, so to me he was an "old man." Living in close quarters—huts housed about twenty men—you got to know people, like them or not, quickly. Mike was from Philadelphia, 3045 Thompson Street, in fact, and was a die-hard booster of his city. Just a plain Joe, but tough. As we were in the same squad of the first platoon we buddied-up digging foxholes, two together to help in the digging. There we were, entrenching tools in hand, preparing to spend the night. But Mike thought we had not gone deep enough, as he stood at the edge of the hole. The next thing I knew he had tumbled and fell partly on top of me. I looked at him in the face and his eyes had set, he died instantly from a bullet to the head. Mike was a big man, weighing probably 200 pounds with all his gear, too heavy to be lifted out. Result, I spent the night with Mike, or his body anyway, and wondered and wondered why Mike. And as I looked at him his wife, now widow, came to mind. He had no children but nonetheless when the private insurance hawkers descended on Claiborne once word was out that the division was shipping out, Mike took out a death policy for an additional $10,000 to supplement the $10,000 government insurance which was standard for all members of the armed forces. Question: the government paid off for sure, but that "fly-by-night" insurance company, did it ever pay?

Despite the pillboxes and the interlocking fire, the regiment was able to make progress in penetrating the extreme western German frontier. The hilly terrain gave way to flatter land, making a general advance possible. Late one afternoon resistance flared up suddenly and G Company found itself pinned down. After some minutes Captain Hiatt decided to send a runner off to the right where elements of the third battalion, occupying an area affording some cover, were also in a holding situation. The runner was to tell Major Muhar to try to move forward, thus relieving some of the pressure on G Company. The Captain turned to the man nearest him, and gave him orders to get the message to the other unit. I was chosen as the runner. I took off on the run but realized at once that standup running was impossible, the gunfire was too heavy. So I crawled, I hunched, I rolled, on my knees and then on my belly. The fact is I was quickly confused and lay still for a while to try to get my bearings. Either the third battalion had not been where Hiatt thought it was or had moved on its own, I had no way of knowing. I resumed my moves only to discover as I encountered some American troops that I had ventured into the territory occupied by a different division! It was the 102nd Ozarks. I told them my orders which meant nothing to them and not very much to me. By this time it was on toward dusk and I had to make a decision to stay put until morning or to try to get back to my own company. One of the Ozark sergeants said he thought it unlikely I could find anybody in the dark and told me to stay put for the night and set off when it was daylight. This I did and dug myself a foxhole. It was a long night but I had some rations with me and managed to keep my wits about me. Morning revealed that my unit had clearly moved as the land in that direction was clear of troops. Knowing, or was it hoping, that by going back in the direction I had come, sooner or later I would locate G Company, or some element of the regiment, I wandered a couple of hours before hitting pay dirt. I had stumbled onto the headquarters of the second battalion, my battalion, and the very first person I saw was a man I knew by name. He was the company clerk of G Company, John Manchester. I sure was glad to be back in touch and the first thing I asked Manchester: "Have I been reported missing?" He assured me that was not the case, that he did not know I had been separated from the company.

My next question was: "Where is G Company now and how do I catch up with it?" Manchester replied that he would find out for me, and shortly came back with good news. Griffin was at battalion headquarters and he was preparing to rejoin Captain Hiatt late that afternoon. Two jeeps loaded with ammo and hot food were going up and he would be in charge, and he said to Manchester that I could ride with him. It took a long while to put the plan in operation and it was near nightfall by the time we moved out. There were the two jeeps with Griffin in the lead along with the driver and the follow-up, driven by Corporal Fowler—I would take another wild ride with him a few weeks later—with him and another soldier by the name of Martinez, seated behind Fowler. We had traveled for a couple of miles, maybe more, when we came to a fork in the road. Griffin hesitated for a moment and then ordered his driver to turn to the left. The #2 jeep followed of course. After no more than 100 yards Griffin decided he had made a mistake, we should have gone to the right, not the left fork. The easy thing would have been for the second jeep to turn with Griffin to follow. But, no, Griffin wanted his jeep to lead and so after a difficult maneuver with Fowler backing off road to let the #1 jeep pass we were off again. We could not have gone more than a half mile in the new direction when the lead jeep, Griffin alongside the driver, hit a land mine and was blown apart: driver, Griffin, food and ammo splayed all over. Both Martinez and I hit the dirt as Fowler, ever alert, brought his vehicle to a halt. Griffin was badly wounded, his driver was dead. Fowler took charge. We lifted Griffin into the surviving jeep along with the body of the driver, aware that if there was one mine there could be more. But Fowler pulled it off. Martinez and I were left behind. For a while we just stood there, thanking our lucky stars that Griffin, being Griffin, had insisted on being in the lead. Just as easily that could have been us.

And there was more to come. Martinez and I were on our own. The night was black, no moon, only the occasional flash of artillery fire in the distance. Then we heard voices and the thud of boots on the roadway. It was a small German patrol, five men at most. Both of us dove into the trench along the road and remained deadly silent. There was an animated discussion by the Germans as to what had happened as they surveyed the debris with a flashlight, but its beam never settled on us. Within a few minutes they decided to move further down the road. Over the next hour we waited not sure where the line separating us from the Krauts was established. Then an American patrol came along, it had been waiting for the jeeps to reach them and when there was a no-show, the Captain had sent it out in search of Griffin, only to learn that his executive officer was gone. Three weeks later I received a V-mail from my parents, telling me that "The Secretary of War regrets to inform you that your son, Pfc. David H. Burton 13135222 was missing in action." Of course they were stunned, and of course I was stunned. I wrote the next day, by V-mail, which Manchester promised me would be dispatched at once, telling them that it was all a mistake. It was another three weeks before I had heard back from them. By then, G Company was on its way to Belgium.

Until the move south to Belgium and the Bulge there was the Siegfried Line and beyond. Despite its vaunted reputation as impenetrable the companies of the division managed to help crack it by mid-November. The obstacles encountered thereafter were the small towns and villages, some of which were fiercely defended, like Geilenkirchen and Lindern, while others had simply been abandoned. But fought over or not they all had the same look: rubble, pulverized almost beyond recognition, and altogether emptied of civilians. G.I.s took some comfort from the fact that they could sleep in cellars, but with their rifles along side them. G Company had yet to experience a counter-attack: that's the way the war seemed to be going.

So much so the army tried to pretend, when Thanksgiving came around, by serving the troops a turkey day dinner. Almost forgot what a mess kit looked like but there we were lined up for hot food about noon time. But then mortar fire commenced, incoming mail, and we all hit the dirt. Then it was quiet, but as soon as the line formed again the shelling resumed. Was there in that half smashed church steeple a lookout calling the shots? A detail went over and unloaded a hail of 30 caliber. Thanksgiving dinner was getting cold. After a bit the line was back, the mortar fire ended and I think it may have been apple pie for dessert. We did not fare as well at Christmas.

The weather was foul, grey, overcast, wet, and cold. We were living, or was it surviving, day to day. The mud was thick and it was everywhere. Keeping your M1 clean was a daily task. One day an officer came up from division to look over the situation. At one point he decided he needed a rifle to fire to mark a point on the objective ahead. He turned to the nearest soldier and said, "Give me your weapon." It was handed over, the "rear echelon commando" fired the rifle only to discover the barrel had mud in it. He blew his lid and came close to having the soldier involved court-martialed. At that point the platoon leader, Lieutenant Schaper stepped in, mollified the officer, and told the rifleman to be better prepared in the future. No wonder Schaper was popular with the troops, and had few difficulties getting men to volunteer for patrols. Even so, patrols were dangerous because once beyond your own lines either an enemy patrol, or a mine field, or disorientation in the dark, or all of the above could await you. But Schaper was so confident of himself and so careful in guiding his men that the received wisdom was, if Schaper was the patrol leader, what the hell?

I don't think that the ASTP-ers stuck together much on the battle-field, but when in a rear area they sometimes gravitated to one another. I did not know him very well while training in Claiborne, but Elsworth Seel and I somehow found we had things in common, not the war which was obviously the case, but the post-war years and what we thought we might do, or want to do. It was just such a conversation we had late one afternoon in early December. Strange, but I remember the sun was actually shining and we said to one another that we would probably come out alive, and then take on the world, or some small part of it. It was a rambling talk and closed as I recall on an upbeat note, kind of, "Well I'll see you later." He was killed that night, even though the company was in reserve; artillery fire came in unexpectedly, if that was possible because death was always on the doorstep, but not always a fixation, and Elsworth Seel, a young man so full of promise, died the death. Old men forget, but all shall be forgotten unless they make the conscious effort to remember and so it is with my memory of the life and death of Elsworth Seel.

BELGIUM

Belgium was different. And very unexpected. The Germans had broken through the American lines in the Ardennes December 16, and within forty-eight hours the 84th Division was on the road south. We were loaded on two-ton trucks, one of the most remarkable products of the assembly lines in the U.S. The jeep had the "glamour" or at least the high profile of recognition but the two-ton truck was the workhorse of the road, moving everything from troops to ammo to food to the wounded and always delivering. The move to Belgium was by night with the trucks using only their cat eyes and as there were no speed laws to break, the trip was made in a matter of hours. As the trucks idled, awaiting specific orders for unloading, French was the language of the few civilians to be seen. We were in the town of Marche: it appeared to be little touched by the German advance in 1940 and who should be walking down the street toward the convoy but two nuns? At first we thought we were in France, someone speculated that we must be in France for R&R. But nothing could have been further from the fact; German panzers were reported no more than ten miles to the east. Years later I met a Belgian army officer and we talked about the war, and I told him about my unit being in Marche on December 19th. He said that was impossible because on the situation map the Germans were reported to have occupied the town. I politely but firmly told him the situation map was wrong, we had beaten the Germans to the punch. So much for situation maps when things were happening quickly.

In less than two hours we left Marche, heading east to meet the panzers. G Company was assigned to defend the two villages of Hotton and Hampteau, which lay alongside the river Ourthe. As it turned out the Ourthe made for a natural barrier to a rapid German advance and the company had a chance to dig in, assess the situation, and wait for the attack. There were no American armored troops about and the weight of the defense fell on the foot soldiers. However they managed it, some German tanks got across the river and bore down on one of the platoons which was under the command of Hinsley, who by that time had been promoted from first sergeant to second lieutenant. Hinsley ordered a couple of his men to string some land mines across the road, hoping to disable any tank that came along. Trouble was, not just one but three tanks rumbled down the road. The first one hit one of the mines and blew, but the second kept on coming. Hinsley ordered two of his men to follow him as he approached the on-coming tank brandishing his forty-five. Imagine! Facing a king Tiger tank with a forty-five. Gutsy but foolish, and deadly. Hinsley was cut to pieces by the tank's machine gun. He need not have sacrificed himself. As it kept on coming the tank hit another mine and was disabled with the crew evacuating it. Harold Houston Liddle (he liked to be called "Cabbage" by his friends), lived to tell about it, but good soldier Hinsley was KIA. The third of the Tigers must have decided that it was too dangerous to proceed; actually it probably wasn't, and broke off the engagement.

That was the only action threatening our position during the first days in the snow and cold of a Belgian winter. Things were quiet enough to encourage Captain Hiatt to order up hot food from the company kitchen in Marche for the boys on line. Corporal Fowler was once again in on the action and I was assigned to ride with him as he took the company jeep, trailer attached, the seven miles from Hampteau to the rear. He was an uncanny driver. We caught some German small arms fire as we sped down the road which, come to think of it, was in surprisingly good condition. It was enemy fire for sure, their tracer bullets left a red streak across the sky where ours were more yellowish in color. We kept our heads down and Fowler floored the accelerator. Result? We made Marche safely. It took a while to locate G Company's kitchen where the cooks were more than ready to make hot stew along with soup and real bread. In less than two hours the food was packed in the jeep and trailer and while these preparations were under way Fowler and I were asked all sorts of questions about our front line position. One thing Fowler mentioned was the small arms fire we encountered and that he supposed we would see something like it on the way back. Neither of us made much of it. The C.O. ordered Fowler to tell the Mess Sergeant to remain with the kitchen and to send along First Cook, Herman Reed, who could help to get food to the troops. But Reed had overheard the story about enemy fire and said he wasn't going. Fowler told the Mess Sergeant, Fred Meskiss, who in turn ordered Reed "to do his duty."

Instead one of the other cooks volunteered and we were off, it was probably about eight in the evening. The trip back to Hampteau-Hotton was "peaceful," no red tracers to worry us, so that we were at company headquarters in good time. Apparently the word had gotten out that hot food might be brought up and first platoon was ready to chow-down as soon as the big thermal cans were opened. But the Captain did not see Reed and wanted to know why. Fowler spelled it out for him, pretty much as it had happened: when asked, I said Fowler had the good sense to try to talk Reed into coming with the food but he simply refused. Well, Hiatt was mad clear through. The next day Fowler and the cook went back in the daytime with strict orders that Reed must return with the corporal. And this he did. Whether he knew what was going to happen to him I don't know, but it was apparent that the captain had had it with him. He became private Reed and was handed a M1. It was some days later, maybe as much as a week, because we were in a defensive position, before Reed was put to the test. And, of course, he failed and he became the blabbering half man, half child, begging for his life. What came flooding back to me as I witnessed this spectacle was the morning of June 6, 1944 at Camp Claiborne. I had pulled KP that day and was busy scrubbing the mess tables after breakfast. The cooks were deep in conversation about D-Day, and I overheard Reed say: "Just wait until we get over there, we'll show them how to fight." Ugh.

At the start of the Ardennes offensive German soldiers were found wearing American uniforms and driving captured jeeps trying to sow confusion as the offensive picked up steam. One of the counter measures taken, at least as it was understood at company level, was: take no prisoners. Not exactly in keeping with the wording or the spirit of the Geneva Convention. But what should be done if by chance or by design, a German soldier did cross into our lines, perhaps even with the intention of surrendering? Just before Christmas Day the hypothesis became a real question. That morning Lieutenant Baker brought back to company headquarters a young German who had "wandered" into his area, which is the way the lieutenant accounted for his appearance. Captain Hiatt roared at Baker: "No Prisoners, those are our orders." But Baker replied, firmly and honestly: "Captain, I could not shoot him." And that put the ball right back in the C.O.'s court. It was at this point Hiatt called out: "Sergeant Howdiesheil, take this man back in the woods and get rid of him." "Sure boss," the sergeant answered. And off the two of them went, the German marching ahead of Howdiesheil who had his rifle trained on the man's back. Less than five minutes later a couple of shots were heard and Howdiesheil returned alone. Did he kill him? Or did he fire in the air and tell the Kraut to get lost? You could not be sure, Howdiesheil was so cocky. I like to think that the Christmas spirit prompted him to spare a life. But who even knew it was Christmastime? I didn't. What goes around, comes around, as they say. Leave it at that, for now.

The German offensive in and around Hampteau-Hotton did not resume until Christmas night and preparations for fording the Ourthe were very noisy and worrisome. Sounds of heavy vehicles assembling and even shouted commands made everybody jumpy. Fortunately there happened to be at company headquarters a forward observer from division artillery: higher command apparently had some intelligence of enemy intentions. The impending attack was made the more obvious when heavy shelling began coming in. The F.O. was not sure whether counter-battery fire would reach all of the German assembly area. He called for twenty-five rounds of high-air bursting to get a feel for what our big guns could do to disorganize if not break-up the attack. When explosions beyond the Ourthe were heard, the artillery lieutenant was confident that the big guns of the division could saturate German positions. From then on it was fire at will. There must have been plenty of ammo back at divarty because bombardment went on for many minutes and our side of the river was the place to be. Looking back on it the 155 mm.guns with a steady fire set the Krauts back on their heels, they were going nowhere, at least not that night. Next morning the day was clear and cold and all was quiet. Hiatt decided to send a Schaper-led patrol over the Ourthe to check things out so across the river we went. How did we manage that? There were remnants of a bridge so by skipping from stone to stone, and on iron debris as well it was fairly routine getting to the far side. Schaper was at his best. Just what were we looking for? Good question. And what did we find? A lot of bodies, not necessarily all dead, and a whole lot of wreckage. The artillery had done a thorough job of it. Of the several men still alive, if only barely, we administered some first aid, perhaps enough to keep them going until they could be evacuated. But we stumbled on one very young looking soldier who was still alive, lying on his back, his eyes open and making some effort to speak, in German, of course. Schaper knew a little of the lingo and was able to make out that the wounded man wanted something taken from his jacket pocket. Schaper reached into the pocket and drew out cigarettes. "Nein, nein," came the reply. Further rummaging produced a picture. "Ja, ja," was faintly heard. Some of us said, it must be a picture of his mother, or his girlfriend, he seemed too young to have a wife. He wanted the picture placed on his chest, so that as he lay there, perhaps to die, he would be able to look at the picture. The photograph was of Adolf Hitler. We were all stunned: then Schaper said, "probably Hitler Jugend," that fanatical band of teenage recruits who enlisted to save, not the Fatherland, but the Germany of the Fuehrer. Wounded as he was, he refused any aid, seemingly content to die as Hitler, you might say, impassively looked on. Score one for Dr. Goebbels and the Nazi propaganda machine. As we made our way back to our own lines little was said about the incident and the Captain was able to assure the battalion commander that it was: "all quiet" along the Ourthe.

Something big was happening and it was not just with the weather. Fact is the weather turned clear but increasingly cold, which meant more to us on the ground than the fleets of B-17s which now flew over us daily, headed for the Ruhr, but also we hoped laying down carpets of bombs on enemy troop formations they spotted. Seeing the heavy bombers in action was more a morale thing with us. The something big happening on the ground was the division going over to the offensive, pushing hard against the retreating Germans. The "bulge" in the

American line was all but smoothed out. And as we were to learn anew, offensive actions can be costly. The first major objective for G Company in a maneuver that included the entire second battalion, was to take a mountain stronghold called the Hez de Harz. It had an elevation of 300 feet and gave the Germans a commanding advantage. If towns like La Roche and Cielle were to be taken, the Hez de Harz had to be occupied, driving the enemy further east. In effect we were ready to attack wherever there was resistance. G Company formed up in a safe rear area and got orders to move toward the edge of the steep mountain with the idea of going down the hillside, across the valley floor and up the far side where the Germans were entrenched. Moving on a horizontal line we reached the edge where land fell off, and immediately came under heavy fire. We were pinned down, which must have prompted the battalion commander to come down for a look see. It was at this point that the Colonel, noting the men on their bellies did likewise, flat out. But only for a minute or so. I was not more than fifteen feet to his left when, I have to say, unaccountably, he stood up. Machine gun fire was crackling and he was hit, at least once in the lower belly. Down he went and lay there unattended. His body, if he was still alive and that I don't know, was dragged out but I lost all track of him. The man to my right, lying just as close to the ground as I was, had his left hand ripped apart by some machine gun fire. I had never tried to wrap a wound before but as he writhed in pain I managed to get to his first aid kit, douse on the sulfa and tie the bandage. He crawled away as best he could. The firing from the German side eased up and we slid, dove, or slipped down the hillside and were able to get across the valley floor.

Regrouping, resting really, we began to climb toward the source of the gun fire. Midway up was a roadway and sitting astride the road was a Panther tank. Getting across the road to the top of the Hez de Harz was a no-go as long as the tank was there. Arnal Ryan was carrying a bazooka. He got off one round which hit the track, likely making it hard for the Panther to move. Excited by that shot Ryan re-loaded and as he took aim he was cut down by a burst of fire. But the tank did begin to back away, disappearing around a curve in the road and at least fifteen of us continued our climb. We reached the top, only to find the defenders had pulled out leaving their heavy weapons in place. You could read into this that the Germans were on the run. But they still had to be chased across deep snows lying on rugged terrain. And that is not to say the killing had stopped. In their retreat the Germans frequently offered some resistance, even on occasion a counterattack, more out of pride than from a belief the tide could be reversed. G.I.s had something more formidable to struggle against and that was the weather. The temperatures hovered near zero most of January so that the snow was a constant companion, and frost bite common for the soldiers who were marching, not on their stomachs but on their feet. From what we could tell it was pretty much an infantry show which went on until the end of the month. February saw a return of the 84th Division to familiar territory, just to the east of the Siegfried Line where for G Company it had all begun.

RETURN NORTH

First there was a respite. We arrived at a Dutch town, Eygelshoven, province of Limburg, Holland. The place appeared little damaged by the fighting and the townspeople still occupied their housing. And that housing would do very nicely as a place to billet troops temporarily. Officers went dwelling by dwelling, knocked on the door and told the owners they would have company for a few days, in our case, four men. I remember the address exactly, Volkwhegen 11, and the family's name was Jacobs. Husband and wife and two children, a teenage daughter who was kept secluded from the four G.I.s who took over the front room of the house and a son, Willy, about twelve, was fascinated by the family's "guests." I don't suppose we were there for more than four days but long enough to get an honest-to-goodness hot shower in a facility attached to a local coal mine, and a working mine at that. It should not surprise anyone that it was my first bath in months. The army's efforts to supply portable field showers were limited and simply inadequate. The four "guests" got on well with the Jacobs family. One of the men, a sergeant, managed to "liberate" quite a bit of boxed rations from the company mess to the delight of the family. Almost as soon as I got back to the U.S. in 1946 I arranged to send CARE (Cooperative American Remittances Europe) packages to the Jacobses and Willy wrote to thank me in what was good if plain and simple English. But of course, this idyll had to be short lived. By mid-February the unit was back in a combat area as the generals prepared the assault on fortress Germany.

With the German collapse in the Ardennes, which entailed heavy losses of men and equipment, the prospects of reaching the Cologne Plain, where the armor could lead the way, were inviting. There was one big hurdle to clear before the tanks could roll, the Roer River. As rivers go the Roer was not wide or very deep. But because a dam upstream had been broken the expanse of water to be negotiated required the army engineers to build a bridge strong enough to handle tanks and trucks and some foot bridges to accommodate the infantry. This construction took time so our first few days on line promised to be uneventful. How uneventful? One day as we idled our time a jeep, flying the flag of a two star general, came roaring up the road. Maybe the division commander was aboard, maybe not, but the two gold stars on a field of red told us it was someone important. It was headed to the river and a look-see. Within less than ten minutes the jeep came roaring back down the road. It seems that as the jeep reached the Roer the Krauts laid down an artillery barrage which no doubt inspired the hasty exit. As the red flag passed us someone made the crack it wouldn't stop until it got to Paris. I was reminded of an earlier episode, speaking of rear-echelon commandos. It occurred when we were in the Siegfried Line. An officer, and a shavetail at that, came from division headquarters to ascertain if the Germans were firing some kind of especially lethal shell, maybe even poison gas. Three of us took our visitor to an area where it was thought he might find the evidence he was looking for. Suddenly upon hearing a swish overhead he turned to us and asked: "What is that noise from?" I think we responded in unison: "Why, that's outgoing artillery." With alarm in his voice and body language he exclaimed: "Do you mean we are in front of our own artillery?" He left for the rear almost at once.

There were few enough light touches. Waiting for some days until the Roer could be crossed, I for one felt a sense melancholy "a rendezvous with death" sort of syndrome. A bad thing to have time to ponder, knowing the battle looms ahead in time and space. The gloom was heightened by word of mouth that L.J. Reed had been blown up by a well-placed anti-personnel mine. About nine in the morning Reed had gone down into a field and straddled a slit trench to do his thing. As he took a step he tripped a mine which sent him sprawling. Seeing this happen the call "Aid Man, Aid Man" sounded. One of the company aid men came on the run. He surveyed the situation and immediately began to work his way to Reed, measuring every step as he approached him. Kneeling at his side he attempted to move him and by that action set off a second explosion; the aid man was now wounded as well. Word reached the company commander and he came at once to find the two men, his men, unable to move. Without saying a word to any one of the dozen or so of us who were standing by he laid down his carbine, removed his coat and helmet and headed in the direction of the wounded, whether they be dead or alive. He first picked up the aid man, shouldered him and made his way to safety. Without hesitating he went back into what all of us now believed was a mine field to rescue Reed. The sergeant was a big man, raw boned, who could have weighed 180 pounds. Hiatt was really slightly built by comparison, so that he had to drag Reed out of danger, seemingly indifferent to the possibility that other mines had been planted. But Reed was dead. Captain Hiatt was met by hushed silence, men in disbelief. But having seen it played out in front of them it was a matter of seeing is believing. Truly "fortune favored the brave." Nothing more needs to be said or can be said.

High drama aside, the war went on. The Roer River was there and had to be crossed before the German heartland could be penetrated. G Company was lucky, we crossed on a footbridge, courtesy of the army engineers. But units going over first in boats were badly shot-up. Once we went across the advance went well, resistance was spotty, and for the first time we encountered German civilians being turned out of their houses. The towns along the Siegfried Line were nothing more than piles of rubble, in contrast to these villages which had not seen the war close up before. A few white flags were flying, and older men and women (I saw no children) looked sullenly on as the houses were swept for possible enemy soldiers.

Viewed from a strategic angle, break-through was on, and Task Force Church, named for the assistant division commander, John H. Church, was being formed. With tanks in the lead and infantry transported by the old reliable two-ton truck the campaign had taken on a new look. And the infantry lapped it up. Once as the tanks and trucks were moving along a road the column was strafed by a Luftwaffe jet fighter. I did say jet. It was on the column in a flash spraying bullets before we had time to off-load, and then it took another swipe at us before disappearing. The damage was more psychological than anything else. I guess the Germans did not have jets in production. If they had, it could have slowed the war down. But things were on the move. Or were they?

Tanks and infantry working together make for a combined operation. As long as the enemy is retreating the task force is able to move ahead, but when resistance is encountered the party is over for the foot soldiers. They dismount and take on the machine guns or the 88s in order to clear the way. And that is what happened next for G Company. At the end of a day on the trucks the men spent the night in what was a "model village" built for German workers before the war. What we learned in the morning was that the tanks could not advance because of heavy machine gun and anti-tank fire. G Company was to clear the way. The Germans were dug in at two small towns, Berg and Eiken, which were about five hundred yards apart. The terrain was flat, very flat, and that could only mean grazing fire, the scourge of infantry. I suppose you might say what happened that day was the defining moment in the history of the unit. By that I mean we really did prove G Company was *sans peur et sans reproche*. To recall that day means I must gird the loins of memory, as best I may. It was noon before Berg was taken, and that phase of the day-long battle cost, in killed and wounded, about thirty men, including Howdieshiel. He died pitching a grenade at a German gun emplacement, cut down as he pulled the pin. Within minutes, Reed, B.S. was killed leading the third platoon. Old soldiers do die, they don't simply fade away. The grazing fire was fearsome but if you crawl far enough and stay lucky, eventually it comes to hand-to-hand and the adrenalin is pumping. By taking Berg we were only half-way there. Eiken loomed in the distance. Again we were pinned down. Captain Hiatt was the only officer left and sergeants were in short supply. And we weren't making much progress because enemy fire was murderous. At this point the C.O. realizing the second platoon had neither officer or senior non-com left turned to the two men next to him. He said to the first one, "I need someone to lead the second platoon. Do you want it?" And I answered, "No"; then he turned to the other man, Bill Hawk, by name and an ASTP-er. And Bill said, "I'll take it, Captain." Hiatt ordered him slide into the ditch next to us, and get the platoon moving at all cost. Less than twenty minutes later the report came back that Hawk had been killed by sniper fire. R.I.P.

Simply because the company managed to inch forward enough men were left to jump into the German positions and much to our surprise they were ready to surrender. As it turned out the defenders were members of an elite German parachute division (the Adolf Hitler division?) who had been ordered by the colonel, who was handling the heavy machine gun, to stand and die for the Fatherland. When Captain Hiatt came forward there were the five Germans, standing in a line, their hands over their heads. As he swung around to look at them he seemed to unshoulder his carbine. Was he getting ready to gun them down, after all these men had helped to decimate his men. At the end of the day there were probably fifty killed or wounded and we had barely 100 men as the battle started. But no, he ordered the prisoners to be taken back for interrogation. Task Force Church could once again move ahead. G Company was to receive a Presidential Unit Citation for this worst of days.

With Task Force Church again on the move the breakout was complete and the armor rolled and the infantry followed on foot. Not a bad thing since there was little opposition. But on a particular night, about three or four days after "the worst day" two platoons of G Company found themselves in an open field with too little incentive to dig fox-holes. Things had been going so well, just maybe we thought foxholes were a thing of the past. What followed that night, dug-in or not, was more than enough to test our nerve. What we sensed and heard was a long range tank battle between them and us with the boys of G Company trapped as the opposing sides sent shells whizzing overhead in both directions. The fight must have lasted an hour or more and while the potential for casualties was limited, still at least one cry went up for an aid man. But there was no response and the guy must have been badly wounded, judging his cries of pain. For a long while no one moved to help him. Then quite suddenly one G.I. jumped up, ran to the downed man, picked him up and moved him to a semi-safe (there were no safe spots) area. It was all done in pitch darkness and not until dawn's early light was the rescuer identified: he was a replacement who had been with the unit only about a week. His name was Nathan Schumckler, just an ordinary soldier who did the extraordinary thing. That is how quickly new men, up from the repple-depple often identified with the company.

Once it was daylight we were able to get our bearings and several of us went around to the front of a house, which protected us from enemy fire, tank or otherwise. We stood there for some minutes, maybe a half hour, waiting for orders. Without any warning sound, as was typical of mortar fire, a round hit the macadam road running by the house and threw shrapnel in all directions, much of it coming toward the house. The man on the right of the group, Vince Celetti the company technical sergeant was hit in the jaw, next to him was Red Lynn wounded in the right arm, I was next to Lynn, hit in the left hand and left knee, and the last person, name unknown to me, a replacement very likely, was uninjured. Seeking safety, Celetti ran into the house and down into the cellar, Lynn followed, then I, but as the last of us went through the door another mortar round exploded, killing the fourth man. It could not have been more than ten seconds between my passing through the door ahead of the man who was killed. The pain to my hand was body shattering as I seemed to throb all over. I was afraid to remove my glove convinced my hand had been blown off. There was not much I could do but to pour sulfa powder on the wound, wrap a makeshift bandage around and cry out in pain. It must have been an hour before I realized my knee wound so intense was the pain in my hand. Meanwhile there could be heard heavy artillery duel so we felt marooned in the cellar. Late in the afternoon, the three of us found it safe enough to walk back to the battalion aid station and proper medical attention. In a pained and painful sort of way I bade adieu to my unit, G Company would no longer be my frame of reference.

AT THE LAST

"All of a sudden you've stopped your story. I wasn't prepared for that. How come?" "Simple, this was not intended to be about ME but about me and G Company. Leaving the unit when I did, and as I did, you probably have heard it before, the 'million-dollar wound,' bad enough to get you out of combat, but not so bad as to change your life style—there isn't much more to say." When in an army hospital in England I met someone from the 84th Division and he told me about G Company doing sentry duty at division headquarters. By the way, I was treated "royally," so to speak, once I was wounded. The Army Medical Corps was humane and caring, and Oh, those clean sheets and hot showers, not quite "worth dying for" but the doctors and nurses earned my lasting regard.

Years later, probably in 1952, when I was working as an intelligence research analyst for the Ordnance Corps at the Pentagon I had the opportunity to debrief our military attaché from Madrid. I had been reading his dispatches for a couple of months and recognized his name, Lt. Col. Lloyd H. Gomez, as having been the assistant regimental commander of the 334th Infantry. After the formal debriefing I introduced myself—how things had changed, he now addressed me as sir—and we agreed to have a drink the next day at the Willard. We were both there at the appointed hour, 5 p.m., drinks were served and we settled in to talk about (what else?) the war. But conversation was labored, I thought in retrospect, not by rank, not by the military/civilian divide, but by the fact that what we had held in common was gone, over, done with. The battles fought and won, the sense of togetherness which only a present, pressing danger combined with a present, pressing duty could not be recreated over scotch on the rocks. We sensed this and quickly made polite overtures to go our separate ways. This episode taught me that only in the unit, and then only in the unit as we were fighting and dying or surviving, was G Company a reality. The feel, the spirit could never be recaptured. And I learned from that: never go to a reunion. To do so is to chase the ghosts of battles past which are as irrecoverable as Lyonnesse, so completely do the years close off what once was and is now ineffable.

Summing Up

What must be obvious, and yet it seems appropriate to state the case again, is the interaction of individuals with the history of their times, rendering that history both more complete and more understandable. Either by design or by impulse, and very likely in combination, my very first scholarly endeavor was an article-length study I entitled "Theodore Roosevelt and Egyptian Nationalism." Researched at the time of the Suez crisis of the mid-1950s, my study argued that Roosevelt judged the Egyptian people as then unprepared for a westernized self-governing polity. He urged the British to stay the course in Egypt, in a speech he gave in Cairo addressing the military establishment there. Again in London, in his Guildhall Address, he told the British either "to govern or go." TR was then enjoying the delights of what newspapers termed "the Teddyssey." The year was 1910, that brief moment at the beginning of the twentieth century when it appeared that wars between great Powers had at last ended. Events were to prove otherwise, the century becoming the bloodiest in human history. But looking back to that initial scholarly effort of mine, which was researched using the Roosevelt Papers in the Library of Congress over the summer of 1957, I realized I had found in "the great man theory of history" a modus operandi. I have been faithful to that method for forty and more years, as evidenced in this collection.

Sounding a more general note, what influence in the writing about historical personages, does direct contact or friendship with blood relations of the individual whose life is being recounted, have on the finished product, be it an article or a full length biography? An interesting question, the answer to which must be based on one's own experience. Of the major figures I have written about, Oliver Wendell Holmes, Clara Barton, and Edwin Arlington Robinson died without issue. In contrast Roosevelt, Taft and Spring Rice fathered sons and daughters whose life spans, for me, were within easy memory. My conversations and/or correspondence have involved Alice Roosevelt Longworth, TR's first born, two grandsons of William Howard Taft and one great grandson as well, and the daughter of Spring Rice. Given these contacts, some casual and some in depth, have the influences been positive or negative, and if so how and why?

My hours-long visit with Alice Roosevelt Longworth took place in February, 1970. I was in the midst of writing what has been termed by others, an intellectual biography of her father. Our meeting impacted positively as I brought the study to completion the next year. I was introduced to her by her book-seller, who happened to be a very close friend of mine and whose advice on "what to read" often guided "Princess Alice." She was an amazing individual, a socialite with the common touch, a raconteur with an endless supply of stories about her father's friends as well as her own, and most helpful to me, a willingness to tell all. And she had a sense of humor. She inquired: "Did you know Franklin?" Of course I responded somewhat, sheepishly, in the negative. To which she replied: "The Oyster Bay Roosevelts were not very kind to Franklin. We had the hubris and he came along and proved to be our nemesis." Amen. But what did I really take away from the three-hour exchange we each seemed to enjoy in our respective ways? Her father's storied vivacity seemed to exude through her, his sense of confidence, yes, of hubris which contemporaries experienced when in his presence, I somehow shared in. And I must add the whole of the afternoon was a joyous occasion, as Mrs. L. was to write in thanking me for a copy of *Theodore Roosevelt Confident Imperialist*, a focused study which I had published the year before. It was a rare experience for a fledgling biographer.

Cecil Spring Rice and Theodore Roosevelt were close friends. And they were so to until the end of their lives despite the strain on the relationship when Spring Rice was HM Ambassador to Washington during World War I and Roosevelt was the outspoken and relentless foe of Woodrow Wilson. I had given particular attention to their mutual respect and admiration in *Theodore Roosevelt and His English Correspondents,* the research for which was done in London in 1968. It was at that time that Spring Rice's daughter, Lady Arthur, afforded me complete and unencumbered access to the Spring Rice-Roosevelt letters which were then privately held. The fact is we became good friends and remained so through letters and visits exchanged over the course of twenty years. In 1985 she invited me to do a full dress biography of her father which I undertook in 1987 while on sabbatical leave in England. She and I established a well nigh perfect working relationship. We met bi-weekly to talk about her father's "life in diplomacy," took trips to Cambridge and Churchill College where her father's papers had been deposited. Betty Arthur, as she had become to us over the years, invited my wife and me to various formal and social events. We met many of her friends, including the Dowager Duchess of Buccleuch a cousin of Queen Elizabeth and the 8th Earl Spencer, Princess Diana's father. Again the question must be posed and responded to: did this friendship skewer my judgments regarding her father's diplomatic style and substance? To some extent, very likely. Born Mary Elizabeth Spring Rice, she married Sir Raynor Arthur, a diplomat in his own right and a Knight Commander of the Order of St. Michael and St. George (KCMG), hence her title, Lady Arthur. The more I studied Spring Rice, from his early childhood through university (he did a double first at Balliol) and his career in diplomacy thereafter, the more I saw his characteristics reflected in his daughter. And finding her ladyship kind and gentle, self-sacrificing and intensely patriotic, the more I came to believe these virtues had been handed down to her, almost unalloyed. Everyone who knew "Springey" as Theodore Roosevelt liked to call him, found in him a man utterly devoted to God, King and Country, ready to sacrifice all for these beliefs. In short, having known Betty over the years I wove her attributes into my accounts of Sir Cecil while on diplomatic station and felt free to do so because her father had remained so much with her in spirit. I honestly believe that because of this nexus I managed to identify that elusive phenomenon, the real Spring Rice.

Meeting members of the Taft clan, and to this day it is a large family replete with numerous aunts and uncles, nieces and nephews, still centered in Ohio, has been for me rewarding in ways unique to the Taft temperament. As I was preparing to write a biographical study of William Howard Taft, the year was 1984, my good friend, John Monagan, arranged a meeting for me with "Young Bobby" Taft. He was the son of Robert A. Taft, aka Mr. Republican, and had been named to the Senate to fill his father's unexpired term at the time of his death. When I met "Young Bobby" he was again practicing law in Washington. Our hour long conversation revealed a person who was by nature not forthcoming but helpful nonetheless in giving me some sense of the Taft family temperament. In our conversation he appeared to want to talk as much about his grandmother as his grandfather, the sometime president and chief justice. That struck me as odd but insightful. Once my book, *William Howard Taft In The Public Service*, was in print it sold very well, especially at the Taft National Part Site in Cincinnati. Years later as I prepared to edit *The Collected Works of William Howard Taft* it seemed fitting that I should clear this undertaking with the Taft family. Seth Chase Taft was suggested to me as the man to contact in this matter. He proved to be both enthusiastic and influential, writing to inform me that I had a green light from the Taft family to go forward with the idea, which I proceeded to do. To underwrite the cost of bringing the eight-volume set into print another member of the family came into the picture. Dudley Taft, director of the Louise Taft Semple Foundation in Cincinnati provided the funding needed to transform proposal into reality. Meanwhile Bob Taft, governor of Ohio, wrote "An Appreciation" of his great grandfather which graces the pages of volume one of *The Collected Works* along with a Forward by Seth Taft. This most important evidence of the historical Taft had become, after all, a family affair. But my judgments as the General Editor of *The Collected Works* were never questioned.

May there be a down side to the personal relationship with family members of a biographical subject? The answer may well be yes and no. The danger lies not so much in the profile of the individual as it does in that person's place in the history of his or her times. The biographer may be more tempted to exaggerate the significance of the individual under the glass, either by way of praise or blame, than to tell the story of a life as borne out by the indisputable particulars. For example, the role of the Taft family in the public as well as in the private life of its preeminent member becomes a simple fact of life. But the influence of Social Darwinian ideas on his foreign policy as president or his court opinions while chief justice are subject to interpretation, and that may be favorable or unfavorable.

Would it profit the biographer very much had Oliver Wendell and Fanny Holmes had a family? Holmes's private life would have been different, though one would not care to predict just how. And be it remembered that he and his father were at odds as how best he should lead his life after the Civil War. When the young Holmes announced that he might pursue the law as a profession his father is said to have retorted "If you can eat saw dust without butter, be a lawyer." But is there any way to argue that such a posture had any influence, direct or otherwise, on Holmes, the professor, judge, and justice, or on his reputation as a master and overlord of the law. Or that if he had had children of his own, this could have altered his judgments in matters legal or otherwise. On balance, then, if there are living friends or relatives of the person being studied there is more to be gained than lost if these individuals are consulted. For me, Alice Longworth brought her father to life, no small contribution to my awareness of a more complete Theodore Roosevelt in life and in history. As for a childless Oliver Wendell Holmes, biographers have had little occasion, or need, to stress this fact, so complete was he as a person.

Biography and autobiography, distinct in form, are closely related in fact and in facts. Of the several historically significant individuals whose lives or aspects of those lives are embodied in Animating History only two, Clara Barton and Theodore Roosevelt, tried their hands at autobiography. Barton compiled but a fraction of her life of accomplishment, *The Story of My Childhood*, published in 1907. It was projected as the first in a series of short books which when completed would constitute a full dress account of her life of achievement. Beyond 1907 nothing was forthcoming, Barton was perhaps too old and too deflated by her loss of the headship of the American Red Cross to carry the story forward. Roosevelt's *An Autobiography* was published in 1913, a work he had been at for a number of years. Looking back over his life of strife and success and quite possibly believing that his misadventure in the 1912 presidential race was to bring down the curtain on a great life, TR decided to "cross the is dot the I's" [sic]. Being the multi-faceted individual that he was he had himself written biographies of Oliver Cromwell, Lord Protector, and Thomas Hart Benton, Missouri Senator. He had mastered the craft of biography which promised well for his autobiography. It was written to celebrate a great life, as indeed he had lived one. But there was a curious irresponsibility therein, for which Dr. Freud might well have had an explanation. Roosevelt made no mention of his first marriage to Alice Lee. She had given birth to a healthy baby to be named Alice, only to die almost at once. No mention is made of her in the text. To be sure Roosevelt was overcome with grief at her passing. But to give a detailed account of his life, nearly thirty years after her death, and their daughter, Alice Roosevelt Longworth, having been very much a part of his life, TR leaves one puzzled over so deliberate an omission. All of this leads us back to Disraeli's admonition: read only biography for there is life without theory.

INDEX

versy, 219, 233-49; nominal head of
court system, 257; separation of
powers, 261; Supreme Court building,
280; use of Senate chamber, 280;
White, 254-55, 258, 262, 264, 268; see
Taft
"The Children of the Night" (1897), 64, 68
China, 199, 203; customs, 197; Japanese
invasion, 90, 108; Chinese, 40, 85,
146; relationship with Russians, 185
Chirol, Valentine, 190
cholera, 124
Christianity, 60, 63-65, 69, 77, 223, 231,
228; anti-materialism, 146; Christians,
228, 244; commercialism, 67; ethics,
165; propagation, 231; saints, 165
Christian Science, 115, 169; see
Protestantism
Christmas, 288, 298, 302-03; Barton, 115;
Roosevelt's fireside chat, 110
Church, John H., Division Commander, 309
Churchill, Jeanette (Jennie) Jerome, Lady
Churchill (1854-1921), 80, 82
Churchill, John, 1st Duke of Marlborough
(1650-1722), 79
Churchill, Randolph Henry Spencer, Lord
(1849-1895), 80-81
Churchill, Winston Leonard Spencer, Sir,
British Prime Minister (1874-1965), 3,
77, 79-96; accomplishments, 79;
administrator, 79; ambition, 89;
American Congress, 80; American
ladies, 215; ancestors & lineage, 79-81;
Anglo-American, 79, 81, 93; army
career, 79, 80-82; Atlantic Charter, 110-
11; Battle of Omdurman, 83;
biographer, 79; birth, 79, 81; *Blood,
Sweat and Tears*, 80; Boer War, 83;
capture at Ladysmith, 83; cabinet, 83-
85, 87-89, 91; career, 79-80, 82;
Casablanca conference, 95; chancellor
of the Exchequer, 89; Chinese labor,
84; Conservative Party, 83-84, 88-89;
critical of British Command, 83; Cuba,
82; death, 96; duty, 89; education, 81-
82; family, 89; First Lord of Admiralty,
87-88, 91, 93; Fourth Hussars, 92; free
trade, 84; Gallipoli, 88; general strike,
89; greatness, 80; Grenadier Guards,
88; hero, 83; historian, 79, 90-91;
hobbies, 89; Home Secretary, 86;
honorary citizen of the U.S., 96;
honors, 96; House of Commons, 80,
83-85, 99, 90, 92; humanitarian, 86;
imperialism, 83-85, 87; imprisonment
in Pretoria, 83; India, 82; Irish home

rule, 93; Iron Curtain speech, 80, 96;
Iroquois blood, 80; Journalist, 79, 82-
83; Kitchener expedition, 82-83;
Knight of the Garter, 96; lectures, 89;
Liberal Party, 84-86; London, 82;
Manchester, 86; meeting with FDR, 94,
110; military planning, 87-88; Mines
Act, 86; Minister of Munitions, 88;
Minister of War, 88; Naval War Staff,
87; nationality, 80; Nobel Prize, 79;
opponent of Russian Communism, 90;
parents, 80, 82; Parliament, 83, 88;
paternal imitation, 81; patriotism, 87;
personality, 82, 85; political connections, 82; politics, 79, 83, 85, 88,
92-93, 96; polo, 82; Prime-Minister,
79-80, 83, 91-92, 94-96, 110; prison
reform, 86; pro-American, 79, 91-93,
96; public life & offices, 79, 81, 86-87,
96; reporter, 82; reputation, 90;
retirement, 89; Roosevelt, 79; Royal
Scots Fusiliers, 88; sense of history, 80;
sense of purpose, 80; South Africa, 83-
84; South African Light Horse, 83;
speeches & oratory, 79, 80, 84-85, 92-
93, 96; statesman, 79; Sudan, 82;
thinking, 91; traitor, 84, 86; trip to
Washington, 93-94; Twenty-First
Lancers, 82; Under-Secretary of State
for colonies, 84-86; victory speech, 80;
War Cabinet, 88, 91; warmonger, 90;
Whitehall, 82; World War I, 87-88;
World War II, 79, 90-91, 93, 95;
writings, 79, 82-83, 89, 93-94; Yalta, 95
Churchill College, England, 317
Church of England, 46, 293; bishops, 89,
126; see Protestantism
Church of Rome, see Roman Catholic
Church
Church of St. George, New York, 188
Church of St. Joseph, Philadelphia, 219,
226, 229, 232; funerals, 229; pastors,
219, 222, 228
Church of St. Mary, Philadelphia, 232
Cicero, Illinois, 288
Cielle, Belgium, 305
Cincinnati, 257, 259, 318
Cincinnati Law School, Cincinnati, 257
citizens, 50, 52, 105, 277; Adams, 50, 52;
Beard, 134;
Churchill, 96; citizenship, 93, 134, 265;
citizen soldiers, 293-94; diversity, 265;
honorary U.S. citizens, 96; military
training, 205; naturalized, 293;
personal freedom of, 70; privacy of,
279; Prohibition, 70; rights of, 277;

District of Columbia, see Washington, D.C.
The Divine Comedy (1308-1321), 144
divine right of kings, 231
divinity, see theology
doctrine, see theology
Doneraile, Ireland, 141, 145; Doneraile
    Court, 141, 153
Douche, Jacob, 227-28
Duchess of Baden, 122
Duchess of Nucleic, Dowager, 317
Durand, Henry Mortimer, Sir, Diplomat,
    Civil Servant in Colonial India (1850-
    1924), 198, 215
Duke of Baden, 122
Duke of Devonshire, 226
Duke of Marlborough, 79; ducal family, 80;
    see Churchill, Winston
Delaney, Daniel, 228
Durant, William James, Philosopher,
    Historian (1885-1981), 66
duty, 30, 33, 35, 52, 74, 87, 122, 151, 205;
    character, 26-27; Churchill, 89;
    Holmes, 238; military, 283, 287-88,
    291-92, 302, 312-13; Taft, 254, 266
Dryden, John, English Poet (1631-1700), 47

E

Earhart Foundation, vii
The Ecclesiastical Review, 140
economics & finances, 41, 53, 59, 66, 103-
    06, 130, 209, 266; Bank Holiday of
    1933, 105; banks, 104, 106-07;
    business, 66-67, 103-04, 106-07;
    capitalism, 72, 103-04, 130, 146, 169,
    207, 209; crisis, 277; deficit spending,
    105; economists, 231; ethics, 66; FDR,
    104-06; free enterprise, 102-03; Great
    Britain, 84; greed, 72-73, 273; laissez-
    faire approach, 102, 130; Ohio
    Republican Party, 200; relationship
    with government, 103-04, 106; waste,
    67; welfare state, 130; world markets,
    146; see commerce
Eddy, Mary Baker, Founder of Christian
    Science (1821-1910), 115
Edward VII, King of Great Britain (1841-
    1910), 182; abdication, 159; death, 194
Edwards, Jonathan, Congregational Preacher
    (1703-1758), 63
Edwin Arlington Robinson, Haledon (1939), 75
Edwin Arlington Robinson, Neff (1948), 75
Edwin Arlington Robinson, Winters (1948), 75
Egypt, 31-32, 315; democracy, 31; nation-
    alism, 32, 39, 40
Eighth Annual Message (1908), 39

Eileen, Germany, 309-10
Einstein, Albert, Physicist (1879-1955), 5, 10
Eisenhower, Dwight David, General, 34th
    U.S. President (1890-1969), 95
Election of 1910, 13
elections, American, 14-15, 21, 109;
    Campaigns, 21; Candidates, 14
Elgin, Victor Bruce, Lord, 9th Earl of Elgin,
    Viceroy of India (1849-1917), 85
Eliot, Charles William, President of Harvard
    (1834-1926), 31, 39
Elizabeth I, Queen of England (1533-1603),
    223
Elizabeth II (Elizabeth Alexandra Mary
    Windsor), Queen of Great Britain (b.
    1926), 96, 317
Ellenker, Thomas, S.J., 222-23, 231; corre-
    spondence, 232; lectures, 222
Ellis, John, 40
Ellsworth, Oliver, Lawyer, Revolutionary
    (1745-1807), 255
Emerson, Ralph Waldo, Poet,
    Transcendentalist (1803-1882), 60,
    147, 153, 156, 179; idealism, 267;
    intuitionalism, 65
Eminent Victorians (1918), 139
empire, American, 28;
empire, British, 28, 50-51, 82, 84-85, 87, 92,
    184, 207, 231
Emporia, Kansas, 97
Encyclopedia Britannica, 136-37
The End of the Holmes Tradition (1950), 247
England, see Great Britain
English Channel, 289
*The English Jesuits From Campion to
    Martindale* (1967), 223
English language, 179, 129, 229
Enlightenment, 46-47, 56, 225
equality, 70-71, 223-24; equal opportunity,
    103, 130; for women, 127, 137, 273;
    see women
Earhart, Amelia Mary, Aviator (1897-1937),
    135
E.S. Dowell's Private Latin School,
    Massachusetts, 159
Espionage Act (1917), 170
An Essay Concerning Human Understanding
    (1689), 47
Essay on Man (1734), 47, 56
ethics, 23, 61, 66, 68, 74, 165, 237;
    relativity, 267; see Morality
Ethiopia, 90, 109
Trudge, Sergeant Marion, 291-92
Eton College (King's College of Our Lady of
    Eton beside Windsor), England, 81,
    158, 187

eugenics, 166-67
Europe, 12, 34, 39, 50, 58, 90, 109, 121,
222, 224; old liberation, 95; political
power, 109; popularity of Sheehan's
writings, 140; ruin after WWII, 136;
Russian hegemony, 96, 112; source of
science, 171; spread of European
people, 15, 22, 26; world practices,
225, 230; World War II, 110-12, 234
European Economic Recovery Program
(1947), 96
European Theater of Operations (ETO),
284-85, 288
Everest, Mrs., 81
evil, 61, 200, 204, 272; alleviation only
through women in political power,
132; Beard, Mary, 131; Brandeis' power
for evil, 268; canonical and feudal
interference as, 49; defects in
government, 207; exploitation, 131;
Jesuit understanding of, 229; need for
reform, 257; New England's escape
from, 49; Prohibition as, 70; prostitution as, 131; relationship to sin, 72;
Robinson, 61; role of government, 279;
struggle against, 61; sweatshops, 273;
Taft, 257, 273; trusts and tariffs as,
202, 209; unrestrained political power
as, 229
evolution, 21-23, 24-25, 27-31, 33-34, 35-
37, 40-41, 60, 245; creation of man,
37; frame of reference, 26; historical
principle, 37; see Species
Evolution and the Founders of Pragmatism
(1949), 245
Exeter, England, 141
"The Expansion of the White Race" (1909),
39, 203
Ex Prate Grossman (1925), 277
extinction of species, 34
Eygelshoven, Netherlands, 306

F

Faber, Frederick William, Fr., Theologian,
Oratorian (1814-1863), 150
faith, 8, 40, 60, 63, 65-67, 74-75, 139, 141,
143-44, 147-50, 171-72, 225-26, 231,
237; emotionalism, 148; intuitionalism, 148; Judeo Christian, 223;
Relationship with Reason, 144, 148-
49, 172; relationship with science,
170-72; Sheehan, 143-44, 148, 151;
Toleration, 224
Fareham, England, 192
farmers, 45, 102, 128, 265

Federalists, 56-58
feminism, 134, 137; *Encyclopedia Britannica*,
136-37; scholarship, 127, 137-38; see
women
feminists, 128, 133-35, 137-38; criticism of
Blackstone, 137-38; opposition to
archives, 135
Fichte, Johann Gottlieb, Philosopher (1762-
1814), 142
Fireside Chats, 97, 110
First Annual Message (1900), 39
First Church, Braintree, 46
First Continental Congress (Sept. 5, 1774-
Oct. 26, 1774), 50, 229
Fisch, Max, 247
Fish, Hamilton, Governor of New York,
Secretary of State (1808-1893), 121,
123
Fisher, H.A.L., 167, 202
Flanders, 225
Flaubert, Gustave, Novelist (1821-1880),
163
Foraker, Joseph Benson, Governor of Ohio
(1846-1917), 254
force, 22-24, 30, 91, 103, 147, 151-52, 203,
221; feminism, 113, 128, 134, 136 38;
historical, 185; Holmes' use of force,
235-39, 243; Nazis, 235, 239; of
destiny, 175; socialist appeal, 207; see
power
The Force of Women in Japanese History
(1953), 136, 138
Ford, John C., S.J., Fr. (1902-1989), 233-49;
theologian, 237; writings, 237, 240
Formby, England, 228
Fort Sumter, South Carolina, 159
Fortune Favored the Brave (1945), 285
Fourth Annual Message (1904), 39
Fourth Hussars, 92
Fowler, Cpl., 297, 301-02
France, 15, 54, 80, 90-91, 95, 229, 288-89,
300; Algeciras Conference, 15; alleged
Catholic support, 226-27; anti-Jesuit,
229; democratic experiment, 31;
diplomats, 50, 57; Franco-German
confrontation, 15; Franco-Prussian
War, 121-22; French Revolution, 53-56;
German Invasion, 92; "Jesuitical
Emmissaries", 226; Language, 300;
National Assembly, 54-56; Peace of
Paris of 1783, 50; Second Empire, 80;
seizure of American goods, 58; war
with America, 46-47, 49, 58; World
War I, 16, 88, 192, 204-05; World War
II, 95, 109, 288
Frankfurter, Felix, Associate Justice of U.S.

events, 5; interaction with people, vii, 7, 43, 51; Laski, 168, 172; law research, 164; men, 43; newspapers disseminating ideas, 131, 265; Robinson, 64; role of the ideal, 113; Roosevelt, Franklin, 106; Roosevelt, Theodore, 22-23, 182, 200-01, 205; scientific, 174; shared ideas between England and U.S., 179; Sheehan, 144; Social Darwinianism, 319; Stratchey, 182, 205; system of, 9; Taft, 258, 265; temporal political prerogatives, 231; translated into political reality, 200; war of, 245; women, 113-26

Illinois, 277, 288; French Settlers, 227

imperialism, Western, 5, 8, 22, 28-30, 74; American, 202; British, 83, 85, 203; Italian, 90; resurgence, 15; Roosevelt, 15, 19, 22-24, 28-29, 33, 35-37, 38; Strachey, 205

independence, 43, 52-53, 230; Adams, 43, 53, 57;

American, 49, 57, 210, 213, 219, 221-22, 229-30, 231; Beard, Mary, 127; Cuba, 32; English elements, 231; Jesuit response to, 219, 221-22, 230-31; Philippines, 31; professional, 127; supporters of, 229; Supreme Court, 288; tax policies, 49; war, 210, 213; see democracy

Independence Hall, Philadelphia, 222

India, 31, 82, 85, 162, 203, 205, 216; democracy, 31

Indiana, 128

Indianapolis, Indiana, 128

individualism & individuals, 26, 52, 72, 151, 153, 175-76, 206

Industrial Revolution, 103, 113

infanticide, 174

"The Influence of the American West on the Imperialist Philosophy of Theodore Roosevelt" (1962), 39

injustice, 29, 105; see justice

Institutes (The First Part of the Institutes of the Lawes of England: Or A Commentary upon Littleton, Not the name of the Author only, but of the Law itself) (1628), 48

institutions, 27, 52, 55, 113; American, 258; Anglo-American, 200; educational, 177; Great Depression, 104; reform of, 104; social, 236

integrity: Robinson, 66, 73; Sheehan, 152; Taft, 268

intellect, 25-26, 35, 38, 43, 56, 171; English, 147;

intellectual stagnation, 24; 239; Laski, 168; liberty of mind, Merz, 171; role in human affairs, 127

internationalism, 15-16, 23

Interstate Commerce Commission, 274; see commerce

intuitionalism, 65, 148

Iowa, 121, 261

Ireland, 27, 140-41, 143, 148, 153; Celtic idealism, 148;

home rule, 93; Irish immigrants to America, 147; problems, 148; Sheehan on, 141-42, 153

Iron Curtain, 80; see communism; Russia

Iroquois Indians, 80; see Native Peoples

isolation & isolationists, 110; England, 196; New England, 46; Worcester, 48; see neutrality

Italy, 95, 109, 111, 288; Berlin-Rome Axis, 109; invasion of Ethiopia, 90, 109; Italians, 26; neo-imperialism, 90

J

Jackson, Charles, Justice of Massachusetts Supreme Court (1775-1855) 159

Jacobite Uprising of 1745, 226

Jacobs, Willy, Dutch Child, 306-07

Jacobs Family, 306-07

Jamaica, 198

James, William, Psychologist, Philosopher (1842-1910), 5, 140, 235; Holmes, 157, Pollock, 160; pragmatism, 5

James I, Stuart (James VI), King of Great Britain (1566-1625), 211, 223

Japan, 93-94, 111, 138, 240; British ally, 188; economic

competition, 84; history of women, 135; invasion of China, 90; invasion of Manchuria, 108; Peace Treaty of Portsmouth, 15; peace with Japan, 188; Pearl Harbor, 93-94, 111; Russo-Japanese War, 15; World War II, 112

Jasper, heir, 73

Jasper, King, 72-73

Jay, John, Ambassador to France & Spain, 1st Chief Justice of Supreme Court (1745-1829), 50, 56-57

Jefferson, Thomas, 3rd U.S. President (1743-1826), 56, 58, 223-24; Adams, 56-57; patriot, 224; philosopher, 224; propagandist, 224; Second Continental Congress, 57

Jefferson Place (Theodore Roosevelt's house – 1820-1822-Jefferson Place NW, Washington D.C.), 187

Kitchener, Horatio Herbert, Lord, 1st Earl, British Field Marshall, Diplomat (1850-1916), 88; defeat of tribesmen, 83; expedition, 82
Klemenic, Rudy, Soldier, 294-95
knowledge, 18, 28, 35-36, 46, 50, 62, 83, 87, 90-91, 117, 132, 157, 165, 175, 227, 256, 278
Koreans, 40

L

laboratories, 11, 69
Ladysmith, South Africa, 83
Lafayette, Marie-Joseph-Paul-Yves-Roch-Gilbert Du Motier, Marquis de, Major-General, Honorary U.S. Citizen (1757-1834), 96
Lala, Raymond Reyes, 39
Lamarck, Jean-Baptiste Pierre Antoine de Monet, Chevalier de, Naturalist (1744-1829), 27
Lancashire, England, 228
Lansdowne, Henry Charles Keith Petty-FitzMaurice, 5th Marquess, Viceroy of India, Secretary for Foreign Affairs, 188, 196
Lanza, Vito, 277, 279
La Roche, Belgium, 305
Laski, Frida Kelly, 166-67
Laski, Harold Joseph, Economist, author (1893-1950), 57, 139, 157-79; Beit essay prize, 167; career, 167; death, 175; economic problems, 167; education, 166-68; eugenics, 167; faith & religion, 170-72; family, 166-67; friendships, 139, 166-68, 175; Holmes, 139, 142-43, 166, 168-69, 172, 175-76; individualism, 175-76; influences, 167-69, 171, 175-76; intellect, 157, 166, 168, 175; Jewish faith, 166; letters and correspondence, 143, 154, 157, 167-70, 172, 176; liberalism, 176; marriage, 166-67; Marxism, 175; Oxford, 167; personality, 166, 175; philosophy, 173-74; Pollock, 176; professor at Harvard; 167-68; radicalism, 168; reputation, 166; rights, 170; science, 170-71; scientific optimism, 175; skepticism, 173; values, 175; Whitehead, 171-72; wife, 166-67; World War I, 167; writings, 167, 177
Laski, Nathan, British Exporter, President of Great Synagogue (1863-1941), 166-67
Latin America, 109

law, 26-27, 47-48, 52, 73, 149, 169, 175, 222, 224-25, 234, 236, 239, 243, 248, 264, 275, 319; American, 49, 157, 164, 233, 244; Anglo-American principles, 140, 157; anti-trust, 13; business contracts, 258; Canon, 49; Common Law, 158, 162-63, 264, 279; Constitutional, 2, 267, 271, 274; English sources, 49; false philosophies, 234; Feudal, 49; Frankish, 164; Holmes' interpretation of, 141, 162, 164; jurists, 253, 256, 272; influences on law, 235-36, 244; jurisprudence of Founding Fathers, 235; legal philosophy, 234-35, 237-39, 241, 243, 253, 256, 266, 279; legal realism, 233, 235-36, 246; legal values, 234-35; legislators, 134; legislature, 51, 56, 132, 204, 258, 261; logic, 149; Maryland, 225; medieval, 164; moral, 68, 239; nature, 48, 146; negligence, 162; neutrality, 109; opposition to religious support, 171; order, 237; "Our Lady of the Common Law," 139, 158; Laski's understanding of, 139, 174; Penal, 223, 229-30; positive law, 238; positivist, 248; possession, 162; presidential responsibility to uphold, 276; professors, 219; Prohibition, 277; role of experience, 149; Roman, 164; rule under law, 47, 51, 223; schools, 225, 234, 241, 243, 246; scientific understanding of, 162-63; sociological jurisprudence, 236; state law, 271; students, 234; stuffing dockets, 260; Suárez's exposition of, 145; supreme statement of, 157; teaching, 21, 162; theft, 164; treatises & writings, 158, 162, 222, 231, 234; trespass, 162; working conditions, 133; see Chief Justices; Supreme Court
law, English, 2, 48-49, 158, 164, 179, 264; Penal, 223; restricted litigation, 264
"The Law of the Country" (1908), 257
Law of Gravity, 37, 41
The Law in Quest of Itself (1940), 242, 248
Law Quarterly Review, 162
Law Reports, 162
"Law in Science and Science in Law" (1899), 237
The Law of Torts (1887), 159
lawyers, see attorneys
League of Nations, 72, 166, 270
Le Bourget Airport, Paris, 289
Lecky, William Edward Hartpole, Philosopher, 82

N

O

161; authority on English law, 2; autobiography, 174; biography, 176; compared with Nestor, 159; Corpus Professor of Jurisprudence, 162; death, 159, 175; education, 158; family, 158, 160, 176; Fellow of Trinity, 158; fencer, 159; friendships, 139, 158, 160, 162-64, 166, 176-77; Holmes, 139, 142, 162-66, 168, 175-77, 237; honorary degree from Harvard, 177; honors, 162; individualism, 175-76; influences, 158, 175-76; intellect, 160, 163, 175; juridical comradeship, 139; king's scholar, 158; lectures, 162; legal career, 158; legal scholar, 157-58, 162-64, 174; letters & correspondence, 139, 154, 157, 163-66, 237-38; liberalism, 176; Lincoln's Inn, 158; Maine, 158, 163; Maitland, 158; marriage, 162; membership in Conversazione Society, 158; mountain climber, 159-60; mysticism, 160; "Our Lady of the Common Law," 139; personality, 175; philosophy, 159-60, 166; poet, 159, 161; realist, 165; reputation, 163; skepticism, 174; "The Sunday Tramps," 60; thinking, 158, 164; values, 175; writings, 158-59, 162-63

Pollock, Frederick John, Sir, 176
Pollock, Juliet, Lady, 160
Pollock, Walter Herries, Jurist, 160
Pollock, William Frederick, Sir, Queen's Remembrancer, 158, 160
Pope, Alexander, British Poet (1688-1744), 47, 56
Popish Plot (1678-1681), 226, 232
populism, 106
Portland, Oregon, 275
position, 9-11, 13-14, 17-19
"The Positivism of Mr. Justice Holmes" (1951), 241-42
"Paulo Post" (1884), 161
postmasters, 275
Potsdam Conference (July 17-Aug. 7, 1945), 112
Potter, Episcopal Bishop of New York, 126
Poverty: A Study of Town Life (1901), 86
Power and Responsibility: The Life and Times of Theodore Roosevelt (1961), 37
power, 33, 53, 56-57, 61, 67, 69, 73, 84, 90, 151, 315; absolute, 239; balance of, 95; farm buying power, 102; Feminism, 134, 137; higher powers, 155, 231, 238; Holmes, 151; judicial, 260-63; Lord Chancellor, 264, national, 274-75; police, 272; political 51-52; 53-54,

61, 130-32, 229, 231, 243, 257, 259, 272, 278; presidential, 104, 275-77; Roosevelt, 97, 107-08; ruling, 151; temptation, 151; separation of power, 53, 261, 276; states, 272-73; unlimited, 151

Powers, Western, 58, 72, 87, 93, 109-11, 183, 203, 315; imperialist, 8, 15-16; Russian, 185; see imperialism
practicality, 15-16, 19, 23, 27, 32, 36, 141, 190, 198, 224, 230
pragmatism, 5, 24, 108, 110-12, 238, 240, 245; Holmes, 140, 143, 160
"The Pragmatism of Justice Holmes" (1942), 237-38
preaching, 46, 227-28
Presidential Campaign of 1912, 21
presidents of United States, 1-4, 7, 12, 33, 35, 56, 58, 97, 130, 253, 276; campaigns, 200, 271; chief executive, 51, 206; executive removal, 275-76; pardoning power, 277; presidential authority, 275-77; youngest, 8
press, 125, 266; British, 82-83; freedom of, 170, 239; newspapers, 49, 108, 131, 148, 184, 241, 265, 315
Pretoria, South Africa, 83
Price, Dr., English Political Commentator, 53
"Priest as Artist: The Dilemma of Canon Sheehan" (1969), 155
Principles of Contract at Law and in Equity (1876), 159, 162-63
Pringle, Henry, Biographer (1897-1958), 19, 37
prisons, 83; Andersonville, 120; prisoners of war, 120, 302-03, 310; reform, 86; sentences, 277
progress, 5, 21, 23, 25-27, 29, 54, 200; cult of progress, 66-67; hypothesis, 26
The Progressive, 242
progressivism, 8, 13, 15, 18-19, 26, 131, 253, 260, 268, 273, 280; FDR, 100, 102, 106; education, 128; era, 130; Hoover, 266; radical, 14, 106; Taft, 273-75
Prohibition (1920-1933), 70, 128, 258, 260, 277; bootlegging, 278; see Amendment, Eighteenth
The Promise of American Life (1909), 13, 19
propaganda, historical, 2, 224
property, 55, 223-24, 226, 270-74; attempted sequestration of Catholic property, 226; Locke, 223; Jesuit owners, 224-25; private property, 270-73